Bangor
in the Seventies

Written and Compiled
by Terence Bowman

BALLYHAY BOOKS

Published by Ballyhay Books,
an imprint of Laurel Cottage Ltd.,
Donaghadee, Northern Ireland.
Copyrights reserved.
© Terence Bowman 2011.
Contributed texts are copyright of individual contributors.
Photographs are reproduced by permission.
All rights reserved.
No part of this book may be reproduced or stored on any media without
the express written permission of the publishers.
Printed by Gutenberg Press, Malta.
ISBN 9781900935913

Bangor in the Seventies is dedicated to the late Michael J. Foley MA, my O-Level English teacher at Bangor Grammar School. It was only later in life I truly appreciated how much he had nurtured my interest in writing.

Contents

Introduction
by Terence Bowman

Everything was still in place. The Abbey Church with its commanding presence at the main entrance to the town, providing an important link to Bangor's pivotal role in early Christian Ireland. Ward Park with its network of rivers, ponds and its ever-present ducks. Even Barry's Amusements and the McKee Clock at the seafront and Cecil Greenwood's joke shop on High Street.

But as Bangor entered the 1970s the town had lost much of the wide-eyed innocence that permeated through the pages of this book's predecessor, *Bangor in the Sixties.* Although widely seen – for good reason – as a welcoming haven away from some of the worst excesses of the Troubles in Northern Ireland, for a large number of those who lived in the town and raised their families here, the story was different.

If I had to pick a single word that to my mind best summed up Bangor – and most other places in this part of the world during the 1970s – it would be 'loss.' The loss of life and property through the heartless and destructive action of terrorists, the loss of thousands of jobs because of a worldwide economic recession linked to rising oil prices and cheap overseas imports, and the loss of that wonderful sense of freedom that ensured parents in the Sixties never lived in perpetual fear for the safety of their children.

While for the most part this book records information that is already in the public domain, I am very mindful that, despite the passage of so much time since all this happened, wounds can still be very raw. To this end, I attempted where possible to make discreet contact with those local families who lost a loved one during the Troubles. Where I was successful I was very touched by their desire to ensure the person they lost should not be a forgotten statistic.

In a number of instances I have been asked to include additional information about the person, along with a cherished photograph, to show they were real people with families, friends, hobbies and interests, and they will never, ever be forgotten. To all those who have helped me in this way, please accept my sincere thanks. To others who may not have been aware of my efforts, please be assured that any future editions of *Bangor in the Seventies* can be updated appropriately.

Lest anyone should assume this book is dominated by the unrelenting impact of the Troubles, I have made sure the efforts of many groups – youth, artistic and sporting – are fully recognised within the pages of *Bangor in the Seventies*. It was largely through their efforts, more often than not on an entirely voluntary basis, that the heart of Bangor continued to beat.

Once again none of this would have been possible without the support of the North Down Museum and its former manager Ian Wilson. They made available to me editions of the *County Down Spectator* published between January 1970 and December 1979. I also consulted newspaper back issues at the Carnegie Library in Bangor and the Central Library in Belfast and verified information through the authoritative *Lost Lives* (Mainstream Publishing, 1999, 2007) by David McKittrick, Seamus Kelters, Brian Feeney, Chris Thornton and David McVea.

My grateful thanks go to the *Spectator* itself and to its former reporters who so willingly shared their Seventies memories. In similar vein my thanks also go to the many other contributors to this book.

Special mention must again go to Jonathan Coates of the *Newtownards Chronicle*, who cheerfully went about the task of seeking out literally hundreds of pictures from the *Spectator* negative archive, and my former *Mourne Observer* colleague Niki Hill, who took time out from her busy life in France to proof read the copy.

For *Bangor in the Sixties* I recalled many of my own childhood memories, resulting in a section that comprised almost 50 pages. Readers of *Bangor in the Seventies* will doubtless be delighted to know they are spared similar detail this time around. There are some things a teenager growing up anywhere, and not just in Bangor, would be too embarrassed to share.

Terence Bowman, October 2011

Soundtrack
to the Seventies

This is the 'Top Thirty' chart rundown Johnny Walker never read out on Radio One at lunchtime on a Tuesday in the Seventies. It features, in alphabetical order, the favourite songs or album tracks, as selected by contributors to *Bangor in the Seventies.*

Abba – *Fernando/Waterloo/Dancing Queen*

Barry Manilow – *Mandy*

Bee Gees – *Night Fever*

Blondie – *Denis*

Chicago – *If You Leave Me Now*

David Bowie – *Rock 'n' Roll Suicide/Life On Mars*

Don Fardon – *Belfast Boy*

Donna Summer – *I Feel Love*

Dr Hook – *A Little Bit More*

Edison Lighthouse – *Love Grows Where My Rosemary Goes*

Elvis Presley – *American Trilogy*

Francis Lai – *Bilitis* soundtrack

Free – *All Right Now*

John Lennon – *Imagine*

John Miles – *Music*

Jonathan Richman and the Modern Lovers – *Roadrunner*

Kenny Rogers – *Ruby Don't Take Your Love To Town/The Gambler*

Leonard Cohen – *Anthem*

Manfred Mann's Earthband – *Blinded By The Light*

Mud – *Tiger Feet*

Nilsson – *Without You*

Queen – *Don't Stop Me Now*

Richard Harris – *Macarthur Park*

Roxy Music – *Virginia Plain/Love Is The Drug*

Sex Pistols – *Anarchy In The UK*

Simon and Garfunkel – *Bridge Over Troubled Water*

Steely Dan – *My Old School*

Steve Harley and Cockney Rebel – *Make Me Smile (Come Up And See Me)*

T. Rex – *Hot Love*

Van Morrison – *Tupelo Honey*

The Who – *Won't Get Fooled Again*

10cc – *I'm Not In Love*

William Patterson, of 90 Churchill Park, was the new chief officer for Ireland of the National Union of Tailors and Garment Workers. He was a former district secretary of the Northern Ireland branch of the National Union of Hosiery Workers.

Sgt Jack Scully, of 14 Church Avenue, was appointed head of the RUC's drug squad. Married with four children, he had served as a constable in Bangor for a number of years before being transferred on promotion to Willowfield Police Station in Belfast.

Shops in Bangor and Newtownards were hit by an unofficial strike of butchers' assistants who wanted a shorter working week and more pay. A total walk-out of union members was reported, with some businesses closing for a short time and the meat counters at a few supermarkets also being forced to close.

Sgt Jack Scully

A spokesman for the strikers said they were asking for a rise that would lift their minimum weekly wage from £14.10s to £16. They also wanted an end to working on Saturday afternoons and a week's holiday in the winter (bringing their annual holidays to three weeks).

Striking butchers' assistants picket a Bangor shop

A branch of SHELTER was formed in Bangor to raise money for the National Campaign for the Homeless. The volunteer workers, including Nevin Robinson, one of the organisers of the meeting, launched their fundraising activities with a car wash in the car park opposite Bangor railway station. They raised £14 towards their immediate target of £325 – the cost of a house for SHELTER.

The arrival of Belfast Gas ended a tradition dating back 116 years, where the gas was manufactured by burning coal in Bangor.

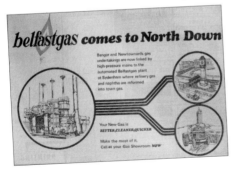

Bangor's Stormont MP Bertie McConnell opposed plans to bring Northern Ireland into line with the rest of the United Kingdom by increasing the cost of a school meal from 1/6d to 1/9d. He called for the rise to be delayed in view of the prevailing economic climate or for an increase in the qualifying line for free school meals. Both proposals were rejected by Education Minister William Long, who said there was "absolutely no alternative" to the increase.

Project Bangor, which offered a new youth centre in Hamilton House and a teenage 'Rave Cave' dance in the Borough Gymnasium, was launched with the Borough Council's approval on Saturday 21 February. It was seen as a replacement for Bangor's only teenage dance, Cloud 9, which had folded the previous December.

Bangor was hit by a spate of bomb scares in March – targets included the Queen's Court Hotel, the Royal Hotel, the Co-Op store at Main Street and Bangor Technical College. The latter's 400 students were evacuated after an anonymous letter was sent to principal George M. Jardine.

The Mayor's chain of office, which had been stolen two years earlier, was recovered on Sydenham rubbish dump on 6 April. The chain, which had been presented to the Borough in 1923 by Sir Thomas Wilson, was undamaged though "a bit scuffed."

Miss Winifred Greaves announced she would retire as headmistress of Glenlola Collegiate in December, ending a teaching career that stretched back more than 30 years. Her first teaching experience, in a temporary capacity, was at Glenlola School during the principalship of Miss Diana Coskery. She then went to Belfast Royal Academy and later Coleraine High School, where she served as vice-principal.

Miss Greaves returned to Bangor in 1951 as headmistress of Bangor Collegiate, succeeding Miss C. M. Weir. It amalgamated with Glenlola School, becoming Glenlola Collegiate, following Miss Coskery's retirement, and Miss Greaves took charge. Her successor at Glenlola would be Down County Education Committee assistant education officer James Hegan, the school's first male principal.

In late April Dr Robert Nixon, North Down's former MP at Stormont, announced he would stand as a Unionist candidate for the constituency at Westminster in the forthcoming general election. He believed the people of North Down needed an alternative Unionist choice, thereby pitting him against former West Belfast MP Jim Kilfedder, who had been selected by the North Down delegates. Others viewed it as evidence of turmoil within Unionist ranks.

The diving boards at Pickie Pool, beloved by generations of children who braved that first terrified leap from the top board, were deemed to have become dangerous and thus were removed completely in May on the orders of the Borough Council.

Cllr Robert Topping succeeded Alderman Bertie Campbell as Mayor at the annual meeting of Bangor Borough Council at the end of May. Alderman Campbell had been the town's first citizen since 1966.

London-based barrister Jim Kilfedder was elected as the new Official Unionist MP for North Down on 18 June. In all five candidates sought to represent the 121,196 electors in the Imperial constituency, with Kilfedder achieving a massive 41,433-vote majority. Kilfedder received 55,679 votes in a 66% poll, with runner-up Ken Young, representing the Northern Ireland Labour Party, the only other candidate to salvage his deposit, having achieved 14,246 votes.

Results for the other three candidates were as follows: Dr Robert Nixon, Independent Unionist, 6,408; Ritchie McGladdery, Independent Moderate, 3,321; and Major Hamilton Simonds-Gooding, Liberal, 1,076.

Newly-elected MP Jim Kilfedder is carried in triumph on Friday 19 June 1970 by supporters including Dr M. S. Smyth, chairman of the Bangor Unionist Association, and Mr Geoffrey Coulter. 227/68/2

Anne McKinnie, of Stanley Road, was awarded a Hamilton Harty Scholarship worth £100 by Queen's University. It enabled her to study music in Rome during July, in advance of joining Bangor Secondary School as a teacher of music and English. Aged 21, she was the third Bangor student in that era to be awarded a Hamilton Harty Scholarship, the others being Norma Burrowes and Suzanne Sloan.

Bangor's first 24-hour cash dispenser was installed in July at the Ulster Bank branch on the Main Street, allowing customers to withdraw £10 at any time of the day or night. At the time there were just 250 cash dispensers throughout England and Ireland.

Top department store Robinson & Cleaver, which opened its new Bangor branch on 31 July, was described as "a great asset to the people of Bangor, for it will cater not only for the tourists of Northern Ireland's premier resort, but also for many of the neighbouring towns." General manager Roger Brewster's team included Jane Arnold (accessories and gifts), George Quinn (men's shop), Isobel Boal (office), Florence Spratt (first floor merchandising), Stanley Rutherdale (linens, soft furnishings and dress fabrics) and Ellen Stewart (first floor departments).

Second Mate Martin McAvoy, from Skipperstone Road, had a narrow escape early on 9 September when his ship, the Glasgow-based *Saint Brendan,* went up in flames off the Welsh coast. The 10-man crew were taken ashore at Milford Haven by a French trawler following the blaze in the engine room.

The North Down Company of the 7th (Belfast) Battalion of the new Ulster Defence Regiment was recruiting platoons in Bangor, Newtownards, Holywood and Comber. The Company had been in operation for six months and was under the command of Mayor Robert Hayes. A number of the men were described as having "Commando, Paratroop Regiment and Ulster Special Constabulary backgrounds."

Borough Council contractors moved in to demolish houses on the north-west side of Castle Square on 2 October, leaving the view into Market Lane completely open in time for Market Day the following Wednesday. Most of the houses had been boarded up in the early 1960s with many of the residents being rehoused at Skipperstone. The short-term plan was to create additional town centre parking, but the Area Plan envisaged a shopping centre, multi-storey car park and market area.

Bangor witnessed the arrival of its first quota of traffic wardens, Messrs. A. E. Johnston, J. Pow, S. Miles and S. H. Rowan. They were under the direction of

Constable T. F. Harmon and formed the nucleus of Bangor RUC's new Traffic Control Division. Although the initial aim was to warn and redirect errant motorists, they had the power to impose £2 fixed fines.

Concorde, undertaking a series of test flights, swept down the Irish coast on 2 October, with the boom hitting Bangor at 10.18am. Despite plenty of advance warnings, the reaction varied between surprise, confusion and anger. To some the sound was not dissimilar to a bomb explosion and both the local police station and fire station were inundated with calls.

James Bowden, from 3 Wellington Gardens, who was head of the heavy crafts department at Bangor Secondary School, was installed as president of the 250-member Northern Ireland Building Trades and Handicraft Teachers Guild.

Bangor's Free Methodist Church appointed its first pastor, the Rev Eric Stewart, with the induction service being held in the church's temporary base, the Co-op Hall, on 3 December.

An action group was formed to press for the restoration of a full 24-hour casualty service at Bangor Hospital. By December the department was being closed at weekends and from 5pm on weekdays. Fears were expressed that the Northern Ireland Hospitals Authority was planning further cutbacks at both Bangor and Ards, with the Ulster at Dundonald being designated an Area Hospital.

A petition bearing 8,000 names, calling for a full-time casualty service in Bangor, was gathered within a week by action group secretary Mrs Jean Foster. It was delivered to Stormont Health Minister William Fitzsimmons by North Down MP Jim Kilfedder.

The first sod for the new £24,000 Kilcooley Presbyterian Church was cut by Mrs Weir, wife of the Rev W. Kenneth Weir, minister of both Conlig and the new Kilcooley congregation. Also in the picture are the Rev. A. H. Graham, convener of the church extension, Mr Weir, Mr H. C. Scott, treasurer, and Mr D. McRoberts, clerk of the interim session. It was hoped the new church would be completed by the end of September. *217/87/1*

First Bangor GB Juniors who won their section at the Ards District PT competition in February 1970. Back (from left): Rosalind Gray, Amanda Dunne, Carole McGowan, Christine Wallace, Anne Hamilton. Front: Shirley Major, Anne Russell, Deborah Wallace and Diane McCullough. *218/54/3*

First Bangor GB Brigaders who won their section at the Ards District PT competition in February 1970. Back (from left): Joan Bickerstaff, Heather Potts, Pat Brewster, Eve Wallace. Front: Isobel Wallace, Rosemary Rea, Barbara Taylor and Anne Preston. *218/54/3*

Mayor Bertie Campbell lays the foundation stone for the new Abbeyfield House at Bloomfield Road. It had cost £18,000 and would be ready for occupation by Christmas 1970. Looking on are the chairman of the Bangor Abbeyfield Society, Mr Hubert Nesbitt, Cllr Mrs Ethel Butler, Mr T. Waddell, builder, Mrs Campbell, and Col John Baxter, architect. 225-23-2

Members of 2nd Bangor (Abbey) Cub Scout pack who received the Meta Caswell Memorial Shield for the best pack in Bangor from the Deputy Mayor, Cllr George Storey. 227/98/3

Cherrie McIlwaine

remembers...

It seems to me now, looking back, that many of my memories of Bangor in the 70s have something to do with change.

That's not surprising I suppose, as the start of the decade began for me with an ending.

Secondary school finished and the big gear-shift between living at home and

Cherrie McIlwaine at Downtown Radio in 1976 90/2/126

moving away to university kicked in as Trinity College in Dublin became my 'other home' for the next four years.

With student life came much to-ing and fro-ing and, in the mix, summer jobs.

My return from my first heady adventure in 1970, having spent the summer working in a hotel in Copenhagen with school friends Julie and Heather, brought with it fresh eyes with which to see my home town.

A new road may seem an ordinary enough thing but

Cherrie McIlwaine was a pupil at Glenlola Collegiate from 1963 until 1970. She then attended Trinity College in Dublin where she studied English Literature, after which, with no clear direction in mind, she found welcome employment in the Civil Service helping to process grant applications for new bathrooms and kitchens for farmhouses.

When local radio came to Northern Ireland in 1976 she joined the team at Downtown Radio, where she set up the station's music library, co-ordinated the playlist and presented music programmes.

In 1983 she left Downtown Radio to join BBC Radio Ulster working in General Programmes as a Producer, initially with Walter Love on *Day by Day* and then with John Bennett on his daily magazine programme.

In 1990 she took a career break to work with the Comber Romanian Orphanage Appeal, returning to Radio Ulster in 1992.

These days she works behind the mic and currently produces and presents *The Late Show* on Tuesday, Wednesday and Thursday evenings. She also presents Radio Ulster's popular Saturday gardening programme, *Gardeners' Corner.*

I'll never forget how altered the local landscape seemed as my Dad drove me home, not along Abbey Street into Main Street and Hamilton Road and past the Tonic Cinema, but instead circumnavigating the heart of the town entirely to travel along the sweeping lines of the brand new ring road. It seemed so very modern and unexpected somehow, as if progress was in the air, and with hindsight, at odds with the changing political landscape unfolding around us.

The following summer it was Amsterdam which beckoned. On the heels of this, new friends made there came to Bangor to see our corner of the world for themselves.

How amazing, it seemed to me then, that my friend Roisin's Yugoslavian boyfriend Mica should be stepping off the train at Bangor station. Yugoslavia came to Bangor via Amsterdam on a dull summer evening and the world seemed smaller and more exciting as we introduced Mica to old Bangor landmarks like Pickie Pool, Queen's Parade and the Marine Bar.

Another summer job took me to Robinson & Cleaver's big new department store to work as a waitress in the Roof Top Restaurant. Customers there were welcomed, greeted and seated by the elegant and charming Mrs Turner whose son was to become the internationally acclaimed florist and floral designer Kenneth Turner.

Mrs Turner helped to make the learning curve easier as did new friends and colleagues like Kathleen and Valerie.

Afternoon teas were a challenge. With the cook off duty, the business of making fresh sandwiches and pancakes and manoeuvring cake-stands was left to us. It's no wonder I treated one poor customer and her pancakes to a liberal helping of salt instead of caster sugar. Thankfully she saw the funny side.

Cherrie McIlwaine today. *Photograph courtesy of BBC Northern Ireland*

With the second half of the 70s came the end of university and back home to decide what to do next.

Working life took me into the Civil Service for a while and then with great good fortune on to Downtown Radio and the exciting early days at the start of Northern Ireland's first commercial radio station. So many people were lucky to have been given the chance to learn the radio ropes at Downtown. It was a case of learn-as-you-go but all the more exciting for that and adding to the excitement were the famous names who came through the Kiltonga gates, among them Brian May, Charlie Pride, Harry Chapin, Barbara Dickson, Chris Rea, The Stranglers and radio hero, The Emperor Rosko.

But the mid point of the 70s wasn't just about finding a job and leaving behind student life. For us as a family the second half of the decade was dominated by the fact that in 1974 my lovely, funny, brave brother Barry was diagnosed with MS.

In Barry's case there was little or no remission from the ravages of his illness and he died in 1979 at the age of 25.

While Barry's life may have been short, and in spite of all he had to contend with, he had the great gift of making friends easily wherever he went. His passions were football and music and we were very grateful to the late Jim Aiken, whom I had met originally through Downtown, for always helping us to have easy wheelchair access and free passes to gig after gig.

A cherished family photograph of Cherrie's brother Barry aged 12.

These days my Mum Liz helps as a volunteer with The Monday Club who meet at The Stricklands Centre to provide a social network for people in the Bangor area with MS. It is of particular sadness to her that 30 years on, the prospect of a cure seems to be no closer.

While I may not live in Bangor any more, I'm in Bangor all the time and as with the many of us who grew up in the town during the 60s and 70s, memories from that time, and in all sorts of ways, are never far away.

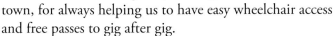

1971

IN THE SPECTATOR

Cyril Oettinger, export sales director at Oneida Silversmiths in Bangor, led an eight-week trade mission to the Australasian markets (Australia, New Zealand, Hong Kong and Japan). Involving 16 different local companies, as well as more from England and Scotland, the mission was the most extensive ever to leave Northern Ireland in search of new business.

Combat Cancer launched a new Bangor group during a meeting in the Royal Hotel on 11 January. Interim personnel included Anne O'Hara, chairman; Cllr Maisie McMullan, treasurer; Alf Eddy, projects officer, and Irene Furney, information officer.

Important archaeological discoveries in a Ballyholme resident's back garden proved the catalyst for the formation of a separate historical society for Bangor in January 1971.

Glastry Secondary School headmaster Eddie Beckett, who lived with wife Sadie and children Peter, Samuel and Judith at 17 Riverside Road, was already a long-standing and enthusiastic member of the Ards Historical Society when he com-

Glastry Secondary School headmaster Eddie Beckett, founding chairman of Bangor Historical Society in January 1971, is pictured showing some of the items he discovered in the garden of his Riverside Road home to daughter Judith and son Samuel. *Spectator picture*

menced a series of searches, which involved digging right down to the bedrock beneath his garden.

During the searches he discovered a number of noteworthy artefacts, including dozens of pieces of Norman pottery, an iron horseshoe – larger than its modern counterpart – an iron plough shoe, and the remains of a fence made from branches which would have surrounded an 800-year-old midden.

This provided ample evidence that a substantial farmhouse had existed at this point along the Ballycrochan River, which ultimately entered the sea at Ballyholme.

Further discoveries at Riverside included Bronze Age marking pegs which would have guided people through a local bog, but the most remarkable find was a polished Stone Age axe head which dated from around 3000BC and offered proof of a settlement going back some 5,000 years. All the finds were subsequently donated to the Ulster Museum.

The first meeting of the new Bangor Historical Society was held in the Good Templar Hall on 20 January, with Ards Society member Ted Griffith giving a brief talk on Bangor – from its earliest settlers to the industrial revolution. He said there was a wealth of history in the area and the town certainly merited its own society.

The meeting was chaired by Mr Beckett, who warned that "the frightening amount of development and redevelopment around the town is threatening to deprive us of our historical heritage."

Issuing Bangor's part-time firemen with pocket radios in February signalled an end to the familiar sound of the fire siren. With more and more firemen living some distance from the fire station, it was less likely they would hear the siren.

The cost of the *Spectator* was halved from Friday 19 February – but this was following the introduction of decimal currency earlier in the week. The paper had previously cost 8d and the new price was 4p (actually an increase as it was the equivalent of 9½d).

It was announced in March that Trinity Primary School would be closing that June, to coincide with the opening of the new Rathmore Primary School. In fact the closure was delayed until June 1972.

The Northern Ireland Tourist Board issued a report proposing a £1m marina for Ballyholme Bay, which it believed could turn Bangor and the surrounding area into a yachting paradise. Proposals included a 350-berth yacht harbour, car parks for around 400 vehicles, an extension to Ballyholme Yacht Club and a multi-storey car park.

Bangor Bay was also considered as it had the advantage of having three sides of the site enclosed. However, the report warned that land space would be restricted unless an area was reclaimed between the piers.

New Prime Minister Brian Faulkner had close links with North Down. His parents, Mr and Mrs James A. Faulkner, lived in Holywood and he had attended Bangor Grammar School before completing his education in Dublin. In addition, he married a Bangor girl, the former Miss Lucy Forsythe.

Lipton's new £200,000 supermarket opened at 90/105 Main Street on 30 March and welcomed 2,400 customers on the first day. In charge was Desmond Niblock, who had been with the company for 15 years.

Mayor Robert Topping invited the people of the Borough to join in a day of prayer for peace in Northern Ireland. It was held in the Council chamber on 31 March.

One-third of the 350-strong staff at the Oneida factory on the Bloomfield Road were made redundant at the beginning of April, with a company spokesman explaining: "What can you do? You've got to live within your income." The American-owned firm manufactured an extensive range of silver-plated and stainless steel knives, forks and spoons but faced intense competition from imported tableware.

Bangor became a target for the IRA bombing campaign for the first time, when a gelignite charge, estimated at 10-15lb, damaged the Strand Hotel at Southwell Road, on 20 April. No one was seriously injured, but the blast destroyed the men's toilet, ripped a hole in the lounge bar ceiling and wrecked much of the lounge and reception area.

Owner George Symonds, who had just announced plans to add a further seven rooms to the 14-bedroom hotel, believed the bar's popularity with off-duty soldiers could have prompted the attack. The premises reopened in early July.

Bangor hoteliers and guesthouse owners faced one of their worst years for business, with bookings down by 50%. By the beginning of May there would usually have been 4,000 enquiries for accommodation, but according to the town's publicity department the figure stood at just 450.

St Columbanus Secondary School secured first prize in the Schools' Gaelic Drama Festival final in Dublin. It was the first time the cup had crossed the border. Pictured with the trophies are Maureen Allen, John Carmichael (narrator and stage manager), Eilish Duffy along with Peter Morris (producer).

The Ministry of Education took over the former Cyril Lord office block at Rathgael and added a new annexe. The buildings were occupied by 400 civil servants, previously housed at Dundonald House outside Belfast. Public representatives hoped the arrival of such a large workforce would boost Bangor's economy.

A major facelift to Bangor railway station meant the 'end of the line' for the outside clock, which for many years had been a part of life in the town. While there was a clock inside the station for the convenience of passengers, Northern Ireland Railways advised Councillors that any external clock would be the local authority's responsibility. Almost two years later, in February 1973, a replacement clock was put in place, courtesy of the Northern Bank.

Back (from left): Mr J. P. Simms, Mr W. J. Irwin, Mr Wilson, the Rev. David Burke. Front: the Rev. R. S. G. Gilmore, the Rev. Ken Newell, the Rev. J. Lorimer and the Rev. W. K. Weir, Moderator of the Ards Presbytery.
243/24/1

The Rev Ken Newell – a future Moderator of the Presbyterian Church in Ireland – was installed at a service in Hamilton Road Presbyterian Church in June to undertake work with the Church's Overseas Board in West Timor, Indonesia.

As the first stage in the provision of a marina at Bangor Bay – preferred to

Bangor resident William Atwell, of Kearney Gardens in Kilcooley, became the first local victim of the Troubles when, on Monday 9 August 1971, he was fatally injured in a nail bomb attack.

It was the day internment was reintroduced in Northern Ireland, sparking an upsurge of violence, with a total of 17 people losing their lives within the space of 48 hours.

Mr Atwell (40), who was survived by his wife and two sons, worked as security officer at Mackie's engineering works on the Springfield Road in Belfast. The nail bomb had been thrown into his office, purportedly by republicans, killing Mr Atwell instantly. He had worked for the company for 22 years, mainly as a machinist. Amid fears of redundancies in the machine shop he had moved to security work just three months earlier.

Interment took place at Clandeboye Cemetery following a service in the Groomsport Road home of his father-in-law.

Mrs Sarah Worthington, 58-year-old widowed mother of Queen's Parade businessman Cecil Worthington and seven other children, was shot dead by a British soldier in her home in the Ardoyne area of Belfast, also on 9 August 1971. An inquest was told she had been the entirely innocent victim of a tragic mistake.

Her son, in a letter to the *Spectator* a week after Mrs Worthington's death, thanked the people of Bangor, on behalf of the family circle, for their expressions of sympathy.

A *Spectator* editorial referred to the two deaths, as well as that of Fr Hugh Mullan, a native of Portaferry, who had been shot in the Ballymurphy area of Belfast while administering the Last Rites to an injured man.

"To the families so tragically bereaved we tender sympathy and express the hope that the loss of innocent and valuable lives will not be in vain – that out of the awful tragedy, somehow, some time, a better community will emerge," it stated.

Ballyholme – it was agreed by the Borough Council that the old wooden section of the North Pier would be "filled in" to create a solid structure. The Council acknowledged the marina project could be undertaken in phases over a number of years.

An IRA firebomb attack on Saturday 26 June failed because some of the incendiaries exploded as staff were still in the targeted premises. In all, 18 devices were found in eight different businesses. High Street targets were the Pink Petticoat, Baillie's and Bell's, the Bookworm and Wilson's Linens, along with the Belfast Co-operative Society store, Wellworth's and Woolworth's on Main Street.

Dunnes Stores opened at 71 Main Street on 2 July 1971.

Crazy Prices opened at the Springhill Shopping Centre on Friday 30 July.

Singer Davy Jones of Monkees fame made a late visit to Milanos on 3 July. After appearing in Lurgan the previous evening, he had returned to London to be with his wife, who had gone into labour. The baby arrived at 7.30pm, whereupon the pop star caught a flight to Belfast that ensured his arrival in Bangor before midnight.

Royal Humane Society Awards were presented by Resident Magistrate Martin McBirney to Gay Wells (18), of 4 Ballyholme Esplanade, and Rosalind McCartney (17), of 4 Dixon Avenue, for assisting a young man who had got into difficulties at Ballyholme Beach.

The Bangor Emergency Refugee Relief Committee, chaired by Cllr Mary O'Fee, was formed in August to help people made homeless by the violence in Belfast. Initially they assisted a family to find and purchase a home in Bangor and they also contributed £50 towards sending 78 children to Liverpool. An outing to Bangor was arranged for a group of senior citizens from the Springmount area, while food and clothing was sent to a refugee centre based in Black Mountain Primary School.

A Bangor branch of the Ulster Loyalist Association was formed in the Ballyholme Hotel on 9 September. Officers included George Green (president), Bruce Mulligan (chairman), David Lyle (secretary) and Beryl Holland (press officer).

They called for the Ulster Special Constabulary to be reformed "to save Ulster from the blood-thirsty Republican conspiracy which has been launched against us" and accused Prime Minister Harold Wilson of "fuelling the fires by his open Nationalist bias."

In early October vigilantes were patrolling at Kilcooley "for the protection of the residents." The *Spectator* reported "this unofficial body of residents is 70-strong, equipped with two-way radios, and claims to be operating with the full knowledge of the police."

A spokesman said the vigilantes were unarmed and he described as "nonsense" rumours that men had been seen walking around the estate armed with cudgels.

Chief Inspector William Gow said there had been no trouble on the town's largest estate and the police were aware of the presence of the vigilantes, "but we sincerely trust the time will never come when they are required."

INTIMIDATION! RUMOUR

IF
YOU NEED
HELP OR ADVICE
CONTACT YOUR
LOCAL POLICE STATION

ISSUED BY THE PUBLIC INFORMATION CENTRE

The decade's first by-election saw former Castlereagh Rural Council vice-chairman Bruce Mulligan being returned in October as Councillor for the Castle Ward. He represented the Ulster Loyalist Association and received 1,025 votes in a 47% poll. Unionist Chalmers Quee received 642 votes and Liberal Tony Coghlan 204.

Central Avenue was made a one-way street from Main Street to Southwell Road, with the stretch from Southwell Road to Princetown Road remaining two-way.

'Damsels demand disco' was the heading over a letter published in the *Spectator* of 10 December. It read: "We are some of the youth of Bangor who are obliged to frequent the Queen's Parade at weekends. Those who complain should realise this is from a total lack of anything better to do.

Skandia

means something special
for you . . . in Bangor !

IT'S MORE THAN THAT, IT'S VERY SPECIAL.

This newest Skandia has been designed to make you relax — you can't help yourself — it's the restful warm glowing decor. You'll appreciate the peaceful cosmopolitan atmosphere while enjoying the delights of SKANDIA's unique international dishes . . . they're really special.

MAKE THAT CELEBRATION DINNER A TRULY MEMORABLE ONE. ENJOY IT AT THE NEW SKANDIA.

It's a new experience in dining out.

The Skandia Restaurant opened above Lipton's at upper Main Street in November 1971.

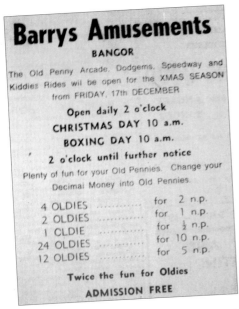

Barrys Amusements

BANGOR

The Old Penny Arcade. Dodgems. Speedway and Kiddies Rides wil be open for the XMAS SEASON from FRIDAY, 17th DECEMBER

Open daily 2 o'clock
CHRISTMAS DAY 10 a.m.
BOXING DAY 10 a.m.

2 o'clock until further notice

Plenty of fun for your Old Pennies. Change your Decimal Money into Old Pennies.

4 OLDIES	for	2 n.p.
2 OLDIES	for	1 n.p.
1 OLDIE	for	½ n.p.
24 OLDIES	for	10 n.p.
12 OLDIES	for	5 n.p.

Twice the fun for Oldies

ADMISSION FREE

"At present two cinemas and one cafe are available to us. We cannot be expected to sit watching films several nights a week. Hanging around on the seafront is bound to breed trouble so why can't those in authority at least provide a dance or disco, which is what we need most to keep us off the streets.

"Surely a large and growing town like Bangor could provide something better than at present for their young people aged between 15 and 18. After all, we are your responsibility."

The letter was signed by Cherry Hardiman, Elinor Conn, Moira Howe, Julia Martin, Gail Martin, Jayne Mawhinney, Caroline McCartney, Mandy Jackson, Ellen McMeekin, Rosemary Hogg, Linda McCormick, Deirdre Goggin, Jennifer Bolster, Jill Milliken and Jan McKee.

There was a second by-election in the Castle Ward within two months and once again there was success for the Ulster Loyalist Association, with George Green beating Unionist Chalmers Quee by 177 votes in a 33% poll on 16 December. Mr Green received 768 votes, Mr Quee 591 and third-placed Tony Coghlan (Liberal) 117.

John Foster, of 59 Brunswick Road, passed his driving test on his 17th birthday – 22 December. Son of a driving instructor, John had only three hours of practice on a public road before sitting the test. Other driving experience was gained in his own garden. Richard Stewart Graham, of 62 Silverstream Road, repeated the feat in October 1974.

Officials and guests of the Bangor Vintners' Association at their annual dinner, which was held in February 1971 at the New Mount Royal Hotel, Donaghadee. Included are Mr and Mrs D. Gillespie (secretary), Mr and Mrs H. Sheenan (secretary of Belfast Vintners' Association), Mr and Mrs M. Lennon, Mr and Mrs H. Caren, Mr and Mrs R. McLaughlin, Mr and Mrs J. Fealty and Mr and Mrs J. Donegan. *237/57/1*

Alan Dunlop (centre, right), of the building firm E. & A. Dunlop Ltd., presents the Building Industry Trophy to Stephen McKeown, of Church Drive, Bangor, in March 1971. The award went to the student with the best record in the Building Department of North Down Technical Area. Included are principal G. M. Jardine (left), J. A. Gunning, head of the Building Department, and S. W. Browne, vice-principal. *238/7/2*

Education Minister and Ards area MP Capt William Long (eighth from left) welcomed a deputation of clergy from the North Down area to Stormont in May 1971. They were protesting over plans by the Ministry of Health and Social Services to integrate local hospital and health services into a large Area Board covering Belfast and the South Eastern area. They were also seeking an assurance that Bangor, Ards and Crawfordsburn Hospitals would not be run down. 240/42/2

Eileen Gilbert, Red Cross deputy president of County Down, presents long service medals to Margaret Mitchell (20 years) and Sybil Mudd (15 years) in June 1971. Included is Mayoress Mrs R. Topping. Not in the picture were Dorothy Bunting and Anne Brennan, who had both given 25 years of service to the Red Cross. 241/32/2

Mr W. Houston, of Bangor Sea Angling Club, whose 10lb 7½oz cod won the prize for heaviest catch at a holiday festival fishing competition in Groomsport in June 1971. *242/76/1*

Frances McKimm, of Newtownards Road, Bangor, with her Irish Setter bitch Trawrickca Golden Ambition, which was judged best of breed at the Newtownards and District Canine Show in June 1971. *242/3/1*

Mr R. Thompson, managing director of the Northern Ireland Bacon Company Ltd., presents a cheque for £130 to Maurice Flowers, chairman of Bangor Round Table. The company was sponsoring Bangor's Learn to Swim Week in the summer of 1971. Included are Northern Ireland athlete Mary Peters, who officially opened the event, and project organiser David Dunseath. *242/19/1*

The 12th Down (Bangor) Troop of the Catholic Boy Scouts of Ireland with visiting Scouters after an investiture ceremony in St Comgall's Church, Brunswick Road, in May 1971.

Gary Devon
remembers...

Schoolboy exhibits in Bangor bookshop

Thirteen-year-old Gary Devon with some of his paintings which are on exhibition in Hugh Greer's Bookshop, Hamilton Road, Bangor.

A ONE-MAN art exhibition with a slight difference is being staged in Mr. Hugh Greer's Hamilton Road bookshop. The oil paintings are all the work of a 13-year-old Bangor boy.

Gary Devon is the youngest son of Mr. and Mrs. Stanley A. Devon, Kensington Park. He is head boy of Rockport School, Craigavad.

Gary has been painting since he was 11. He tried water colours without any great success, but found his medium in oils. He began, like most painters, by copying the styles of other artists; more recently his own style has emerged, and it certainly shows great maturity and promise. His work is impressionist, often surrealist, he paints landscapes — mountains and sweeping moorlands — and seascapes, for which he has a genuine feel. Almost always blue is the key colour, and the mood varies from the gentle tranquility of becalmed yachts at misty evening to the vitality of construction and treatment of some of his landscapes.

Will he follow in the steps of Picasso and Kandinsky? Gary thinks it's a little early to wonder what he'll do when he leaves school.

JOY BANNISTER

When the author approached me about this book he emailed me a copy of the very same *Spectator* article I'd coincidentally only just rediscovered in my mother's collection of family memorabilia. So memories are already stirred.

It was Mum's sentimental habit to cut out any *Spectator* article to do with her offspring. It was no coincidence that Mum and Dad were friends with the paper's owners, David and Lolita Alexander. Further into the 70s my sporting activities were also recorded. Little did I know at the time of Mum's subterfugal part in the articles' coming to be. Truth be told I was only too glad of my celebrity status and confess to the head-swelling eagerness of searching out the headline after a trip to the newsagent.

That article roughly marked the start of the 70s for me and ironically the *Spectator* office was where I would end up at the close of the decade as a would-be journalist. For the most part, however, contact with my home town throughout that decade was interrupted due to my education. Starting with Rockport, I went on to board at Campbell College, thence over (or 'up', as they say) to Cambridge University in 1977.

My previously close childhood relationship with Bangor – particularly my coastline playground between Carnalea

Born Bangor 1958. Educated at Garth House and Rockport Preparatories (1965-71) and Campbell College (1971-76). Abortive attempt at law degree at Cambridge University. Foundation art course at Jordanstown Polytechnic and on to Goldsmiths' College in London to do BA in Fine Art

(1982-85).

Stayed on in London for three years after college, painting professionally. Did commissioned painting of Kensington Palace for HRH Prince of Wales. Returned home to Bangor and has painted full-time ever since, exhibiting in various galleries in the north and south of Ireland, also publishing prints of local scenes and various institutions and teaching privately part-time.

Commissioned works include the 200 sq. ft. mural in North Down Museum depicting the coastline between Ballyholme and Groomsport (1989). Elected Associate Member of Royal Ulster Academy in 2006 and now serving on Council. RUA Conor Prize winner (2002) and Landscape Prize winner (2010).

Hobbies: three children, fishing, golf and growing vegetables.

Gary Devon during his time at Cambridge

and Pickie Pool – was broken. Yet Bangor still catered nicely for my holiday and weekend needs. My interests were also now sophisticated – from boyhood stickleback fishing in Stricklands Glen, I graduated to adult mackerel fishing with a spinning rod and bright orange fluorescent float from the North Pier.

This was a dare-devil activity, carrying not only the risk of death from the imminent collapse of the precariously balanced and rotting wooden structure, but also the possibility of a trespassing offence, involving stealing onto the pier around the edge of the metal gate which arched prohibitively over the edge and was fortified menacingly but ultimately in vain with barbed wire.

I was in even greater peril as I had not learned to swim – the icy waters of Pickie Pool and Andy Johnston's rope technique had seen to that. I had all the arrogance of youth as I sat, feet dangling over the edge, eyes fixed on my bright orange float waiting for it to plunge under the surface and for the ensuing, energetic tugging of a shiny blue/green/silver mackerel, its flanks glinting as it emerged from the deep, deep water, into which I fortunately never fell.

But I did fall for the charms of a certain Miss Josephine. We met the odd night at 7.30 at the North Pier and were sometimes together all day Sunday. She took me to far-away places, such as Black Head or The Gobbins, where she idled away her time, rocking back and forth while I caught herring after herring. *Miss Josephine,* the deep-sea public fishing boat, was captained by salty dog Victor, whose weather-beaten wife Diana could gut and fillet a fish as fast as she could roll a cigarette.

I simultaneously and curiously developed an interest in painting. Bill and Anne O'Hara, owners of the Royal Hotel, and my grandmother unwittingly promoted it. Granny Devon, a remote, venerable Victorian widow, who I cannot imagine had anyone resembling a close friend, found me useful for distraction. It was her occasional pastime to escape the musty confines of her Seacourt flat and to take me out in her Morris Minor (a thousand unnecessary, fumbling gear changes per journey) for lunch or afternoon tea at such venues as The Stables in

Groomsport or Bangor's 'Ritz', The Rendezvous, or the Royal Hotel. The cleanliness and presentability of my face was paramount in Granny's eyes, so she carried a wet flannel in her capacious handbag. One day she had forgotten the flannel, so I was cleaned with a hankie and some surprisingly less than ceremonious spit.

I was ritually paraded to those who came up to bid their hellos and farewells to 'Mrs Devon', never 'Elizabeth'. I was patted on the head and told what a good boy I was. Jelly and ice-cream or lemon meringue was my consolation for such public humiliation. The ladies who served wore their perfect black skirts and pristine, starched white aprons and small white hats. They looked almost as if they belonged to a religious order. Mrs Sharples always served Granny. Molly was another of the waitresses and I had the privilege of meeting her again recently. She's a resident at a care home I visited as an art therapist. I'd no idea who she was but she instantly cottoned on to my name and indeed remembered me – it was a treat to talk about the good ol' days and a fondly remembered Mrs Devon.

Of the venues the Royal Hotel was my preference for on the walls were paintings to which I was inexorably attracted. I had already taken to some daubing of my own after discovering an unused box of oil paints in the house – an unwanted present for my brother. Why as a 10/11-year-old I got a buzz out of art I cannot say to this day, but I was smitten by the look, feel, colour and smell of oil paint and I was enthralled by Kenneth Webb's sweeping, palette-knifed panoramas of glowing white gables of thatched cottages under dramatic cobalt skies and impossible landscape reds. Norman McCaig's harbours and boats also appealed.

Perhaps there was something already built into my system which allowed me to appreciate the plasticity of paint, particularly the thick impasto variety. A brickie's trowel and a palette knife are after all cousins and as a seven-year-old I recall my strange fascination for cement. Our neighbours in Kensington Park, the Collinsons, employed a handyman whom I'd 'help'. He showed me how to crazy-pave. Blue Circle Cement and I were instant friends. Aware of my craze for crazy paving, Dad once bought me a bag of cement and a brickie's trowel for my birthday, so pretty soon other neighbours had some of my crazy paving in their garden.

When my interest in and the demand for crazy paving died out, I began to paint pictures with a vengeance. I voraciously copied postcards, images from *Teach Yourself To Paint* books, magazine photographs, etc. At times Mum would sit and paint along with me. Without a moment's tuition she was a natural then and still is. Today she comes to my classes and is one of my best students.

From the point of view of my career it was a stroke of fortune perhaps that I ended up at Rockport. It was an eccentric place which, by dint of its beachside location, felt fun but also because of its ethos, as promoted by headmaster Eric Tucker. Extra-curricular and very Rockport activities were to the fore. Education was as much to do with what went on outside the classroom as in it: helping school groundsman Eddie gather the spuds from the field up the driveway (I now grow my own spuds), rifle shooting (I love clay pigeon shooting), music (I can listen to Mahler, Chopin et al all day) and 'kick the can' on the beach (don't bother so much with that these days).

Eric, who was also our Latin teacher, had some novel ideas for drumming that strange language into us. To this day I can recite *Waltzing Matilda* in Latin: 'Tendit in fusis amnis ero lacibus, Quis comit ambliclatella mihi. Cecinit qui tuens dum fervit igne cacibus...'

Of all the opportunities Rockport provided, the hobbies competition was tailor-made for me. Winning it set me on fire. I 'turned professional' at 11, selling my first work to another neighbour, surgeon Bill Bassett, for three guineas. Edwin Dunlop of Dunlop Properties, a business friend of my father, happened to know my hero, Kenneth Webb, and arranged a meeting. From that point on I was hooked.

Arthur McFadden, who used to sell art materials on High Street, let me exhibit a painting in his shop window. I remember the huge pride I felt at seeing it lit up when I passed at night. After that, local bookshop owner Hugh

Greer – another friend of my parents – offered me an exhibition.

Another bug I caught in my teens was golf. The juveniles' hut, fairways and practice ground of Bangor Golf Club were my second home. I could not get enough, often playing 36 holes per day. Ernie Jones was the Pro and later David Jones, whose wife, Noreen, made bespoke trousers. Whacky flares were in vogue and I sought out the zaniest coloured, checked curtain material I could find. What a clown I must have looked.

Mum, a 4-handicapper herself, encouraged my golf. Some fellow but better juniors also inspired. Garth McGimpsey, later a Walker Cup player, and big Stu Irvine impressed me with their power and control. On a good day I was once able to match future Ryder Cup star David Feherty stroke for stroke. But the swing I always tried to bear in mind when addressing the ball was that of now retired Bangor solicitor and fellow Campbellian Graham Neill. It was sheer elegance, poise and simplicity and it served me well as a model to bear in mind when I probably played the best golf of my life, the year I made it through to the semi-finals of the Ulster Boys Championship.

Until the semis I couldn't miss a fairway or a green. I destroyed an Irish schoolboy international 7/6 in the quarters but, golf being golf, I fell apart in the semis against future Pro Jimmy Heggarty. I may have had the swing but my nerves got the better of me and I myself was trounced. But my trousers were nicer than his.

Art took a back seat at Campbell as more academic studies prevailed. No one ever suggested there was a possible life/career in art. However, I can only blame myself for not thinking specifically of art as a career choice for I never considered at all at that stage what should have been the wider and burning question: "Whadda you wanna be?" Sheep-like, I followed a line of other intelligent, articulate Campbellians who'd studied languages, went 'up' to Cambridge to study law and made a success of it.

To this day I wonder what possessed me. I hadn't a clue what it was all about, but presumably I'd crack it. However a year's worth of agonised and abortive study was as far as I got down that particular road. The amassed and various tomes required for my first year's study were a truly awesome proposition to me. Never having been a great reader I baulked at their number and thickness and I don't believe I had the necessary composition of grey matter to store legal case history then recall it in an instant, applying the appropriate principle to the case at hand. Or was I just lazy?

I eventually collapsed under the strain of the workload. I remember sitting in the afternoon summer sun on the steps of the Senate House Library, taking a break from the impossible 11th hour revision before the first year exams, and saying to a friend I was doomed. His jaunty reply was that no one ever failed those exams. How right I was and how wrong he! As someone later joked to me by way of consolation: "Sure, you didn't want to be a policeman anyway."

I can partly blame hockey for my lack of commitment to my studies. It was at the same time a contributory factor in and an escape from the nightmare of the drudgery and mounting backlog of work. At Rockport hockey had been one of the sports on the menu and I loved it. Tony McMillen, a former pupil and ex-international, came to play one day and I recall his astonishing aerial flicks and the graceful way he controlled the ball.

Hockey became a big part of my life. At Campbell I went on to play at international schoolboy level and later at Irish Under 21 level, captaining the side at a World Cup tournament in Paris. I played my way straight onto the university 1st X1 and enjoyed the sporting high of playing at Lords in the annual varsity match against Oxford, winning my much prized Cambridge Blue.

Gary Devon in his hockey playing days at Campbell College

My humiliating academic failure was my much needed wake-up call after a privileged and cloistered upbringing. The option was to return to try to repeat the exams, but I knew that wasn't going to work out, so I stayed put in Bangor. But what to do then became the question. An interim solution was a summer job as a greenkeeper with Johnny Mooney and his gang on the golf course. The work was hard and, almost literally, back-breaking. My favourite job was cutting the greens for I got to operate the five-headed, sit-on mower. One day at the 18th, with my concentration on the mower head closest to the edge, I let the back wheel fall into a bunker. Somewhat embarrassed by my mishap in full view of the members watching from the clubhouse and too proud to go for help, I got down on my hunkers and inched the rear of the mower back onto the green. I didn't notice the strain until the following morning when I was barely able to move for the pain in my lower back. That was the start of serious back trouble for many years, resulting eventually in an operation by Donaghadee surgeon Alistair McAfee to remove part of a vertebra impinging on the nerve. It was a great success, so much so I was up playing sport again only months afterwards.

Thanks to the injury my green-keeping days were over, so another, lighter job had to be found. Wellworths provided. The job was not that much lighter and neither was it going to be my vocation, but my new role as storeman was a job and it got me by. In fact I enjoyed it. There was always plenty to do off-loading the regular 40ft lorries at the loading bay at the car park off King Street and squashing the hundreds of cardboard boxes in the adjacent giant squasher machine. Oh, how good it felt to press that button.

I enjoyed the company of my workmates too. There was the odd moment of stir-crazy, storeroom madness involving toilet roll hurling between us, including others my own age and Tommy, a 70-plus ex-welder from the shipyard, who told us of the days when people would cycle from Millisle to Belfast to work there.

During my time off I became curious about Dad's long-abandoned photographic darkroom set-up in the downstairs cloakroom/ loo. His old black and white family photos were stored in a wooden cabinet he'd made himself. They were great and I wanted to know all about photography. I'd got myself a cheap as chips but very reliable 35mm Russian Zenith camera and a £100 black and white home development kit, including an enlarger, from Chris Ward's shop in High Street. I picked Dad's brains, blacked out the tiny room for the second time in its life and got stuck into another enduring pastime, which in turn put me in mind of approaching the *Spectator*. Photographers were not in demand as such, but proof-readers, van-drivers, gofers, and general hands-on-deck were, so I ended up doing just about everything.

Gary Devon during a recent visit to the North Down Museum (previously the Heritage Centre), where his mural remains a popular attraction.

When questioned by editor Annie Roycroft about my life thus far, I was persuaded to consider reporting. I thought: "Why not?" Perhaps my attempt at the weekly canine report – "the worst that ever appeared in the *Spectator*", according to the doggy person who'd submitted the results and complained bitterly – should have been a warning. On reflection I might have made a decent journalist. While I may not have known my Shih Tzus from my Lhasa Apsos, I could string a sentence together, but, true to form, I opted out of the *Spectator* after a year and much to Annie's annoyance after she had persuaded me and possibly pulled a few strings for me to join a pre-entry journalism course in Belfast. I lasted but a day and came home thinking: "Now what the hell will I do?" I wasn't proud of myself but I knew I hadn't yet found my "thing." Good ol' Mum to the rescue: "You used to like to paint," she said. "What about art college?"

Four years later I had my degree in Fine Art from Goldsmiths' College in London. I've painted professionally ever since, I'm back in Bangor, I fish for trout these days, usually with Josh Reynolds, fellow pupil and now teacher at Rockport (we both grow spuds and veg), I still visit Stricklands Glen with my kids and shimmy across the cast-iron railings above the waterfall at the lower pool, looking out for sticklebacks, I met Johnny Mooney twice recently, I get very frustrated that I can't keep the ball on the fairway as regularly as I used to, I couldn't run the length of myself these days, so hockey is not an option, but I cannot imagine a better life.

1972

IN THE SPECTATOR

Borough Councillors were advised that 280 Bangor applicants were awaiting Council houses. Mindful of the need to help those made homeless by the Troubles in Belfast, they were also anxious to see fair treatment for long-term residents.

Mr and Mrs James Woods, owners of the Redcliffe Hotel on the Seacliff Road, were bereaved when their only son, Peter Gerald (Gerry), was shot dead by three men who broke into his Belfast home on Saturday 8 January.

The murdered man, who was 29 and the father of two young children, lived at Lowwood Park, off the Shore Road, and was part-owner of the Gibraltar Bar on nearby York Street. The motive appeared to have been robbery, with speculation that the UVF was responsible.

The funeral service in St Comgall's Church, Brunswick Road, was followed by interment at Clandeboye Cemetery.

BANGOR FAMILY'S TRAGIC BEREAVEMENT
Son murdered in city

A BANGOR COUPLE were tragically bereaved on Saturday when their only son, 29-year-old Peter Gerald Woods, was murdered by armed men who broke into his home in Belfast and stole £500.

Mr. Woods, a married man with two young children—Jim aged four and Christine aged three—lived at 38 Lowwood Park, and was part-owner of the Gibraltar Bar in York Street.

His parents, Mr. and Mrs. James Woods, own the Redcliffe Hotel, Seacliff Road, Bangor.

Around 1.30 a.m. on Saturday three men broke into Mr. Woods's home where he and his wife Eilish were counting the takings from the bar.

It is believed that the men followed Mr. Woods from the bar to his home. The robbers broke a glass panel in the front door with a hatchet and burst into the living room one carrying a gun.

Mr. Woods was shot in the head and died instantly.

During the incident the two children were asleep upstairs.

DECENT MAN

Friends of the family living in the Lowwood Park area described Mr. Woods as a quiet, decent man, who would have done anything for anybody.

The public bar had only recently been redecorated after it had been severely damaged by a petrol bomb. Since the beginning of the disturbances in the City several attempts have been made to destroy the

premises—the only one left at the railway station end of York Street. Others had been destroyed by explosions and others pulled down as part of a new road scheme.

The funeral took place on Tuesday to Clandeboye Cemetery following Mass in St. Comgall's Church. Many of the mourners were unable to get into the small church and stood outside in heavy rain.

Mr. Eddie Houston retires

A POPULAR member of Bangor Gas Undertaking's staff, Mr. E. E. Houston, Beatrice Road, has retired after over 30 years' service.

Eddie, as he is known to his gas works and bowling colleagues, was installations inspector.

The Rev Ian Paisley, a frequent visitor to Bangor for religious meetings, made his first trip to the town to speak on politics. His talk in Hamilton House on 24 January was entitled "The Ulster crisis and the way out." He opposed the Government's ban on parades, declaring that loyalists had to march in 1972 or they would never march again.

It was announced that a branch of the new Democratic Unionist Party was being formed in Bangor. Amongst its first members was Beryl Holland, who announced her resignation from the Ulster Unionist Party. She served as secretary, with David Browne chairman and Raymond Beattie vice-chairman.

The same venue was chosen for a meeting of the Ards/ Bangor branch of the New Ulster Movement, which had been formed in 1969 and campaigned for political, economic and social reforms in Northern Ireland. The speakers included Nationalist MP Austin Currie – a founder member of the new SDLP – and Richard Ferguson, former Ulster Unionist MP for South Antrim.

The venue was changed to a Belfast hotel after the organisers learned loyalists intended to protest over Mr Currie's presence on the platform.

An acute shortage of junior medical staff at Ards and Bangor Hospitals led to the temporary closure of the casualty department in Bangor, prompting fears it would become permanent. The department reopened at the end of August but closed again within weeks.

The Borough Council opened Brice Park, on the High Donaghadee Road, on 8 February without any formal ceremony. It was named after Fred Brice, who had given the ground to the authority 30 years earlier.

Bangor businessmen, commuters and those involved in the tourist trade welcomed an announcement in February that Belfast's Central Railway Line would be restored, with a new station being constructed at Maysfield to replace the Great Victoria Street and Queen's Quay stations. The scheme meant that once again excursion trains would reach Bangor directly from Dublin and places along the line such as Lisburn, Portadown and Newry.

Bangor MP Bertie McConnell, along with colleagues Tom Gormley (Mid-Tyrone) and Phelim O'Neill (North Antrim), joined the Alliance Party, thus becoming its first representatives at Stormont. Mr McConnell, who was also a Bangor Councillor, had stood for the seat as an Independent Unionist, beating official candidate Bertie Campbell.

Some 2,000 loyalists, under the banner of the newly-formed Ulster Vanguard movement, packed Castle Park on 19 February to "reaffirm their allegiance to the Crown and Constitution and to state that, if necessary [failure to restore Stormont with increased powers], they would establish an independent British Ulster."

The speakers included founder William Craig MP, George Allport, Official Unionist candidate for Bangor at Stormont, Loyalist Councillor George Green,

Members of Ulster Vanguard stand in line awaiting inspection by William Craig MP

Capt Austin Ardill, former Unionist MP for Carrick, and Billy Hull, of the Loyalist Association of Workers.

Former Mayor Fred Tughan officially opened 1st Bangor Scouts' new hall on the Donaghadee Road. A former 1st Bangor Scout himself, Mr Tughan was among a large number of contributors whose generosity ensured the new hall was completely free of debt. It replaced their previous 'hut' in Ward Park, home to the Scouts for 41 years.

Mercifully no lives were lost after terrorists left two car bombs in Main Street on Friday 24 March. They caused extensive damage, with windows shattered at locations as far apart as the Royal Hotel, Queen's Parade and Hamilton Road.

A woman caller at 12.30am had warned there was a bomb in lower Main Street. An hour later the first of the two explosions occurred, after the police, aided by civilians, had evacuated all residents from the Main Street/ King Street area. Four hours later the Army detonated the second bomb. Again there

The damage was extensive – as far as Bridge Street (above) and Queen's Parade (below). *Pictures donated to North Down Museum in 2004 by Maurice Boal*

Unattended parking advert – 7 April 72

was widespread damage.

Among businesses forced to close or move to temporary premises were the dry cleaning firm of H. McRoberts and Son, opticians Harris Rundle Ltd., Femina Hairstyles, and Lennon Bros., whose fruit shop was completely destroyed along with the Rendezvous Restaurant.

Loyalists succeeded in bringing Bangor to a virtual standstill on 27 and 28 March, following a call from Ulster Vanguard to protest at the imposition of Direct Rule from Westminster. Some shops that remained open had their windows broken and the police received a number of reports of intimidation. On the second morning over 1,000 loyalists took part in an unlawful parade around the town.

A bomb containing 30lbs of gelignite virtually destroyed the Feedwell pet food factory on the Belfast Road on 29 April, wrecking cars and breaking many windows in the process. Debris landed on roofs and in gardens in the area and also on the railway line, causing trains to be stopped and traffic diverted. The factory had been out of production since an earlier fire.

Ulster Plastics on the Clandeboye Road was closed by its Manchester parent company at the beginning of May, with the loss of 120 jobs. Efforts by the Ministry of Commerce to find a suitable replacement tenant proved successful, with the factory reopening under new management in June. They hoped to have 80 employees on their books within two to three years.

Seven members, including two Bangor Councillors, were expelled from the Bangor Unionist Association in early May for actions deemed incompatible with membership of the party. The expulsions, by the executive committee, followed George Green's election to Bangor Borough Council, despite the presence of an official party candidate.

Along with Cllr Green and his son Paul, those expelled were Cllr Mary O'Fee, Neil Oliver, Cecil Black and George Dickson and Hannah McCalmont. Two weeks later George Allport, a founder of Ulster Vanguard, was similarly expelled from the Association – although he insisted he remained the party's official candidate for Bangor at the next Stormont election (an election that would never happen).

Also in May, the Bangor Loyalist Association formally offered its allegiance to Ulster Vanguard, thereby becoming its Bangor branch. By the summer a second branch was formed in Kilcooley.

Saturday morning talent shows, so popular at the Tonic Cinema in the early 1960s, were revived at the rival Queen's Cinema between June and August 1972. The programme included Safety First films, cartoons and music by Ken Gillen's band City Sound, along with guest performers.

The Parent-Teacher Association of Glenlola Collegiate rejected, by a substantial majority, a suggestion by the Down County Education Committee that it could be amalgamated with the town's new Girls' Secondary School to form a "non-selective, comprehensive structure of education for girls in Bangor."

The erection of barricades in Bangor by the Ulster Defence Association over the weekend of 10-11 June was described as "magnificent" by Cllr Bruce Mulligan at a Vanguard meeting in the town. He further declared: "If anyone suffered inconvenience it was for the good of Ulster."

You wouldn't give a terrorist a gun... so don't let him have your car!

Remember! All car bombs are left in stolen vehicles, so...
Make sure your car is securely locked at all times.
If it doesn't have a steering column lock, fit an anti-theft device.
If your house has a garage use it and keep it locked.
Be careful where you park.
Should your car be stolen, report it to the police immediately.
Use the 5-point plan to beat the car bomber

Official barricades, with the aim of stopping the car bombers, were erected in Bangor overnight on 22/23 June. Lower Main Street, High Street, the east side of Bridge Street and Quay Street all became pedestrian precincts.

Although the ban also applied to taxis, vehicles owned

by employees of town centre businesses and commercial travellers, buses were still permitted up and down Main Street and High Street.

Four families, one Protestant and three Catholic, moved out of the Skipperstone Estate in late June/ early July following the first instances of serious sectarian strife. A mother-of-eight was dragged from her home in Lisnabreen Walk before her furniture was piled high in the front garden and set alight. The incident had involved about 20 masked men who also assaulted a 15-year-old boy. In a separate episode a Catholic family left the estate after shots were fired into their Lismore Avenue home.

The Ministry of Education opened discussions on the provision of a new central library for Bangor Borough. Reports on possible sites were submitted to the Council's Library and Museum Committee in July, with the most suitable location being the site of the Carnegie Library at Hamilton Road.

Fifty Belfast families, all Protestant, were illegally occupying houses in the Kilcooley Estate, after being moved there with the help of the local Vanguard group. A spokesman said they had acted because they were worried about an "unequal number of Roman Catholic families moving into the estate." He added: "We are just trying to make sure this estate will be one which is peaceful to live in."

Severe structural damage was caused to the Bangor Girls' Secondary School assembly hall by an accidental fire which broke out on 18 September. The Castle Street blaze was one of the most spectacular witnessed in the town for many years.

Bangor Borough Council objected to the Ministry of Development's decision to make Downpatrick the centre for the new North Down, Ards, Castlereagh and Down Councils, with public health and building control staff being based there.
Alderman Bertie Campbell told colleagues on 7 November that Newtownards was more central, given that North Down had such a large population.

Cllr Bruce Mulligan resigned as chairman of Bangor Vanguard on 20 November, to be replaced by vice-chairman Campbell McCormick.

Alderman Bertie Campbell became a Freeman of Bangor on 23 November. He was presented with a parchment declaring him to be an honorary burgess of the Borough and his portrait was unveiled after Town Clerk Richard Wolsey read out the resolution which conferred the honour on their former Mayor, who had served on the Council for 20 years.

Constable Gordon Harron (32), from Drumglass Avenue in Bangor, became the 27th member of the RUC to be murdered during the Troubles and the 404th victim of 1972. He had been shot on 17 October after stopping a stolen car on Belfast's Shore Road and died in hospital four days later. A native of Co Donegal, he had lived in Bangor for some years, playing rugby for the RUC and the Bangor club.

Constable Harron, who was survived by his wife and two-year-old son, worshipped in Bangor Abbey. Senior curate the Rev William McMonagle gave the address at the funeral service in the border village of Pettigo on 23 October.

Constable Harron's killer, a member of the UDA, was convicted of capital murder and sentenced to death. A reprieve was granted by Secretary of State William Whitelaw, with the sentence being commuted to life imprisonment.

Former Belfast man John Mullin became the 675th victim of the Northern Ireland Troubles when he was shot dead on the Clandeboye Road on 23 December while waiting for a lift to work. It was the first sectarian killing in Bangor, with suspicion falling on the Red Hand Commandos.

Aged 25 and a Catholic, Mr Mullin lived at nearby Tudor Park with his wife and four-year-old child. He had moved to Bangor a year earlier after obtaining work at Donaghadee Carpets.

His parents lived at North Parade, Belfast, and the funeral service at Holy Rosary Church on 24 December was followed by interment at Milltown Cemetery.

Bangor senior citizens pictured outside their headquarters in Castle Street before setting off on a day's outing to Kilkeel in June 1972. *256/40-3*

Vanguard leader William Craig addresses a meeting in Bangor on 14 August 1972. Included (from left) are: Hugh Johnston (treasurer), Claire Boal (assistant secretary), Cllr Bruce Mulligan (chairman) and Richard Weir. *20/5-57*

Children who competed in a fancy dress competition organised by Bangor Borough Council's Recreation Department on 10 August 1972. *12/7/57*

Five children from Knockdene, off the
Bloomfield Road, held a garden fete and
raised £10.70 for Bangor's Save the Children
Fund branch. Secretary Mrs R. W. Hamilton
receives the money from nine-year-old
David Graham. Included (from left) are: Peter
Smyth (8), Nicola Graham (6), Michael Smyth
(10) and Cherie Graham (11). *258/21-3*

Spectator printer Jimmy
Connolly examines a nylon
'newspaper' umbrella Bangor
native Dr James Martin
brought home during a visit
to see his parents, Mr and Mrs
J. Martin of 28 Bellevue, in
August 1972. Included are Mr
Martin (sen.) and *Spectator*
office girls Liz McNamara,
Annette Cuthbertson, Irene
Cooley and Jennie Atkinson.
62/5a-57

One of two sets of the Von Trapp children from Bangor Amateur Operatic Society's production of *The Sound of Music* in September 1972. Back (from left): Colin Reid, Shona Hall, Christine Mulvenna, Vanessa Campbell, Dex McGloughlin. Front: Liane Radcliffe and Mark Hedgeley. *69/10-58*

The first assembly for pupils and staff of Bangor's new Boys' Secondary School was held in the open air on 4 September 1972 because the Gransha Road school, for the time being, did not have an assembly hall. *16/1a-58*

Kilcooley Ladies' Club members entertained children from Kyle House at a Hallowe'en party on 30 October 1972. *60/9-59*

Olympic gold medal winner Mary Peters receives a rapturous reception as she switches on the Christmas lights at the Springhill Shopping Centre on 16 November 1972. *45/18-60*

The Rev John Turner, of Hamilton Road Presbyterian Church, opens a service for peace in Castle Park on 1 October 1972. Over 1,000 people attended the service, at which all the major denominations were represented. Other participating clergy (standing behind Mr Turner) were the Rev. C. Kerr, the Rev J. Mercer and Fr. B. Murray. Special prayers were read by schoolchildren Lorraine Dickson and Phillip McWilliams. *82/17a-58*

Brenda Claney buys an autographed copy of cartoonist Rowel Friers' new book *Pig in the Parlour* at Stewart Miller's Bangor shop on 2 December 1972. Included are artist Lolita Alexander, Mr Miller and members of the public. *81/20a-60*

The Brunswick Players performed *The New Gossoon* in the Little Flower Hall in December 1972. Producer Tony Coghlan (left) is pictured with Bill Henry, Bill Pollock and Harry Dornan, along with (front, from left): Lillie Morgan, Marie Gildea, Molly Crossey, Danny Taggart and (front) Pam Stamford. *94/12-60*

The male chorus from Bangor Amateur Operatic Society's production of *Sinbad the Sailor* at Christmas 1972. Back (from left): Jeffrey Johnston, David Feherty, Simon Mercer, Robert Hutchinson. Front: Christopher Spence, Colin Petherick and Mark Hedgley. *81/7a-61*

Geoffrey Bowman

remembers...

On the night of Thursday 23 March 1972, I was lying in bed reading a book. It must have been a very good book because I was still reading it well past one o'clock in the morning. Perhaps I was trying to expel the less agreeable images from my mind that had poured from the television screen throughout the month.

The Provisional IRA had certainly been busy. Two people died and dozens were injured in the Abercorn Restaurant at the beginning of March. Six died in another no-warning blast in Lower Donegall Street. It wasn't just Belfast. Provincial towns were also being hit, with a bomb causing widespread damage in Lisburn in the middle of the month. It was easy to imagine a creeping pestilence spreading across Northern Ireland; indeed only that evening Bangor Borough Council had voted to introduce a parking ban in the town centre to prevent Bangor becoming the next victim of terrorism.

Too little, too late. At around twenty-past one, as I closed my book and contemplated six hours' sleep before school, the heavy, old-fashioned sash-window near my bed rattled violently as the large pane of glass was forced inward by an advancing shock-wave. A split-second later a massive concussion shook the house and from the direction of the town centre I heard a deep, heavy "ker-WUMMP", a two-note prelude to a symphony of destruction.

Geoffrey Bowman is the older brother of the author of this book. Born in November 1954, he was educated at Bangor Grammar School. He then studied law at Queen's University, before taking up legal practice with the firm of C & H Jefferson in Belfast, where he is now a partner specialising in asbestos litigation.

As a decade the 1970s shaped Geoffrey's future career, spanning the journey from schoolboy to practising lawyer. But the journey was not limited to study and education: in the early years of the decade photography occupied much after-school time and the Apollo missions were a source of endless fascination.

Geoffrey still has photographs of astronauts walking on the Moon taken off the TV screen with an ancient camera and printed in the school darkroom. Occasionally the Moon-landing missions clashed with school. Apollo usually won. When the Apollo 14 lunar module touched down in February 1971, the whole of Jimmy Driscoll's Latin class heard it live on the transistor radio perched (with permission) on Geoffrey's desk.

The transition from school pupil to university student is not always easy, but finding a sport or hobby to pursue with passion helps to divert attention from the horrors of the Equity tutorial and what passes for food in the Halls of Residence. Gliding at Ards airfield became Geoffrey's passion, and he indulged it at every opportunity over the span of his university career and beyond.

This passion even survived a serious crash… but not marriage (Geoffrey occasionally persuades his wife Sandra to let him have a flight for old time's sake at

It was the first time I had heard the detonation of a car bomb, but I was in no doubt about what had happened. It sounded very close, but I could see nothing in the blackness outside my window. Making my way to the bathroom, I gazed to the west, where the glow of streetlights indicated the general direction of the town centre. Silhouetted against the dull orange radiance, a sinister black column of smoke poured skywards.

I had to suppress a crazy adolescent thought that I should get dressed and make my way to the town centre to "do something." Instead, I forced myself to return to bed and eventually weariness overcame adrenalin and I managed to fall asleep.

Three hours later my window rattled again and a second "Ker-WUMMP" shattered my sleep, among other things. A further trip to the bathroom revealed another column of smoke. After that, my sleep was fitful and I awoke at least once more, convinced I had heard a third detonation. A few hours later I turned up at school with sleep-rimmed eyes. The lessons of the day were all but forgotten as pupils and teachers discussed the IRA attack. Fortunately, no one had died and, thanks to the prompt action of police officers who evacuated residents from several Main Street premises, no one was injured.

After school I rushed home to collect my Uncle Edgar's cine camera (which I had on temporary loan) and made

my way to Main Street. The clear-up operation was well under way as I shot a few jerky sequences of colour film, which to this day preserve the after-effects of two huge explosions in a town centre. Woolworths, ravaged by the first blast but salvageable, had already been boarded up. The building that housed Lennon Brothers' fruit shop and the Rendezvous Restaurant was little more than a pile of rubble and was later pulled down. On the opposite side of the street, unseen damage lay behind the new hardboard façade of Millsopp's Stores and the adjacent businesses had been gutted. I couldn't even remember what they had been. One of the most graphic indications of the violence of the attack on Bangor was a large piece of mangled metal – a fragment of a disintegrated car – which had pierced the sign of Warner's shoe shop, just to the left of the W.

My probing lens zoomed in on a hole in the road, roughly filled in with gravel: the site of the second explosion. A short distance away, the gap-toothed windows of Trinity Presbyterian Church provided ample explanation for the 'POSTPONED' sign across a placard advertising a music recital.

Scattered around Main Street, among the remains of honest traders' shattered livelihoods, lay jagged shards of metal and shredded car tyres: evidence of the delivery mechanism for this brutal assault on our town. No, not just an assault. A violation. This was the day the Troubles visited Bangor, the day the pestilence arrived. This was childhood's end.

Both bomb damage pictures by Geoffrey Bowman

the Ulster Gliding Club's site at Magilligan.)

A reasonable athlete at school, Geoffrey took to running to counterbalance the sedentary lifestyle of a lawyer and completed three Belfast Marathons in the 1980s, twice under three and a half hours.

In later life Geoffrey has enjoyed travelling and writing. He has contributed two chapters to a book on the Apollo missions *(Footprints in the Dust:* Nebraska University Press, July 2010). His travels have taken him to Alaska, Easter Island, the Falkland Islands, Chile, Greenland,, Spitsbergen and China, but on a recent visit to Bangor he also enjoyed the simple pleasure of a stroll along the promenade at Ballyholme Beach.

The grains of sand have been rearranged many times but the beach hasn't changed in 50 years.

Geoffrey Bowman on a recent visit to Greenland

1973
IN THE SPECTATOR

THE New Year dawned with petrol bomb attacks on three Catholic-owned homes in the Whitehill Estate. Two of the houses sustained damage and a woman suffered slight burns to her arm.

David Adams, of Brunswick Road, retired from the *Belfast Telegraph* after a career spanning 68 years. Mr Adams had joined the paper as a 14-year-old copy boy earning four shillings and sixpence a week.

County Down's first teachers centre opened at Seacourt, off the Princetown Road, in January. Director of Education Mr F. H. Ebbitt said the centre's success depended on the teachers of the area and how they would make use of its facilities.

The first annual meeting of Bangor Credit Union, held in January at the Royal Hotel, heard that loans totalling £1,064 had been paid out to 21 members. Outgoing president Patricia Fox announced a recruitment drive (at the time there were 63 members). The organisation moved to permanent premises at 10 Abbey Street in 1978.

Bangor faced widespread violence and disruption during a 24-hour loyalist strike on Wednesday 7 February. Police were stoned in Main Street, petrol bombs were thrown at a number of private houses, shots were heard around the town and there was a small explosion on the Clandeboye Road. Most shops and factories closed their doors, some after receiving threatening calls.

Hundreds of young 'Tartan Gang' members protested outside the police station as part of a province-wide picket of RUC stations. A number attached loyalist flags on top of the 20ft-high fence. They then moved to the Abbey Street/ Main Street

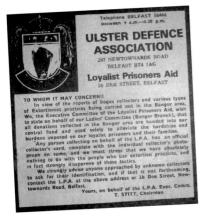

roundabout, where they blocked traffic.

Petrol bombs were thrown into Whitehill's sub-post office and a house at Beechwood Avenue, while fires were started in grass at Ballysallagh and Pickie. Police answered more than 200 calls, including many diversionary and hoax calls.

The first sod was cut in late February for a new church hall at St Andrew's Presbyterian Church, Clandeboye Road. The hall would replace a Nissen hut which had been in use for 25 years. The minister was the Rev. C. W. D. Kerr.

Bangor couple Mr and Mrs William Ernest Watt celebrated their golden wedding anniversary on 28 February at their London home with their six children and 13 grandchildren. Mr Watt and his wife Rosa (née Gribben) were married in Bangor Abbey in 1923. For many years he ran the Bangor Car Laundry in Central Avenue. Their eldest daughter, Mrs Louis McClean, still lived in Bangor.

Fifty-two per cent of homes in the Bangor area had telephones by March 1973, which was twice the Northern Ireland average and 10 per cent higher than the United Kingdom average.

Five hundred people were on the Post Office's Bangor waiting list.

A Samaritans branch was launched in Hamilton House on 9 March. The Rev. John Turner served as director, along with deputy directors Fr McAnally and Mrs Lorna Connor, while Bill Bailie was financial director. The branch commenced a 24-hour service based at 92 Dufferin Avenue from 18 October.

Sir Robin Kinahan (right) opens the Dufferin Avenue headquarters of the North Down Samaritans, watched by North Down Mayor Jack Preston and financial director Bill Bailie. *85/1a-75*

Work commenced in mid-March on the £600,000 dual carriageway to Newtownards. The three-mile roadway had first been mooted in 1966, when the average traffic flow on the road was 6,000 vehicles each day; by 1973 the figure had risen to 9,000.

Plans for a motel at Cleland Park, off the Newtownards Road, were turned down by the Council's Planning and Traffic Committee. Developer Edwin Dunlop's proposal met with strong local opposition.

Widespread violence in Bangor was blamed on hooligans who accompanied Orange lodges and bands on their Easter Monday (23 April) visit to the town. Thirty-nine police officers were injured, along with members of the public, including children. The trouble initially involved rival gangs, mainly from Belfast, fighting among themselves but they eventually came together to attack the police with bottles and stones.

Bangor's casualty unit, which had been closed some months earlier, was reopened to help cope with the riot victims.

The first pupils were welcomed to the new Towerview Primary School at Bally-holme on 30 April. There were 114 pupils in four classes (P1-4).

Bar a couple of by-elections, the reorganisation of local government saw most Bangor voters going to the polls for the first time since 1967 to elect Councillors to the new North Down District Council (Borough status would follow later in the year).

North Down comprised four areas: A, for Groomsport, Churchill, Ballyholme, Ballymagee and Bangor Harbour; B, Conlig, Whitehill, Rathgael, Clandeboye and Silverstream; C, Bangor Castle, Springhill, Bryansburn, Princetown and Crawfords-burn; and D, Craigavad, Loughview, Cultra, Holywood Demesne and Priory.

Forty-five candidates sought the 20 seats under the new Proportional Represen-tation voting system on 30 May – 18 Unionists, 12 Alliance, 10 Loyalists, three Independents, one Labour and one 'Abolish the 11-Plus' candidate (future Green Party MLA Brian Wilson). Nine Unionists were elected, along with seven Alliance and four Loyalist members.

In area A outgoing Mayor Robert Topping topped the poll, being joined by fellow Unionist Maurice Butler, Cllr Bertie McConnell (Alliance), Eddie Mills (Unionist) and Alderman James Hamilton (Alliance). Area B: Cllr Jack Preston (Unionist), Cllr George Green (Loyalist), Albert Magee (Alliance), Amy Corry (Unionist) and Tommy Braniff (Loyalist). Area C: Alderman Bertie Campbell (Unionist), David Belshaw (Unionist), John Calvert (Alliance), Cllr Mary O'Fee (Loyalist) and Jean Foster (Alliance). Area D: Rev. John McConnell Auld (Unionist), Keith Jones (Al-liance), Jim Shannon (Alliance), Maureen McClure (Unionist) and Ian Kerr (Loy-alist).

Although the new authority did not take over from the four it replaced until

October, at their first meeting, on 7 June, Cllr Preston was elected as chairman, with Cllr O'Fee as vice-chairman.

Due to a continuing drought Bangor's water supply was turned off each night for approximately 12 hours from 2 June. The decision, taken by the Borough Council, was blamed on declining levels in local reservoirs. Efforts were made to maintain a 24-hour supply to Bangor Hospital, Bangor Dairies and local industries.

Voters returned to the polls on 28 June to elect seven North Down members to the new Assembly, which followed the British Government's White Paper on the future of Northern Ireland.

North Down MP Jim Kilfedder (Ulster Unionist – Anti-White Paper), topped the poll with 20,684 votes, while Bertie Campbell was returned as an Ulster Unionist (Pro-White Paper), along with Bertie McConnell (Alliance). The other four North Down Assembly members were Captain John W. Brooke, later to become Lord Brookeborough (Ulster Unionist – Pro-White Paper), Lord Henry Dunleath (Alliance), Major William Brownlow (Ulster Unionist – Pro-White Paper) and Charles Poots (Democratic Unionist – Loyalist Coalition).

Among the defeated candidates were Vanguard Unionist Loyalist Coalition representatives George Green and David Trimble, the latter losing his deposit after receiving 446 votes (the lowest number cast for any of the 18 who stood in North Down).

Top pop band Mud became the first English chart act to visit Bangor since the beginning of the Troubles. They appeared at the King's Club in the Queen's Court Hotel on 6 July. The following week saw the return to Bangor of early Sixties favourites Emile Ford and the Checkmates, while The Tremeloes appeared at the same venue on 11 August and Vanity Fayre on 24 August.

Two Bangor mothers were fortunate to escape from the seven-storey Summerland complex at Douglas on the Isle of Man, which was destroyed by a raging inferno on 2 August. Fifty people lost their lives, including Newtownards man Wilbert Hamilton, and 80 others sustained serious injuries.

Mrs Sidney Wilson, Fourth Avenue, and Mrs Kay Watterson were on the top floor when the fire started and were among a handful of people who managed to escape through an emergency door. Members of the Nesbitt family, from Brunswick Road, were about to enter Summerland but stopped to buy some souvenirs, while another Bangor family, Mr and Mrs Robert Moore, Millisle Gardens, their daughter Helen and her friend Lorena Hughes, Elmwood Drive, had been looking forward to attending a disco in Summerland. They decided to do some packing first and avoided the tragedy.

Bangor was named 'Best Kept Large Town' by the Central Gardens Association for the fifth time, with Town Clerk Richard Wolsey advising Councillors that a largely unloved landmark had played a major part in Bangor's success.

"One of the things that influenced the judges was our attempt to do something with the gasholder by painting it in a mild silver and picking out the staircase and rail in white, like a Christmas cake," he explained.

Bombers targeted St Columbanus Secondary School on 6 September. They threw a can of petrol into a classroom, followed by a 5lb bomb which caused extensive blast damage. The resulting fire was quickly extinguished by members of Bangor Fire Brigade.

Echoing events from a decade earlier, there were vacant desks at Bangor Grammar School in early September after a number of Lower and Middle Sixth students refused to have their hair cut and were sent home. Following incidents at the end of the previous school year headmaster Randall Clarke had insisted a new standard of discipline would be enforced.

At one stage just three boys were left in one class with between 20 and 30 in the entire Sixth Form. The episode ran for some days, attracting the attention of the local and city press and television news.

Fred Tughan CBE became the seventh man to be given the Freedom of Bangor – and the last to have the honour conferred by Bangor Borough Council before it went out of existence on 1 October.

He had served on the Council from 1952 to 1961, was Mayor from 1956 to 1960, and held a County Council seat following his resignation from the Borough Council.

A bomb was thrown towards the crowded Ormeau Arms public house at High Street on 22 September. However, it struck a Venetian blind and fell onto the street where it exploded, breaking windows in both the pub and a nearby chemist's shop.

A hall serving as St Columba's Parish Church in Kilcooley was formally opened and dedicated on 6 October by the Bishop of Down and Dromore, the Rt. Rev. George Quin.

The appointment of local hotelier and former Bangor Borough Councillor Bill O'Hara as the BBC's new chairman and National Governor for Northern Ireland was approved by the Queen in late October.

There was a close result in a by-election held on 5 December for a Bangor Area C seat on North Down Borough Council, following the resignation of Alliance representative Jean Foster. The seat was won by Unionist Frank R. Gill, who defeated Oscar Rollins (Alliance) and David Trimble (Loyalist). Gill received 943 first preference votes, with Rollins runner-up on 934 and Trimble third with 887. After Trimble was eliminated and his transfers were distributed the final totals were: Gill 1,278 and Rollins 1,000.

Bangor Chamber of Trade cancelled a special pre-Christmas shopping night, scheduled for 21 December, because of energy restrictions imposed from Westminster as a result of the global oil crisis. Shops were permitted to open during the day without using electric lighting or heating.

Industrial and commercial premises were permitted to use standby generators but had a limited allocation of oil. Food shops, restaurants, chemists and public houses were exempt from the restrictions. Television stations closed down at 10.30pm.

Ringing in the New Year in the belfry of Bangor Parish Church are (back, from left): Rev. George A. Mitchell (rector), Tom Huggins (churchwarden), Brian Tracey, Jim McBride, Joan Tracey, John Marshall (verger), Rev John Scott (curate), T. J. McConkey (former bellringer). Middle: Mrs T. McBride, Tom McBride, David Filmer, W. T. Feherty. Front: Barbara Humphreys, Heather Manning, Stephanie Hamilton and Lorna Humphreys. *89/3a-61*

Hostesses at a ball at Milanos in January 1973, organised by the Royal National Lifeboat Institution, were (from left): Mandy Thompson, Rosemary Lyons, Karen Simpson, Brenda Houston, Sheelagh Rensen and Dana Coote. *14/7a-62*

Members of the chorus from Bangor Amateur Operatic Society's production of *Mame*, which was performed in the Little Theatre in late March 1973. *53/11/65*

Bangor's first woman traffic warden, Mrs Lelia Pollock, of Belfast, is pictured in March 1973 with 'victim' Mrs Lorna Agnew and Constable Jim Stevenson, who looked after the town's wardens. 42/6a-65

Competitors at Bangor Music Festival in late March 1973 included (from left): Diane O'Fee (Pringle Cup for scripture, 13-16 years), Dawn Kielty (runner-up), Linda Milling and Sheelagh McManus (joint third). 52/7-65

Rathmore Primary School U9 and 9-11 choral speaking teams were placed first and second in their respective age groups at Bangor Music Festival in April 1973. Included is Mrs McDonough, who was in charge of choral speaking at Rathmore. 100/3a-65

Kilcooley Presbyterian Church's new organ was dedicated on 15 April 1973. Included with choir members are organist Mrs Vera Craig and minister the Rev W. Kenneth Weir. 71/6-66

Pupils of the Winifred Ashcroft School danced *Over the Rainbow* in Bangor Technical School in May 1973. 8/11a-68

Children who
took part in the
Bangor Christian
Workers' Society
95th birthday
celebrations at
Pickie in July 1973.
19a/2-72

Bangor Salvation
Army's Singing
Company took
part in a junior
harvest service in
Newtownards on
7 October 1973.
267/93-3

Aileen Hull, outgoing president of the Soroptimist Club of Bangor, invests successor Edna Nicol with the badge of office in October 1973. 76/1a-75

Four generations came together on the occasion of Mrs Sarah Jane McNeill's 100th birthday on 25 November 1973. Mrs McNeill, from Park Drive, is pictured with (at front) son Kenneth, youngest great grandchild Roger Kerr and granddaughter Mrs Barbara Plester. Back: grandson Donald McNeill, daughter Miss Noreen McNeill and Donald's wife Paula. 41/7-77

Glenlola Collegiate Old Girls' Association committee members with Miss Betty McConachie who was in charge of the canteen for their annual dinner on 23 November. From left: Heather Slane, Karen Morrison, Lorna Brown, Morva Brown, Miss McConachie, Betty Dunlop, Sheila Hall and secretary Yvonne Barnes. 11/2-77

Pupils from the Adele Sloan School of Dancing took part in a charity fundraiser at the Little Theatre in December 1973. *60/9a-77*

Trinity Girls' Brigade Company (8th Northern Ireland) won – for the first time – the Explorers Cup for choral speaking at the Northern Ireland finals. Their captain was Miss Pearl Hassard. Back (from left): Sandra Boal, Jill Whittle, Karen Davis, Sonnya Porter, Jackie Adams, Morny Colville, Nicola Wilson. Middle: Sian McCully, Audrey Wilsdon, Diane Yourston, Sandra Gillespie, Janet McConnell, Coleen Armstrong. Front: Lynn McCreedy, Beverley Parker, Susan Lovell, Judith Welsh, Simone Lemon and Ruth McGaughey. *89/12-77*

Babbity Barwick

– known in Bangor as Eileen Blackie – remembers...

We arrived in Bangor in September 1966 after fleeing Uganda in its post-independence turmoil. We watched from our hilltop home as tanks and soldiers took control of the streets of the capital, Kampala, in the valley below.

My father's company offered to move us to Ireland where we had family connections in both the North and the South. Our first home was No. 31 Beverley Gardens, Bangor. Shortly after arriving in the town we watched, from the sitting room sofa, the news as people demonstrated on the streets of Belfast and heard of murders and violence. We'd arrived just in time for the start of the modern Troubles!

My first school was Ballyholme Primary. It was there I learnt about religion. On our first day at school my brother Richard and I were asked by a teacher if we were Protestant or Catholic. We had absolutely no idea what to

Eileen Blackie – now Babbity Barwick – aged 17

Babbity's last Christmas in Bangor was in 1978. In 1981 she finished at St Martin's Art College and freelanced as a Graphic Designer in London for a couple of years.

Her first permanent job was for a colourful character called Alex Herbage who turned out to be a Ponzi fraudster and was finally arrested and deported to the USA in 1986. Babbity realised that all was not above board and left before his demise in 1984.

She went back to London and found work with PA Design (part of the Michael Peters Group) and eventually found her way to BBC News Graphics at Shepherds Bush.

"In 1987 I was whisked away from the UK by my new Kiwi expatriate husband and taken to the Cayman Islands where we set up a small advertising and brand agency and have lived ever since. Cayman is home for the family although our daughters now work in London."

Babbity Barwick (Eileen Blackie) is pictured with husband Simon and children (from left) Jack, Amy and Joanne at Ndarakwai ranch in Tanzania, which was once owned by Babbity's grandparents.

say, having never heard those words before. The teacher pronounced us 'Heathens', another new word, and shot us a look of total disgust. We were sent home in disgrace to find out what religion we were.

It hit me then that we were out of place and had a great deal to learn about this strange, cold, grey place. In Africa skin colour was the differentiator; in Bangor the differences were more subtle. It mattered which street you lived in, which school you went to, which church you attended, what job your Dad had and who your friends were.

Initially we were an oddity: blonde-haired, Swahili-speaking 'jungle bunnies'. I spent my first year at school ostracised by the children and picked on by my teacher. I had no idea why I was being subjected to this treatment but perhaps it was because I was a Heathen. My brother was experiencing the same issues – he was six and I was seven.

Over the next few years we picked our way through the social minefield, learnt to use the local accent, developed a sense of sardonic humour, learnt to fight, learnt to ignore insults, learnt about the differences (and similarities) between Catholics and Protestants, and found a way to enjoy life.

After a slow start at primary school I squeaked through the 11+ and started at Glenlola in 1970. Bangor was a happy home for me in the 1970s, although life there was punctuated by regular reminders of the Troubles.

One memorable day our history teacher locked the classroom door to teach us 'the truth about the British involvement in Ireland'. Her brief, in a predominantly Protestant school, was to teach us an artificially positive view. She took a risk by giving us a more balanced perspective and asked us not to talk with our parents about what we'd learnt that day.

There was the night in 1972 when we were woken by the blast of the High Street bomb followed a couple of years later by firebombs in the Main Street, signalling a change in the way we used town.

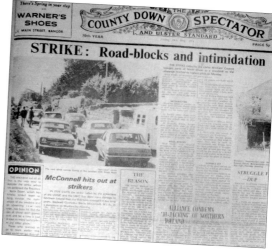

I recall one afternoon on the Main Street when three soldiers on weekend break appeared at the top of the hill. Everyone in the street stopped to stare because one of the soldiers was black. He was jeered at by some which I found embarrassing.

There was also the surreal experience of the 1974 UWC strike, which happened just before my O-Levels. It meant revision by candlelight and nights spent exploring the streets made unfamiliar by the total lack of illumination.

My grandfather was in hospital in Portadown, having just had a heart attack – we had to queue for hours and beg for a couple of pints of petrol to be able to visit him.

A year before starting at Glenlola we'd moved to Ward Avenue close to the sea. While my mother had been welcomed into many neighbourhood homes for coffee, a Catholic family we knew moved

The view from the family home at Ward Avenue

in a couple of years later and were quietly ignored and disapproved of.

My brother and I spent most of our afternoons and weekends with our neighbourhood friends Mark Robson and Christine Coulter. We messed around on the beach,

Brother Richard Blackie at Ravenhill in March 1979, playing for Bangor Grammar School in the Schools Cup final

sailed at Ballyholme Yacht Club and played tennis and golf at the park across the road.

In our early teens evenings were spent playing pool at the church youth club in town or risking life and limb at the Blue Lamp Disco close by. In our late teens we'd spend sunny days at Pickie Pool, weekends at Bangor Rugby Club socials or at the Royal Hotel disco.

Bangor in the 1970s offered us many opportunities to explore our passions and to roam safe and carefree from the chaos of the Troubles just 10 miles away in Belfast. It wasn't until I left Northern Ireland in 1977 to go to Art College in London that I realised how the issues of prejudice and hatred fuelled by the Troubles cast a gloom over the whole country – profoundly affecting life in our otherwise happy seaside town.

Babbity's father Alan Blackie on the beach at Ballyholme in the 1970s

The teenage sailing enthusiast at Ballyholme Yacht Club

Charlie Quin

remembers...

My time in Bangor came to end when I left Bangor Grammar School after completing my A-Levels in June 1969. However, three years later, in 1972, on a home visit from Southampton University I went to see my old headmaster, the redoubtable Randall Clarke.

I had a healthy respect and a high regard for Randall. I remember his advice on my applying to Voluntary Service

Charlie Quin pictured by the *Spectator* on a home visit to Bangor in 1973

Charlie Quin (front, third from left) with other major prizewinners from Bangor Grammar School's sports day in May 1968. Back (from left): D. Brennan, B. McCready, J. G. McCay, R. A. Milliken, S. B. Johnston. Front: D. Sim, G. Robinson, R. Lightbody, P. McKinnie and R. Parker. 185/2/2

Son of the late Rt Rev George Quin, Bishop of Down and Dromore, and Dr Norah Quin, Charlie was educated at Garth House Preparatory School, Bangor Grammar School, Southampton University and Queen's University in Belfast.

He was called to the bar of Northern Ireland in 1978, where he practised law until 1981. He served as a Crown Counsel in the Attorney General's Chambers in Bermuda from 1981 to 1984. He was admitted as an attorney of Grand Cayman's Grand Court in January

1985, and was called to the Supreme Court of the Eastern Caribbean in September 2005.

He also acted as Attorney General of Montserrat. He was appointed Queen's Counsel in 2004.

Justice Quin QC was recently appointed the fourth judge of the Cayman Islands Grand Court.

Married to Diana (née Robinson), they have three sons: Nick, Tom and William.

Overseas (VSO) was that if I did go I would find myself "poisoned for the rest of my working life."

I didn't quite understand this advice as I hadn't even started working nor, at that time, was I showing any particular promise or aptitude – for work of any sort!

What I think he meant was that I would remain somewhat restless in future. Randall was prophetic because my experience on VSO in Africa did make me restless. After practising as a junior barrister in Belfast I then moved on to work in Bermuda, Montserrat and the Cayman Islands.

What I can say of my time spent in Bangor was that I had the most wonderful education with great teachers and some very good friends.

Justice Charles Quin QC, recently appointed the fourth judge of the Cayman Islands Grand Court

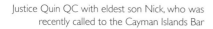

Justice Quin QC with eldest son Nick, who was recently called to the Cayman Islands Bar

1974

IN THE SPECTATOR

Celebrating her 100th birthday on New Year's Day was Sara Jane Patterson, who lived with her daughter Moysie at 25c Ballyquinton Gardens, Kilcooley. A native of Upper Balloo, she had married John Patterson, from the Skipperstone area, when 17 – he predeceased her by some 60 years – and she held the distinction of being the oldest parishioner of Bangor Abbey.

Hamilton House hosted a 'United Unionist Rally' on 10 January against the new power-sharing Executive, headed by Brian Faulkner, which followed the signing of the Sunningdale Agreement the previous month. Members of the packed audience were urged by David Trimble to support an anti-Sunningdale, anti-Council of Ireland petition.

It was also announced that Loyalists and Unpledged Unionists had joined together as the United Ulster Unionist Council (UUUC).

Environment Minister Roy Bradford was chosen by the North Down Imperial Unionist Association as their candidate for February's General Election – beating sitting MP Jim Kilfedder by three votes (303 to 300). Kilfedder claimed two of his supporters had

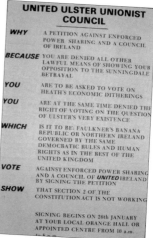

UNITED ULSTER UNIONIST COUNCIL

WHY   A PETITION AGAINST ENFORCED POWER SHARING AND A COUNCIL OF IRELAND

BECAUSE YOU ARE DENIED ALL OTHER LAWFUL MEANS OF SHOWING YOUR OPPOSITION TO THE SUNNINGDALE BETRAYAL

YOU   ARE TO BE ASKED TO VOTE ON HEATH'S ECONOMIC DITHERINGS

YOU   ARE AT THE SAME TIME DENIED THE RIGHT OF VOTING ON THE QUESTION OF ULSTER'S VERY EXISTENCE

WHICH   IS IT TO BE: FAULKNER'S BANANA REPUBLIC OR NORTHERN IRELAND GOVERNED BY THE SAME DEMOCRATIC RULES AND HUMAN RIGHTS AS IN THE REST OF THE UNITED KINGDOM

VOTE   AGAINST ENFORCED POWER SHARING AND A COUNCIL OF UNITED IRELAND BY SIGNING THE PETITION

SHOW   THAT SECTION 2 OF THE CONSTITUTION ACT IS NOT WORKING

SIGNING BEGINS ON 26th JANUARY AT YOUR LOCAL ORANGE HALL OR APPOINTED CENTRE FROM 10 a.m.

United Ulster Unionist Council

The Ultimate Reason
FOR REJECTING ENFORCED POWER SHARING AND A COUNCIL OF IRELAND

★

PATRICK DUFFY, S.D.L.P. Assemblyman, and Party Adviser at Sunningdale said recently:

"No better body can be devised FOR DEVELOPMENT INTO A FEDERAL IRISH GOVERNMENT, THAN A COUNCIL OF IRELAND AS AGREED AT SUNNINGDALE."

★

REJECT YOUR BETRAYERS BY SIGNING THE PETITION AT YOUR LOCAL ORANGE HALL OR SIGNING CENTRE ON SATURDAY, 9th FEBRUARY BETWEEN 10 A.M. AND 8 P.M.

Your Last Chance

been locked out of the meeting, others had not received the admission circular and some of those casting votes belonged to branches outside the redrawn North Down boundary.

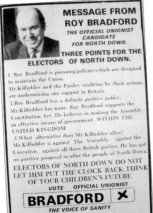

Three Bangor boys saved a local man from drowning in the Rathgael School swimming pool. Stephen Patton (14), Stephen Hall (13) and Brian Hall (9) went to the aid of a man who had suffered a sudden stomach cramp.

In the Westminster election Jim Kilfedder, standing as 'Your Official Unionist Assembly Man', with UUUC backing, defeated both Roy Bradford and Dermot Curran (SDLP). The Alliance Party had declined to put forward a candidate, not wishing to endanger the already fragile Executive.

Kilfedder polled 38,169 votes against the 21,943 and 2,376 cast for Bradford and Curran respectively. His majority was down by some 25,000 on the 1970 figure.

While accepting the verdict of the voters, Bradford stated: The policies on which I stood in this election – those of reconciliation in place of conflict – will be vindicated in the days ahead."

Bangor tool manufacturer Belzer Works (NI) Ltd. announced it would be shutting at the end of March, with the loss of 48 jobs (44 men and four women). The closure of the factory at Rathgael was blamed on a recession in the tool industry.

The IRA targeted Bangor's main shopping area on Saturday evening 30 March with devastating consequences. Three major stores – Woolworths, Wellworths and the Co-op – as well as a number of smaller shops, were gutted after incendiary devices exploded in lower Main Street.

A caller to Bangor Police Station and the Samaritans at 5pm warned that 15 two-pound bombs had been planted and would go off in half an hour. The police began a sys-

tematic search of premises, with the first device, in Woolworths, being detected at 5.15pm. The first of two devices in the Co-op detonated at 5.20pm, just after it had been evacuated. Within minutes the whole store was ablaze.

Then, from the bottom of the street, successive devices detonated in Woolworths, Wellworths and smaller shops on both sides. In addition to the big stores, Stewart Miller's newsagency and Hazletts TV rental business were destroyed – with the bill running into millions of pounds. At the height of the conflagration flames from the Co-op and Woolworths/ Wellworths stores met in an arc over firemen's heads.

A number of the businesses quickly reopened in alternative

Picture: Terence Bowman

23/8a-81

Picture: Desmond Bell

premises, including the Co-op which used its own Co-op Hall in Market Square. By September it was also operating a food store in Holborn Avenue, while Wellworths opened temporary premises off Clifton Road.

For the second successive Saturday a section of the town centre was sealed off – on 6 April – due to terrorist activity after a cylinder bomb was found on the roof of a bookmaker's premises in Mill Row. Given the close proximity of the Bangor gasometer, the area was evacuated. Army bomb disposal experts dragged the potentially lethal object to the beach, where a controlled explosion shattered a number of windows on Queen's Parade.

The network of security gates in Bangor was extended to include upper Main Street, in addition to lower Main Street, Bridge Street and High Street, from the beginning of May. Castle Park Avenue became a late night by-pass.

A strike called by the Ulster Workers' Council following the rejection of a UUUC motion against the Sunningdale Agreement at Stormont paralysed much of Northern Ireland between 15 and 28 May.

As the strike entered its second week road blocks with masked men, acts of intimidation and damage to property were widely reported. A blast bomb was thrown at a Catholic-occupied house in the Whitehill Estate, while a similar device was lobbed over a wall at the rear of The Helmsman bar at High Street.

Bin collection services were suspended, train services were interrupted by hoax bomb calls and those schools which opened reported a fall in attendances.

Just before the strike officially ended, following the collapse of the power-sharing Executive, the *Spectator* reported that the UWC's local representative was warning Bangor Chamber of Trade it had a list of businesses that remained open and would impose sanctions on them. This claim was later refuted by Belfast Committee chairman Harry Murray, a Bangor resident, who declared that as far as the UWC was concerned "the slate was clean."

The Bangor office of the Ministry of Health and Social Services dealt with approximately 4,500 unemployment benefit claims, largely arising out of the strike.

A welfare committee operating from disused shops at Kilcooley ensured that pensioners received a hot meal every day and milk was delivered free to all those requesting it. According to a caller to the *Spectator* the same men who manned the barricades emptied every bin on the estate and delivered coal to old people.

A weekly direct cargo service linking Bangor with Peel on the Isle of Man was launched on 19 June, prompting hopes the town could become a viable commercial port. The *MV Orlock* was capable of carrying 300 tons of general cargo. The service was run by Inter-Island Shipping, based at 5 Crosby Street.

The Rev. Ian Paisley addresses a rally in Castle Park on 29 June 1974.
41/14-87

During a Democratic Unionist Party rally in Castle Park on 29 June, a number of speakers, including party leader Ian Paisley MP, called for a Home Guard in Northern Ireland. Harry Murray, of the Ulster Workers' Council, declared that "only Ulstermen will save Ulster," while Assembly member Charles Poots added: "We will stand together and work together to save Ulster."

Within days Mr Murray had resigned from the UWC after attending a conference convened by the British Irish Association and indicating he would talk with the IRA if they put down their guns and bombs.

There was a similar call for a Home Guard – or Third Force – at a meeting in Hamilton House the following month, which was convened by the Ulster Special Constabulary Association.

Teenager Michael Bernard Browne, son of Mr and Mrs Edmund Browne of Abbots Walk in the Whitehill Estate, was murdered at the Valentine Playing Fields early on 12 July. The 16-year-old Catholic, one of a family of seven, was shot a short distance from an Eleventh Night bonfire.

The funeral, which took place four days later from his home to Clandeboye Cemetery, was largely attended. Michael, who had recently started work as a car sprayer with Gael Motors at Ballyholme, was a former pupil of St. Comgall's Primary School and St. Columbanus Secondary School.

Two men, one from Bangor and the other from Newtownards, were jailed for life that December for what was described in court as a "particularly callous murder." Responsibility has been attributed to the UVF.

Glenlola PE teacher Ann Davidson and sisters Jacqueline and Charmaine Cottam, from Ballymaconnell Road, were among hundreds of tourists trapped in Cyprus following the Turkish military invasion on 20 July. The trio travelled home once relative calm was restored.

Bangor's oldest resident, Miss Margaret Steenson, formerly of 28 Windmill Road, died aged 102 at The Banks, Groomsport Road, on 22 July. She had enjoyed a long career in nursing, receiving a CBE in 1924.

A branch of Brian Faulkner's New Unionist Party (later the Unionist Party of Northern Ireland) was formed in Bangor on 19 August. Two Assembly members, Alderman Bertie Campbell (North Down) and Peter McLachlan (South Antrim), addressed the meeting, the latter declaring: "We leave behind those who pay lip service to the union, while selfishly working for Protestant supremacy. We also leave behind those who advocate the formation of private armies and thereby foster civil strife."

Colleen Dunn (13), of 20 Stanley Road, won the Adele Sloan Cup for the most promising dancer in the ballet section at Bangor Music Festival in 1974. 24/12a-83

A week later around a dozen members of the executive committee of the Bangor Unionist Association, who had attended the pro-Faulkner meeting, were expelled for disloyalty.

It was announced that the Bangor engineering firm of McKee & James would be closing in October, leaving 70 skilled production workers, all male, along with five female office staff facing redundancy. Blame was placed on continued trading difficulties in Northern Ireland.

The redundancy notices were subsequently delayed until mid-November while takeover talks were being held. It was believed that employment totals could be restored to around 100 under a new owner but these hopes proved unfounded.

There was widespread sympathy for the wife and family circle of Resident Magistrate Martin McBirney, who was murdered by the IRA in his Belfast home on 16 September.

Mr McBirney had presided at court sittings in Bangor from 1969 until the time of his death. Outside his legal work, he was a member of the Northern Ireland team in the BBC *Round Britain Quiz* with Helen's Bay rector Dr Michael Dewar. Their success in the 1974 competition was due to be announced that week.

The new and old owners and staff members of the newsagents (from left): Mr and Mrs Ferguson, Joan McAllister, Ivy Duff, Evelyn Rowan, Mrs Flood, Pat Mooney and Mr Flood. Missing is schoolgirl Karen Hayes, who assisted part-time. *82/9-92*

Bangor's oldest newsagent, Corbett Flood, retired after running his shop at Church Street for 31 years and being involved in the business for nearly 50 years, having started as a newsboy. The new owners were Mr and Mrs William Ferguson, of Groomsport Road, both natives of the town.

North Down voters returned to the polls on 10 October after Prime Minister Harold Wilson decided to seek a majority at Westminster, the February election having resulted in a hung parliament. Jim Kilfedder (UUUC) successfully defended his seat against two other candidates – Major William Brownlow (UPNI) and Keith Jones (Alliance).

Speakers and members of Bangor's People Together steering committee in October 1974. Back (from left): Gary Bower, David Thompson, Thelma Shiel, John Murray, Clifford Creighton, Judy McClelland. Front: Canon Padraig Murphy, Harry Murray, Sadie Patterson and George Reid. *86/0a-93*

Kilfedder received 40,996 votes (72% of the total valid poll), with Jones on 9,973 (17.5%) and Brownlow 6,037 (10.5%).

A local steering committee for People Together was formed on 11 October in the Good Templar Hall. The speakers included former UWC chairman Harry Murray, Canon Padraig Murphy, from West Belfast, and Miss Sadie Patterson, chairman of Women Together.

Mr Murray declared that no cause justified what was happening in Northern Ireland and asked: "Do you want another five years of this? God will damn each one of you if you do not do something about it."

Making a welcome return to playing the Tonic's famous Compton organ, which had a new home at Bangor Boys' Secondary School in November 1974, was Louise MacDonald, the long-serving resident organist at the Hamilton Road cinema.

Louise MacDonald is pictured with (from left): Rodney Bambrick, who was responsible for the restoration work, singer John Lorimer, Dr Donald Davison (Belfast City organist) and Stanley Wylie (last resident organist at the Ritz Cinema in Belfast). 3/16-96

The Exorcist was screened for a fortnight during December at the Queen's Cinema, prompting *Spectator* correspondent Campbell McCormick to denounce local Councillors for allowing it to be shown in Bangor. Describing the film as "revolting and evil", Mr McCormick claimed many of those who had seen it "have been so spiritually and emotionally upset that they have needed medical or hospital treatment."

Donaghadee man Robert Brown was appointed Bangor's first litter warden, assigned with the task of preventing the dropping of litter and also the fouling of footpaths by dogs. His beat was mainly Main Street/ High Street and Queen's Parade.

Following a slump in the textile industry 39 men were laid off at the Gainsborough factory, leaving 80 per cent of the staff still employed. The Rathgael-based company was upbeat about the future but indicated that a further review would be carried out in the New Year.

First Bangor Seniors, winners of their section in the Ards District PT competitions in January 1974. From bottom: Rosalind Gray, Cherie Graham, Jennifer Hamilton, Muriel Stewart, Ann Russell, Deborah Wallace, Shirley Major, Brenda Houston (officer) and Lorraine Crothers. 24/14-79

Producer Joe Cavan (back, second from left) with the cast of Bangor Abbey Players' production of *Beside the Seaside*, which was presented in the Abbey Hall in February 1974. Back: Gerald Watson, Sheila Oliver, Ernie Craig, Barry McFadden. Front: Olive McKillop, Anne Cree, June McGlennon, Maud Thompson and Delia Davidson. 39/3-79

First Bangor GB Explorers were acclaimed the best in Northern Ireland at the Explorer PT competitions on 16 February 1974. With officer Brenda Houston they are (back, from left): Karen Smith, Julie McGowan, Andrea Watts, Julie Mateer, Linda Gowdy. Front: Donna Revie, Glenys Tolley, Sara Henry and Julie Hall. 71/4-79

Girls from St Columbanus Parish Church Sunday School formed an entertainment group called 'Children at Play', under the guidance of Mrs Dorothy Magee, in March 1974. They hoped to visit hospitals, old people's homes and schools for handicapped children with a programme of singing, dancing and games. *65/12-79*

Pupils of St Columbanus Secondary School who passed with honours the Grade I Theory examination of Trinity College, London. Their teacher was Sister Alacoque McDonagh. *90/4-79*

Wendy Fair (14) with her *Old Woman in a Shoe* arrangement which won second prize at the Bangor Horticultural Society's annual show in the Abbey Hall in April 1974. Looking on are her brothers Terence and Gary (aged 10 and 12), with Philippa Clegg (7), Susan Clegg (11) and Vanessa Burrowes (9). *33/3-81*

Gavin Barnes and Judith McDowell (at front) won bicycles in a Sukie Sunkap colouring competition organised by Bangor Dairies in April 1974. They are pictured with the runners-up, as well as Mr Rainey Stewart, retail sales supervisor with Bangor Dairies, and Mr J. Toy from Grange Park Primary School. *40/9-81*

Mr D. G. Baird, chairman of the RNLI's Bangor branch, receives a sponsorship cheque from Derek Tughan, a director of the Ulster Scottish Assurance Group, towards a Lifeboat Ball in Milanos on 10 May 1974. Included are George Rolston, branch secretary, and Jim Claney, treasurer. Manning the inshore rescue boat are (from left): Roger Killiner, Jim Ellesmere, Ernie Lyness and Mervyn Gill. *5/4a-82*

Connor House pupils who received special awards at the preparatory school's annual prizegiving in May 1974 are pictured with headmaster Gordon Thomson. From left: Peter Cunningham, Michael Smyth, Kenneth Thompson and Christopher Capper. *53/15/84*

Organisers behind the new Sergeant Pepper's Disco Club for over-21s at the Royal Hotel in June 1974. From left: Ian Wilson, road manager; Christine Hare, hostess; John Mac, DJ; Liverpool Lue (alias Ann Mulligan), billed as Ireland's only female DJ; Leo Cunningham, bar manager; Richard Morrow, disco manager; Mary Hewitt, hostess, and Terry Swanston, DJ. *66/8-86*

Boys and girls who received cycling proficiency certificates from Mayor Jack Preston at Bangor Town Hall on 19 October 1974. *7/9-94*

Members of the Bangor Parish Choir pictured in November 1974 at the retirement of John F. Walsh after singing in the choir for 35 years. Mr Walsh received an inscribed blackthorn stick from Helen Williamson, while Mrs Walsh received flowers from Gordon Hamilton. *21/4a-95*

Members of Bangor Grammar School's choir with the cups they won at Bangor Music Festival in November 1974. Included are conductor Ian Hunter and headmaster Randall Clarke. 45/9-96

Hamilton Road Presbyterian Church GB Explorers who won the Ards Area choral speaking competition for five to six-year-olds in December 1974. Back (from left): Mrs John Burns (team coach), Rachel Guy, Diane Lee, Tara Davison, Pamela Todd, Heather Brown. Middle: Alison McCullough, Lyn Forshaw, Deborah Lindsay, Heather Welsh, Janet Sloan. Front: Louise Andrews, Lorraine Webster, Shirley McClelland, Carol Graham and Joan Martin. 1/3a-97

Towerview Primary School choir entertained friends, family and elderly guests at a series of pre-Christmas services in December 1974. Conductor was Miss Margaret Matthews, with piano accompaniment by Miss Daphne Sheppard. 51/2-97

Lembit Öpik
remembers...

I was born in Bangor on an ice cold, clear morning in March 1965. A snow shower had recently passed through, leaving a fresh glistening cloak of virgin white, and the sun shone for my good fortune. Of course, these details are not my own; I'm told it was so and have no reason to doubt my source.

What I need not take from another's recollection is Bangor in the 1970s. In that erratic,

Lembit Öpik (centre) with fellow RBAI pupils who were successful in the National Essay competition. He attended the school between 1976 and 1983. *Picture courtesy of the Belfast Telegraph.*

uncertain decade I spent most weekends there, visiting my grandparents in their residence: 99 Clifton Road. They lived in that old, enormous, cubic box of a house, next door to the distinctive and striking towers of the Royal Ulster Yacht Club. Side by side, these imposing grand designs gazed out across Belfast Lough, their aged windows bearing silent witness to the ever-changing moods of the sea. When the wind blew hard from the north-east, the spray from the waves would drift up across salty lawns, coating the glass with a misty sheen. The window frames rattled in humble respect for the ocean's wrath.

At night, distant lighthouses blinked patiently, warning

Lembit Öpik was born in Bangor in 1965 to Estonian parents. After his schooling at the Royal Belfast Academical Institution, he studied Philosophy at Bristol University, graduating in 1987. He was president of the Student Union (1985-6) and national student politician after that. In 1988 he joined American soap giant Procter and Gamble in Newcastle upon Tyne, rising to the role of Global Corporate Training and Organisation Development Manager.

In May 1997, he was elected as MP for Montgomeryshire,

Lembit's grandparents' home at 99 Clifton Road, Bangor

The view across Belfast Lough

serving as Liberal Democrat Spokesperson for Northern Ireland for 10 years. He was Leader of the Welsh Liberal Democrats and a Shadow Cabinet member.

In 2010 Lembit lost his seat in the night's most unexpected election result. Characteristically, he turned his difficulties into opportunities, and has appeared on programmes as diverse as *Newsnight, Have I got News for You* and *Celebrity Come Dine With Me.*

Lembit's interests include astronomy, aviation and motorbikes. He speaks fluent Estonian, and some French and German.

west-bound mariners of their approach to a perilous seaboard. Passengers steaming east for Liverpool, with Belfast lost in their wake, stood on deck. Peering starboard from three miles out, they would catch the shimmering lights of the town, bidding its whispered farewell to departing souls.

Walking into Bangor in that era was, for me, an adventure loaded with the excitement of childhood and exploration. Rambling down High Street, my heart raced with thoughts of visiting McCulloughs, the toy store opposite where Queen's Parade turned its dramatic right angle. All along that front resided the tired penny arcades with their moody proprietors: the woman who always looked ready to blame you, but for nothing in particular; the men who sat inside, whatever the weather, as if the sunshine had long ago lost its lustre to their weary eyes — as if the darkness was in some way preferable, an escape from the elemental nature which rose and fell with the swell of the tides.

And out there, rising and falling with those long ocean breaths, were the fishing boats. My aunty would walk us along the front to stare at trawlers, often idle, sometimes the focus of repair, or of conversation between ruddy-faced mariners (and always they were men). Further along, the little boats of private citizens sighed with the gentle undulations behind breakwaters... or rested on their sides, waiting for the moon to again release them from their beached discomfort.

Sometimes we'd arrive by train. Bangor bound, we were transported past a shipyard in its prime and an airport in its infancy – and back in time, gliding high above the grandeur of Crawfordsburn Country Park, across its exquisite viaduct. As the carriages halted, we'd 'alight' and walk along the platform, my father and I. For me, the station held a particular fascination – its terminus a quiet final destination, a world away from a bustling and troubled city, a peace at the end of the rails. And I'd spy that sign on the wall exhorting the virtue of sobriety – 'be teetotal and free!' – though whether would-be revellers en route to hostelries took any note, I'll never know.

We'd invariably walk from there. To me, Main Street seemed a mountainous slope, as if the whole town had been folded down the middle – to mischievously slide visitors down to the lowest point by the harbour. And what then? Having unwittingly arrived, they were encouraged to stay in the town's warm heart by the prospect of inclines in every direction, in steep contrast to the level sanctuary of the front itself.

I was not afraid in Bangor. The Troubles were somehow not welcomed there. While it must be said the town had its share of sectarian tragedy, it seemed to me this place had been granted a partial respite, an unspoken amnesty from the heat of the strife. In Bangor my parents discussed the Troubles as if they occurred elsewhere... away... and the measured angst in their words prayed it would remain so.

Bangor in the 1970s did not presume to be a dandy town, a place of ostentation. The boats in the water were small. The lines clinking against masts opposite Caproni's Ice Cream Parlour marked a disappearing age when time itself felt more in abundance; and on rainy days along the shore, often as not you could pursue your own thoughts and footsteps in undisturbed solitude. And Caproni's itself was an incongruous contradiction to all of this – an exotic taste of Italy, its exquisite ice creams in ironic contrast to the

Lembit Öpik at Westminster

Lembit is also tipped to be the first Lib Dem Prime Minister since the 1920s – according to the *Times Almanac* – in 2023. He claims to regard his current spell away from Parliament as the essential 'Wilderness Years Period' any true statesman requires.

Lembit's optimism about the human race combines with his wish to engage with the public in a lively and approachable fashion. He says his observations about life – and Bangor – are sincere and evocative of an era when people still had time to notice the world – and people – around them.

Caproni's on Seacliff Road

grey sheets of rain resentfully lashing the adults and children braving the elements for the sake of a frozen delight.

Bangor made do with its lot. Its uncomplaining and undecorated humility was in a sense epitomised by Pickie Pool – a public gesture of icy opportunity, its chilly waters tinged with marine oil and hints of seaweed. To its last days, it remained a place of congregation for a stoic generation professing their loyalty to the sea, in preference to the seductive temptations of a heated, indoor pool.

So much of it has gone. My grandparents' house has been replaced with a profitable new development. The penny arcades have been evicted, their proprietors' weathered expressions turned out into the daylight, to squint at sunshine and seasons. Their copper-based empires were long ago replaced by desirable restaurants and places where pennies buy you nothing, and which my family in the 1970s could not have afforded to frequent. And Pickie Pool, in all its idiosyncratic splendour, was swept away by the tides of opulent progress, caused to crumble in deference to this irresistible force.

Bangor, like my grandparents and my aunt – and my father – has moved on. There are roads I dare not visit for fear of dissolving fond impressions which still inhabit that era of my mind. And with those reside quiet murmurs of regret that things do not stay the same; that progress, with its financially-motivated forward march, will redevelop those Bygones-by-the-Sea, selling new vistas to those who never knew the particular past which was sacrificed for their present.

But even now, when a north-east wind howls and the lines clink against the masts opposite where Caproni's used to be – as boats adjust themselves restlessly on ocean swells tamed by breakwaters – the spirit of decades passed lives on. Their memory can still be heard in the mutterings of the solitary widow, homeward bound, through punishing December squalls. The soul of those days sighs in every wave that crashes on the deserted rocks, opposite where my grandparents used to live. Our history looks on, knowing that whatever the future holds, for better or worse, our past can never be undone.

1975

IN THE SPECTATOR

Two Bangor families had an unexpected New Year stay at the Royal Hotel after a storm blew the roofs off their bungalow homes at Cairnsville Drive, a new development off Ballycrochan Road.

Miss Ann Dexter, who lived in one of the houses with her father, was in bed when the incident happened,

Jack Coey receives assistance with the removal of furnishings from his damaged home. *36/14a-98*

but fortunately she was not injured. Next door, where Mr and Mrs Jack Coey lived with their two teenage sons, Mr Coey suffered a head injury, but after treatment he was back out with family and neighbours shifting furniture and moving to their temporary accommodation.

The houses were of an unusual design with roofs of mineralised felt. The developer blamed a design fault which affected just the two bungalows in question.

Ulsterbus withdrew the last double-decker buses from service in the Bangor, Newtownards and Donaghadee areas at the beginning of January. Coinciding with the decision, two long-serving members of staff decided to take early retirement

Rev. Cecil Newell, chairman of the Bangor Council of Churches, leads the march for peace towards the town centre. 14/14-100

– John Lucas, 46 Rugby Avenue, and John Johnston, 3 St Gallen's Court (both 28 years' service).

More than 1,000 people took part in the latest march for peace on 2 February 1975. Participants gathered at the flagpole in Castle Park, venue for a service of prayer for reconciliation and peace. It was organised by the Bangor Council of Churches and the local branch of Protestant and Catholic Encounter (PACE).

The Tonic Cinema regained its famous name in early March, having been part of the Odeon chain since April 1969. Belfast Cinemas Ltd. acquired a number of local cinemas, including 'The Show Place of Bangor', and immediately restored the name by which it had been known since opening in 1936. Manager Eric Crossan said they wanted to bring back stage shows as well as "really good films."

The Department of Commerce announced a £900,000 facelift for Bangor seafront at the beginning of May, including marina accommodation for 400 pleasure boats. The Borough Council welcomed the scheme, with Mayor Jack Preston declaring: "This will revitalise our whole seafront area which is becoming completely out of date and shoddy."

Voters returned to the polls on 1 May to select seven North Down representatives out of 12 candidates for the new Northern Ireland Constitutional Convention. Its aim was to find a form of government that was likely to command the most widespread support throughout the community.

There were three candidates each for the Official Unionists (Jim Kilfedder, John Taylor and Neil Oliver), the Alliance Party (Lord Dunleath, Keith Jones and Bertie McConnell), the Unionist Party of Northern Ireland (Lord Brookeborough, William Brownlow and Bertie Campbell), and one each for the Vanguard Unionist Party (George Green), the Democratic Unionist Party (Charles Poots) and the SDLP (Sean Hollywood).

Bangor was again plunged into grief following the murder of 26-year-old Woman Reserve Constable Mildred Harrison on Sunday evening 16 March. Millie, as she was popularly known, was on duty in her home town when a bomb, which had been left on the windowsill of the Ormeau Arms public house, exploded as she was passing the Albert Street junction with High Street. A piece of debris pierced her chest and she died in

the arms of a male colleague who was on patrol with her.

Mrs Harrison, who was married with two young children, was the first policewoman to die through terrorism in Northern Ireland. Following a service in St Comgall's Church, Brunswick Road, she was buried at Clandeboye Cemetery with full RUC honours. The Bishop of Down and Connor, Most Rev. Dr William Philbin, presided at the Mass and the mourners included Chief Constable Jamie Flanagan, Mayor Jack Preston, politicians and other civic and church leaders.

Tony Coghlan, brother of the murdered police officer, responding to the reaction from the 'ordinary people of Bangor,' stated: "To these people I would say, in my sister's death you were united in your genuine grief. Politics and religious differences were forgotten, you were united as one people: please try to hold on to that unity. Don't let her death be in vain; let her young blood wash away the misery and hate of the past six years. It would be a fine legacy to her two children if we could forget the past and go forward to the future in peace and love."

Speaking in 2011 Mr Coghlan added: "Let us hope with the new political situation in Northern Ireland that peace has finally arrived and no one will be drawn into joining dissident organisations. The cause of a United Ireland was set back by the actions of the IRA; it might have happened without the Troubles as things were very definitely changing here."

Low prices are back in fashion

Penneys are opening in the new
Clandeboye Shopping Centre Bangor
on Tuesday 10th June

PENNEYS

CLANDEBOYE SHOPPING CENTRE BANGOR

The five Official Unionist, VUP and DUP representatives all had UUUC backing. Four of them won seats, namely Kilfedder, Taylor, Green and Poots (although Oliver could have joined them with better management of Kilfedder's transfers), along with Lord Dunleath and McConnell for Alliance and the UPNI's Lord Brookeborough.

Kilfedder topped the poll with 21,693 first preference votes, while Campbell, who received 901 votes, was the only candidate to lose his deposit. Hollywood achieved the fourth highest number of votes (3,988), beating three of the ultimately successful candidates, but failed to attract transfers.

Over in South Belfast David Trimble, standing as a Vanguard Unionist, gained his first election victory – and a seat in the Convention.

A by-election took place on 29 May in Area B (Conlig, Whitehill, Rathgael, Clandeboye and Silverstream), following the resignation of Cllr Tommy Braniff,

Three-year-old Debbie Hardy, of Linden Gardens, Kilmaine, won the Miss Pinta beauty contest at Ballycrochan Country Fair in July 1975. 89/9-111

who had won the seat in 1973 on a Loyalist ticket. Ulster Unionist (UUUC) John Shields secured 1,509 votes, which was more than the other three candidates added together – Andrew Templeton (Independent), 441; Harry Murray (Alliance), 400; James McKibbin (Independent), 268.

Siobhan Lennon (14) was named St Columbanus Secondary School Personality Girl for 1975. Sister Paula (8) was the reigning Miss Bangor Camera Club, while another sister, Joanne, was a past Little Miss Northern Ireland.

Hosiery firm Welrex, which had started life at Queen's Parade in 1958 with just three employees and had become one of Bangor's biggest companies with several hundred workers, became the latest victim of the recession. By July Welrex employed 68 people at its factory on the Clandeboye Road, with a further 164 in Newry. General manager Mr W. J. Bradley announced they were going into receivership and would close both factories by the middle of the month.

The Debretta textile company extended its traditional two-week Twelfth holiday to three, but staff were unpaid for the third week.

The era of the Blue Lamp Disco was born at the Borough Gymnasium on Saturday 26 July. The RUC, while wishing to clamp down on teenage drinking, accepted they needed an alternative to public houses.

Sgt Spiers Wilson, the local Community Relations Officer, stated: "If there is a big turn-out we will run a similar disco every Friday and Saturday night."

Young people dance to the sounds of the Blue Lamp Disco in the Borough Gymnasium in July 1975. *32/3-113*

Future venues included First Bangor Presbyterian Church's Guild Hall (Main Street), the Methodist Church's Epworth Hall (Bingham Lane), and Milanos (Seacliff Road), with attendances numbering into the high hundreds. Blue Lamp Discos also spread to Holywood, Newtownards and beyond following their success in Bangor.

Ulster Television's new *Lunchtime* magazine programme was presented by Robin Dunseath and Hilary Maxwell, both from Bangor. He worked in public relations and she was a graduate of Manchester University.

The Crosby Flats complex on the High Donaghadee Road, which provided 32 self-contained flats for elderly residents, was opened by Housing Minister Don Concannon on 27 September. The scheme, along with renovations to the adjoining Sunnyside House, was undertaken by the Shankill Road Mission of the Presbyterian Church.

Two Convention members from Bangor, George Green and David Trimble, along with Vanguard Unionist Party leader Bill Craig, were suspended from the United Ulster Unionist Council in mid-October after Craig voiced support for voluntary power-sharing. Another Bangor man, Campbell McCormick, resigned as chairman of the town's VUP branch, citing "power-sharing proposals in relation to our enemies, the SDLP."

North Down Borough Council chief executive Richard Wolsey announced he would retire at Christmas. Mr Wolsey, who had joined the local authority in 1952 as assistant Town Clerk, wanted to devote his energies to his other role as secretary of the Association of Local Authorities in Northern Ireland. He was succeeded by second-in-command Jack McKimm.

The Council rejected an application from Belfast Cinemas Ltd. to screen films at the Tonic on Sundays and to operate a licensed restaurant within the complex. The planners also vetoed the restaurant proposal, claiming it would result in a "considerable increase in traffic to and from the premises."

Chief Constable Sir Jamie Flanagan, Mayor Jack Preston and other guests with teenagers who attended the Blue Lamp Disco in Milanos on 25 October 1975. 6/6-119

RUC Chief Constable Sir Jamie Flanagan, Supt. Trevor Forbes, head of the RUC's Community Relations Branch in Northern Ireland, and Mayor Jack Preston visited the Blue Lamp Disco at Milanos on 25 October. The Chief Constable described it as "a truly worthwhile venture" and commended the Bangor team behind the Blue Lamp initiative.

There was a by-election success for the Alliance Party in Area C (Bangor Castle, Springhill, Bryansburn, Princetown and Crawfordsburn), following the resignation of Cllr David Belshaw, who had been elected as a Unionist in 1973. Three candidates stood on 6 November – Maisie McMullan (Official Unionist with UUUC backing), Archie Pollock (Vanguard Unionist Party) and Oscar Rollins (Alliance).

In a 21% turnout Rollins topped the poll with 928 votes, with 757 being cast for Mrs McMullan and 368 for Pollock. The transfer of the latter's votes saw Rollins' total rise to 1,033 – 121 ahead of Mrs McMullan. This increased the Alliance team on the Council to eight.

Work on the new Skipperstone Hall, serving the people of Whitehill, Lisnabreen and Clanmorris, was completed ahead of schedule and it was handed over to the Council on 7 November. The hall would become the home of the Skipperstone Community Association, formerly the Tenants Association.

The Roads Service suggested converting lower Main Street and possibly both High Street and Bridge Street into a pedestrian shopping precinct. Councillors welcomed the proposal in principle after receiving an assurance that the DoE would consult widely before any decisions were taken.

The Gainsborough factory finally succumbed to changing fashion trends, with its imminent closure being announced by parent company Carrington Viyella on 2 December – putting 256 men and 24 women out of work by early in the New Year.

John Knipe, of 24 Ballyholme Esplanade, visited Buckingham Palace with his wife Phyllis and son Christopher to receive the MBE from the Queen for his services to drama in Northern Ireland.

The Blue Lamp Disco's future was in doubt after Bangor business H. Cowan Ltd. won a planning appeal in December against a previous refusal to use Milanos for a furniture store. The company agreed to consider alternative proposals from those wishing to keep the Blue Lamp Disco at its Seacliff Road home.

Off to see the Bay City Rollers in Belfast on 22 December after winning double tickets in a *Spectator* competition were Nicola Fyffe (12), of Moira Drive, with friend Cheryl Glithero (13), of Park Avenue, and Irene Bishop (14), of Cleland Park Central, with friend Lynn McAleer (14), of Whitehill Avenue, all Bangor.

Les McKeown of the Bay City Rollers on stage in Belfast at Christmas 1975. *58/19-123*

Former Bangor Mayor Charles Milligan and his wife Marjorie celebrated their 60th wedding anniversary on 29 December. Mr Milligan, by then 87, devoted much of his time to promoting his native town. His then recently published reminiscences were entitled *My Bangor from the 1890s.* He served as Mayor from 1963-66, received the OBE from the Queen and was made a Freeman of Bangor.

Members of the P1 class at the new St Malachy's Primary School, off the Clandeboye Road, which opened its doors on 6 January 1975. Included are principal Gerard O'Loan and teachers Patricia Gallagher and Mary Fealty. 65/7-99

Members of the Bangor Abbey Church Lads' Brigade in front of one of two stained-glass windows they provided for the Abbey. Included are Alfred Henderson, CLB captain, Canon R. C. Ellis, Dunmurry, who preached at the dedication service in January 1975, and the rector, Canon James Hamilton. 98/9-99

There was an appropriately Dickensian setting for the visit of Cedric Charles Dickens (left), great grandson of the famous novelist, to Bangor in March 1975, when he met Robbie Lightbody and Peter Barry, who shared the title role in Bangor Amateur Operatic Society's production of Oliver! at the Little Theatre. Included are the two Artful Dodgers, Keith Murray and Paul Donley, Jimmy George, who organised the visit, and Denby Bell, Operatic Society chairman. 94/6a-101

Twelve-year-old Raymond Seenan, of 3 Owenroe Drive, was acclaimed by the *County Down Spectator* as Bangor's first 'Kojak' in March 1975 after paying 40p to have all his blonde hair cut off by a local barber. He was a pupil at Bangor Boys' Secondary School. *53-4a-102*

Principals in Bangor Harmonic Society's presentation of *The Rebel Maid* in April 1975 at the local Technical College. From left: Robert Howell (tenor), Philip Walden and Geraldine Roberts (pianists), Frank Morwood (baritone), Janette Simpson (soprano), Ernest Browne (conductor), Lorraine Wilson (mezzo-soprano), Desmond Cole (baritone) and Eric Hinds (baritone). *115/18-104*

Bangor couple Mr and Mrs Norman Shaw, of 156 Seacliff Road, with members of the family circle at a celebration to mark their 60th wedding anniversary in April 1975. *24/3a-106*

Members of the Bangor Good News team who won an inter-club Bible quiz at 2nd Newtownards Presbyterian Church in May 1975. Pictured with the Rev. and Mrs Eric Stewart, of Bangor Independent Methodist Church, are (from left): Barbara Taylor, Angela Hill, Alan Robinson, Valerie Young and Paul Robinson. *53/5-107*

Worshipful Master Sammy Mellon (centre) is pictured with Sons of Ulster LOL 1027 before leaving for the field in Holywood on 12 July 1975. *45/5A-112*

Young people who received certificates for completing the inaugural Mourne Ramble, promoted by the RUC's Community Relations Branch and North Down Council's Recreations Department, in September 1975. Included are Mayor Jack Preston, Sgt. Spiers Wilson, Deputy Mayor Mary O'Fee, and Chief Inspector D. Turkington, Bangor. *86/6-115*

Tommy and Sally Robinson took their first ballroom dancing class of the season – for children – in the Borough Gymnasium in October 1975. *4119-117*

Mrs Spiers Wilson receives a bouquet from Patricia Stanfield, secretary of the Brunswick Road Youth Club, at the official opening of their new hall in October 1975. Local police representatives, youth leaders and youth club officials are included. *50113-117*

Pupils from Bangor Boys' Secondary School visited Kent in October 1975 as guests of Ashford Rotary Club. From left: teacher Rodney Bambrick, Rhys Boyd, Ian Gordon, Simon Walker, Brian Tipping, Peter Vernon, Stephen Courtney, Barry Christie, Jim McCullough, principal. Front: Andrew Watson, David Blaikie, Laurence Upton and Andrew Sweeney. *9121-118*

In November 1975 four-year-old Timothy Lennon became the sixth child of Malachy and Dympna Lennon, 24 Bryansburn Road, to leave Bangor Nursery School for St Comgall's Primary School, Brunswick Road. From left: Dympna, Timothy, Dympna Marie (7), Helen Porter (past principal), Paula (8), Jean Shannon (former assistant), Joanne (15), Siobhan (14), Malachy (5), Irene Irvine, principal in 1975, with (at back) Malachy and Anne Harbinson (former assistant). 69/7-118

The Clifton Special Care School band, under the baton of Mrs A. Chambers, won the Deveney Cup at Bangor Musical Festival in November 1975. 69/2-120

P1 and P4 classes at Glenlola's Preparatory Department who presented a nativity play in December 1975. Included are Sorina Morrow (Joseph), Jane Pritchard (Mary), Michelle Andrews (Gabriel), Shirley Martin and Caroline Jemphrey (Readers), Leslie Whittle (Star), Shirley Lorimer (Angel), Barbara Hull, Judith McCormack and Julie McKay (Wise Men). 49/0-22

Suzy O'Hara
remembers...

Suzy O'Hara today

I began the 1970s aged 12 with a Saturday job washing hair and brushing floors in a hairdressing salon in the Royal Hotel. The Tickle Pink was the first mixed salon in Northern Ireland to operate in a hotel. It offered me my first chance to work in my family's hotel and I wanted to do it well so I took my job very seriously.

Our family's involvement in hospitality in Bangor began in 1886 when my great grandmother Annie, a widow with four young sons, together with her brothers opened a pub on Bangor seafront. When the Town Council subsequently wanted her site on which to erect the McKee Clock, they offered her premises across the road which became the Grand Hotel, later Barry's Amusements and more recently the Marine Court.

In 1908 my grandfather, Willie O'Hara, decided to follow his mother into the business purchasing modest premises at the end of Quay Street called the Royal Hotel. In 1932, in the middle of the great depression, he took the bold decision to add two storeys to the building, making it the familiar landmark it is today.

In 1951, his son and my father, Bill O'Hara, took over the business. Following his marriage to Annemarie Finn in 1953, the two began an innovative partnership which was to transform the hospitality industry, in Bangor and

Suzy O'Hara worked in the Royal Hotel until she moved to the Cayman Islands in her mid-20s. Then followed a three-year spell in London as Public Relations Manager at the London Tara Hotel.

On her return to Bangor with her daughter Claire at the end of the 80s she joined the BBC, where she remained for 20 years. She currently works in Worthingtons Solicitors in Belfast.

Her life revolves round her family, work and golf.

beyond, with a brand which became known simply as Bill & Anne.

By the end of the 60s, O'Hara's Royal Hotel in Bangor had become well established as a central part of the social scene for the town's residents with the ground-breaking Half Door Club, the Grill Bar, unique in Northern Ireland in that it served food from 11.00 – 11.00 and Bangor's first coffee shop. It was also popular with tourists who flocked to the town during the summer months to stay by the sea.

As the 70s began and the Troubles took hold, Northern Ireland was no longer a desirable destination for tourists. However, during this turbulent time Bangor was seen as being a safe and convenient distance from Belfast and it offered an attractive option for people to relocate to and so the seaside resort became a city suburb. My parents, already faced with the closure of several of their pubs in Belfast, concentrated their efforts on the Bangor business.

They were able to attract travelling representatives who were no longer prepared to stay in hotels in the city and the Royal was thus transformed into a business hotel, a second home for people who still had reason to do business in Northern Ireland at this time.

The Royal Hotel in the 1970s

My parents recognised that the younger element seemed to have more money in their pockets and, as there was an increasing degree of reticence about socialising in Belfast, they saw an opportunity to provide a venue for that age group in Bangor. Thus, The Viking was born. Bangor's first disco quickly became iconic, with anniversaries still celebrated to this day. I wonder how many families exist as a result of relationships formed at the Viking Disco during the 70s?

Unlike my younger brothers, I was not allowed to work

there and was very envious when they bragged about seeing Ireland's first punk rockers who had begun to frequent this groundbreaking club.

The rest of the hotel continued to attract an older clientele, with the restaurant and Grill Bar being very busy most of the time. I know just how busy it was because by this time I was 14 and working in the kitchen doing starters and desserts. The Royal was a wonderful place to work with true

Popular couple Bill and Anne O'Hara, who were at the forefront of tourism promotion in Bangor during the 1970s.

camaraderie amongst the staff, which was predominantly made up of three families, the Lennons (the hotel was often referred to as *Lennongrad,* such was the number of the family working there), the Storeys and the Delargys.

There were, of course, many others who worked in the Royal and there are few catering establishments in the wider area today that do not employ either a person who worked in the Royal or their descendant. Mum loved the fact that many attractive girls chose to work in the Royal and on occasions, such as the opening nights of performances with the Bangor Amateur Operatic Society which were traditionally devoted

Dolly (Laura Carr) and her 'dollies' – all Royal Hotel staff members – help to promote the opening charity night of a 1970s production of Hello Dolly by Bangor Amateur Operatic Society. Among the Royal girls are Annemarie Lennon, Valerie Blue, Patsy McAleer, June Gamble and Mary O'Neill. *Spectator picture*

to a charity, Mum would get her 'girls' out with the collection boxes. A sure-fire way to make more money for the charity!

I attended these evenings and thus began my interest in drama. When I was 15 I was encouraged by Ian Kennedy, a teacher in Sullivan Upper School, to enter the Bangor

Pictured at the close of Bangor Verse Speaking Festival in April 1974 are (from left): Mrs V. Sloan, holding the bouquet she received from Lindsey Thompson, Miss F. Newell, general secretary of Bangor Music Festival, Jill Thompson, who presented flowers to Deputy Mayor Alderman Mary O'Fee, adjudicator Mr William Bennett, and Mrs Babs Pinkerton with the flowers she received from Suzy O'Hara. Suzy won the Gloria Joy Cup for Shakespeare and the Baxter Cup as best of the senior prizewinners. *93/1-80*

Festival with two monologues from Shakespeare. Until that time, despite entering numerous festivals in verse and dance over a seven-year period, I had never won a medal for anything. I never once got even shortlisted! So it was with some trepidation that I went along to the first competition playing the part of Launcelot from *The Merchant of Venice*. The adjudicator tore me to shreds and I was devastated. He said I should not have chosen a male part as there were many female Shakespearean roles to choose from and he was not impressed by my outfit – I had dressed like a clown because this was a comic character.

I went home feeling extremely dejected and was quite determined to give the second competition a miss. It was to take place exactly a week later, on the final day of the week-long festival. I was clearly persuaded to go but I stood my ground on the subject of dressing up, insisting I would play the role of Juliet in my trousers – under no circumstances was I prepared to wear a dress which would, of course, have been more appropriate.

Up I got and did my piece and, lo and behold, the same

adjudicator thought it was brilliant but he kept going on about the fact that a Juliet shouldn't be wearing trousers. I was awarded first place and got the cup. What a moment! I was so excited I really thought I would burst with pride. There was no one from my family with me because I didn't want to suffer the humiliation of the week before in front of anyone who knew me.

Then I was informed that, as a prize-winner, I had to enter the Prize-Winners competition which was to take place immediately. This involved every first prize-winner of the entire week. So I had to do it again and blow me down if he didn't give me first place in that too. I walked out of Hamilton House with two big trophies and I was the happiest person ever. So unexpected was this achievement that when I got home, the family honestly thought I had borrowed the trophies from someone and was having them on!

Although I have great memories of this period of my life, I was always aware of the terrible events taking place with increasing regularity across the Province. It was a sad day when Dad, as a key holder for the Abercorn Restaurant in Belfast, had to attend the devastating scene after the bomb went off.

Even before these tragic events my father had believed segregated education was aggravating an already divided society. This is why my three siblings and I spent the 70s in state schools rather than the Roman Catholic schools we would have been expected to attend. This did not make my Dad universally popular but he was determined to do his bit to bridge the religious divide in Northern Ireland.

Suzy O'Hara (left) with sister Jane and brothers Bill and Stephen (right)

During the 70s Dad sat on a committee whose main purpose was to relocate people whose lives were under threat from paramilitary groups. Dad had become quite prominent in the community through business and public appointments and after one such meeting future Chief Constable Jack

Hermon, who had access to the lists of persons being targeted, advised Dad that his name, quite unusually, appeared on the hit lists of both the Provisionals and the Loyalists. From that time I noticed extra security around the house. I also recall that at one time Dad had to change his car following a tip-off to the police.

I went off to Drama School in London in 1976 and for the next three years my involvement in Bangor was confined to holidays when I continued to work in the Royal as a Grill Bar waitress. My most abiding memory over this period was that, almost without fail, the inside of the hotel would look different each time I came home. Dad, who always had a penchant for knocking down walls, had lost so many businesses with the Troubles that he was left with only the Royal through which to satisfy his architectural ambitions. Our reception desk was relocated so many times, my brother Stephen suggested Dad should put it on wheels! In many ways it was a difficult decade but we appreciated all that we had and I have many happy memories of that period of my life.

A final memory of my father. When I was in my last year at St Comgall's Primary School I was entered to play the recorder at a music festival in Belfast along with the other girls in my class. It transpired a few days before the event that I was performing the same piece as another girl in my year. Sister Brendan asked me to find another piece of music. I came home very worried because I had no idea how to find something new at this stage.

Suzy as a pupil at St Comgall's Primary School in the mid-1960s

My Dad took an unusual interest in helping me out. He didn't play the recorder himself but he was able to guide me through the notes until I had the music in my head and then I went off to practice. I worked very hard and had it perfected by the next morning, playing it completely through for Dad before leaving for school. When Sister Brendan asked me to play for her I did so with gusto. I didn't understand her reaction when she shouted that it wouldn't do and I was to revert to the original music, until I was told by my Dad when I got home that he had taught me, and I had played in total innocence, *The Sash My Father Wore*. Forty years on and I can still play it!

1976
IN THE SPECTATOR

A former Glenlola Collegiate student became the first woman to be ordained to any church in Ireland. The Rev Ruth Patterson was ordained on 2 January at Gardenmore Presbyterian Church, Larne. Her Groomsport-born father was the Rev. T. A. Patterson, minister of Portaferry Presbyterian Church, while her mother, Dr Ruth Patterson, was well known in the medical profession.

Bangor's new eating out experience, the floating restaurant *MV Balholm,* was moored at the North Pier from mid-January. However, it was a short-lived experiment, with the 240-ton vessel ultimately heading to Dublin for a refit and then disappearing from temporary moorings off the Welsh coast in January 1979, never to be seen again.

The Tonic was put up for sale by Belfast Cinemas Ltd. with a £125,000-plus price tag. The 1.5-acre site included space for 175 cars, living accommodation and four shop units. Many believed the decision stemmed from the refusal of planning permission for a licensed restaurant.

Almost immediately a planning application for a change of use to a furniture showroom was submitted on behalf of H. Cowan Ltd., the same firm that had previously expressed an interest in Milanos. This was opposed by the Borough Council which instructed officers to investigate the property's potential for civic purposes.

Irene Edgar (16) and Karen McCormick (15) hold the petition they organised in the hope of keeping Kilcooley Youth Club going, following a closure announcement at the end of January 1976. 85/9-125

The last Blue Lamp Disco in Milanos was held on 31 January, coinciding with the closure of another youth facility in the town, the three-year-old Kilcooley Youth Club. Blue Lamp Discos resumed in the Dufferin Hall at the end of February but future dates during the year proved intermittent.

More than 30 town centre traders, in an open letter to the 6 February edition of the *Spectator*, called for the reopening of Main Street during business hours.

"As far as security is concerned," they wrote, "everyone knows the gates are a completely useless exercise and the police would verify this. Would they not be better employed, along with the traffic wardens, in patrolling Main Street and High Street to ensure cars only park if someone remains in them? This is the practice in Belfast and elsewhere."

While it had no authority over the security element, the Borough Council responded by replacing barrels at Quay Street and Bridge Street with plant containers.

Bangor native John Edward McCready (56) died in hospital on 6 February, 10 days after he was the victim of a random sectarian shooting on the Cavehill Road, near his Old Westland Road home in Belfast.

A member of an old Bangor family, he was born in the Mill House, Windmill Road, and subsequently attended the Primacy School and then Rowandene School on Hamilton Road.

After moving to the city Mr McCready retained many of his links with Bangor and this was reflected by the large local attendance at the funeral, which took place to Clandeboye Cemetery following a service in St Barnabas Parish Church, Belfast.

A weekend spate of loyalist-inspired violence in early March included an incident in which an elaborate hoax device was thrown through the front window of a Catholic home in Kilcooley's Ballyquinton Gardens. The resulting bomb alert led to the evacuation of some 30 families from their homes for nearly four hours. Elsewhere a beer keg was left on the railway line near Bangor. A carriage was seriously damaged when the Army carried out a controlled explosion.

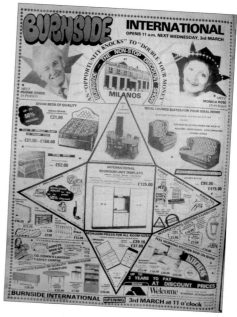

Opportunity Knocks host Hughie Green and 'sidekick' Monica Rose visited Bangor on 3 March to open Burnside International – the discount furniture warehouse located in the former Milanos ballroom.

A UUUC rally was held in Hamilton House on 8 March, four days after Secretary of State Merlyn Rees announced the dissolution of the failed Northern Ireland Constitutional Convention and the restoration of direct rule. Speakers included the Rev. Ian Paisley, former DUP Convention member Charles Poots, Ernest Baird, leader of the United Ulster Unionist Movement, and Captain Austin Ardill, former Official Unionist Convention member for South Antrim.

Trinity Presbyterian Church bade a fond farewell to the Very Rev. Dr John Carson, who retired in March. Trinity's large upper hall, part of a suite of buildings erected during his ministry, was renamed the Carson Hall.

The opening of Belfast's new Central Station in April and the restoration of the Central Line once again linked the Bangor and Portadown lines and made possible travel between Bangor and Dublin without needing to change stations.

The town's youngest Church of Ireland congregation, St Columba's in Kilcooley, broke a male stranglehold in the town by appointing its first female churchwarden, Mrs Myra Stronge, a mother-of-two from Kircubbin Gardens.

Pop Prom '76, staged at Clandeboye Park on Wednesday 26 May, was Bangor's first-ever outdoor music festival. Organised by Bangor Young Men FC, it brought together a host of Ulster bands, all providing their services free of charge. However, despite admission costing just 75p, only 700 attended, rather than the thousands that had been expected.

Headline acts were Teddie Palmer and the Rumble Band, Clouds and the Young City Stars (without Ian Mitchell who had joined the Bay City Rollers earlier in the year). Local acts included Gypsy, Chalkie, Zodiac and Pace.

There was a Bangor interest in July's trial in Angola of Greek-Cypriot mercenary Costas Georgiou, alias Captain Callan, for his part in the Angolan civil war. Georgiou, when serving in the British Army in Northern Ireland, was convicted of robbing Clandeboye Post Office in early 1972. Jailed and dishonourably discharged, he later became a mercenary in Africa, where he was captured, tried and executed for killing innocent civilians and unarmed captives.

Bangor man Dave Stewart, a member of the North Down branch of the British Sub-Aqua Club, joined a diving expedition 200 miles inside the Arctic Circle. The group was hoping to recover a midget submarine, the X5, which was lost during an attack on the German battleship *Terpitz* at Kaafjord in Norway in 1943. The search proved unsuccessful.

A working model of the proposed marina for Bangor seafront went on display at Queen's University in July. It measured 40ft by 20ft and was built to scale, complete with waves to test tides and currents.

The scale model of the proposed marina, with Pickie Pool in the foreground. *61/17-10*

Investigations were undertaken in August to determine the condition of Bangor Parish Church's late 19th Century spire, amid fears the top would need to be removed. Among the 'casualties' were the bellringers who had to cease their weekly trip to the belfry.

Bangor's new health centre, located on the Newtownards Road, welcomed its first occupants on 23 August, when the clinic moved there from Central Avenue. All the Bangor doctors made a phased move to the new building during the first two weeks of September.

Some 3,000 people attended a peace rally in Castle Park on 28 August 1976. Organised by a group of housewives following the deaths of the three Maguire children in Belfast earlier in the month, it marked the beginning of the Peace People movement.

For the first time in 21 years, and only the second time in their history, 2nd Bangor Scouts won the County Down Challenge Flag. Team members were Michael Moorehead (Patrol Leader), Robert Wilson (Assistant Patrol Leader), George Roe, Nigel Benson, Chris Murnin and Gary McGifford.

In advance of a Bangor Peace Day Rally in November, area peace groups were established during a meeting in Hamilton House on 21 October. Kilcooley housewife Mrs Margaret Taylor, who chaired the Bangor Organising Committee, said they were ordinary people from different parts of the town who wanted to "understand each other a little better."

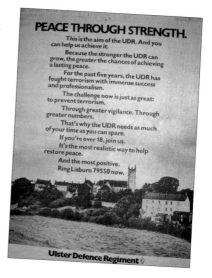

David Trimble, deputy leader of the Vanguard Unionist Party, said Unionism would benefit enormously from the inclusion in government of Catholic representatives who would accept the will of the majority, support the law and seek change only within the law.

The inaugural meeting of Bangor Youth Council was held in the Seacourt Teachers Centre in early November. The executive committee was chaired by Donald Hayes, with Sam Wilson as vice-chairman and Maurice Henry as secretary, along with Tricia Stanford, Margaret Simpson, Sandra Jordan, Wilfred Boucher, David Johnston, Spiers Wilson (RUC Community Relations Department), Marion Taylor (South Eastern Education and Library Board) and Ken McKinnon (North Down Borough Council's Community Services Officer). The leaders' sub-committee was chaired by John Bushell, with Pat Stanfield as secretary.

Plans were made for inter-organisation sports competitions, along with a Gala Night for Youth early in 1977.

Harry Davis, of Beechwood Gardens, was celebrating at Crufts in 1976, after his Irish Terrier bitch Duncairn Mirabelle won two titles – Limit Open Dog or Bitch and Open Bitch – along with the Challenge Certificate for Best Bitch. *15/3-126*

Myles Christie (14) from Ward Avenue, who had been breeding budgerigars for three years, displays his many trophies, diplomas and awards. He was a member of the Bangor and District Cage Bird Society and the Northern Ireland Budgerigar and Foreign Finch Society. *80/14-2*

Bangorian Harry Grindle became the first Irishman to be elected to an Associateship of the Royal School of Church Music. His family had a long association with Bangor Abbey and it was there he made his musical debut, as a choirboy. For several years in the 1960s Mr Grindle was organist and choirmaster at St Comgall's Parish Church, before being appointed to the same positions at St Anne's Cathedral in Belfast, where he remained for 11 years.

Bangor housewives went head to head on 11 November in the only local poll of the year – a by-election in Area C (Bangor Castle, Springhill, Bryansburn, Princetown and Crawfordsburn), which followed the death of Alliance Councillor John Calvert. The candidates were Louise Devlin (Alliance) and Maisie McMullan (Official Unionist). In a 21% turnout Mrs Devlin came out on top, receiving 1,113 votes to the 1,052 cast for Mrs McMullan. Mrs Devlin (32) became the youngest member of the 20-strong local authority.

Bangor Youth Council sought a meeting with Education Minister Lord Melchett in December after hearing that crime involving young people had increased dramatically following the closure of the Blue Lamp Disco in Milanos earlier in the year. Sgt Spiers Wilson said efforts to identify a local venue to cater for the 1,400-strong club membership were continuing.

Pupils of Towerview
Primary School
whose seasonal
pantomime at the
beginning of 1976
was *Dick Whittington*.
7/13/-122

Children at a new
youth club located
in Kilmaine Primary
School from January
1976. 85/2-124

Teachers from Bangor
Technical College at
their annual dinner
dance, held jointly
with Newtownards
College staff. 97/4-125

Some of the Bangor Girls' Secondary School cup winners at the annual prizegiving in March 1976. Back (from left): Julie Hall, Lorraine Menary, Ruth Farr. Front: Dawn Jolley, Anne McAneney and Dawn McKillop. 66/6-126

Kilcooley Primary School pupils visited the Ardglass Activity Centre during March 1976. Included are teachers Mr and Mrs Lloyd and principal Charles Bayly. 70/20-127

Members of the recorder ensemble from Bloomfield Road Primary School were first in their class at Belfast Music Festival in March 1976. From left: Janet McConnell, Susan Lovell, Gail Donnelly, William Mayne, Joanne Russell, Lesley Fulton, Janice Reid, Nicolla Graham, Morna Murphy, Alison Webb, Michele Hawkins and Tracy Kennedy. 85/11a-127

Mrs Margaret Murphy, appeals organiser with the Royal National Institute for the Blind, accepts a cheque for £200 from St Comgall's Primary School pupil Michelle Abbott, who organised a collection for the charity. Holding the certificate presented to the school is Margaret Doherty, while the other pupils include Ann Lennon, Helen McKenzie, Clare Crawford, Gerard McGuinness, Michael Morgan, Stephanie Taylor, Leisha O'Doherty, Pamela Dickson and Gerard Lavery. *7111a-127*

1st Bangor GB Company broke local records with nine members receiving the Duke of Edinburgh Gold Award in one session. Captain Jean Thompson is pictured with (back, from left): Shirley Major, Stephanie Major, Christine Wallace. Middle: Lorraine Crothers, Amanda Dunne, Alison Bell. Front: Angela Scully, Ann Russell and Rosalind Gray. *4118-3*

Bangor Girls' Secondary School bade farewell to vice-principal Peggy Ferris, who was guest of honour at a function hosted by the Former Pupils' Association in June 1976. She is pictured receiving a bouquet from Susan McGregor, while seated beside her is school principal Marie Brownlee. Former pupils include Gloria Butler, Julie Hamill, Moira Dillon, Carole McGowan, Janeen Corbett and Gail Burns. *6110-7*

Members of the St Gall's playgroup at their end-of-term party in July 1976, along with leaders Carole Jackson (left) and Valerie Robb and helper Gloria Stockton. *29/14a-8*

Mrs M. I. Norman (left), who donated prizes for free expression at Bangor Horticultural Society's show in August 1976, presents cups to winners Mrs R. Sterling, Churchill Park, and sisters Romilly and Vanessa Burrowes, Bryansburn Road. *91/8-12*

Ballyholme Playgroup supported the RNLI flag day in September 1976, raising £9.30 through the sale of coathangers. Pictured with supervisor Mrs G. Ralston and Mr J. R. McDowell, secretary of the RNLI fundraising committee, are (from left): Sarah Duffin, Claire Thompson, Dane Ralston, Jeffrey Ralston and (front) Helen Thompson and Mark Greenaway. *6/10-13*

Two pupils of St Columbanus Secondary School – pictured holding the new Company flags – gained their Queen's Badges as members of the 11th Bangor (West Church) Guide Troop. Picture shows (from left): Judith Allen (captain), Rosalind Nevin, Carol Murray (14), Clair Lynch (14), Edna Pherson and Denise Elliott. *49/1-16*

Kilcooley Primary School infants pictured in November 1976 with the harvest produce they collected for Ravara House in Kilcooley. Included are Alan Glenn (principal), Mrs Kirk (P1 teacher), Miss Wood (deaconess at Kilcooley Presbyterian Church) and Elizabeth Buckley (head of infants). *37/6A-15*

The cast of *Bangor Gang Show '76*, presented by Scouts from all the local troops in November 1976 in the Little Theatre. *85/4-17*

Malachy Lennon moved from the Royal Hotel to Furey's in King Street, where he was general manager of the pub, restaurant and off-licence complex. He is pictured (second from left) with staff members Rosemary Beattie, Paul Storey, Barbara Black, Ingrid Magreechan, Hugh Hanna, Pat McKee and Kathleen McConnell. 60/4-18

TV personality Jimmy Savile visited Northern Ireland on 13 November 1976 to take part in a Peace Walk from Belfast to Crawfordsburn Country Park. He met these children and youth leaders from Bangor, including Rev. Raymond Devenney, St Columbanus Parish Church, teacher John Quinliven and Susan McGregor, Project Bangor Youth Club. 22/16-18

Cast members from the Bangor Girls' Secondary School production of The King And I in 1976. 94/1-20

Tommy Boal
remembers...

At the height of the Troubles in the early Seventies, Bangor, although by no means the most difficult of areas in a political sense, did have its own problems. There was always pressure, particularly on teenagers, from various sources.

Evening activities were partly curtailed but despite all of this life went on in a relatively quiet way. However, there was pressure on some young people to become involved in paramilitary activities. It was then that the Bangor Youth Council was set up. A few people led by Donald Hayes got together and inaugurated the group and tremendous encouragement was provided by Cllr Mary O'Fee. The object was to provide activities and programmes for young people and to encourage existing youth groups, regardless of religion or the area in which they were based, to come together for fun and to get to know each other better.

Competitions were organised such as five-a-side football, fun runs, Easter egg hunts, chess and draughts competitions, table tennis championships, skateboard demonstrations and competitions, and what became the highlight of those years in Bangor – the Youth Expo.

Alongside these activities was the very popular Blue Lamp Disco. The RUC were anxious to ensure young

Tommy Boal, the third of a family of four boys, was educated at Bangor Grammar School before taking up a career in the construction industry, first in architecture, next civil engineering, and then holding a quarry manager's post before opening a precast concrete and road construction company.

Sixteen-year-old Lesley Harvey was named Miss Bangor in the Bangor Youth Council-run competition at Caproni's in June 1977. Included are runners-up Charmaine Finnegan and Fiona McCoubrey. *45/14/33*

Following graduation in Economics from Queen's University, he became technical manager for a large construction company. He later was appointed Industrial, Commercial and Tourist Development Officer in North Down Borough Council and set up Enterprise House in the Balloo Estate, where he was appointed manager.

Tommy was, from a very early age, a member of 4th Bangor Boys' Brigade Company in Trinity Presbyterian Church and is currently a member of Session of that church.

Hobbies include calligraphy and the study of ancient manuscripts – and he is a supporter of Arsenal.

With a keen interest in local history – being the seventh generation of Boals in Bangor and having ancestors buried in the Abbey graveyard – he now acts as "The Mad Monk" at the North Down Museum, talking visiting groups through Bangor's early Christian history.

people did not get drawn into unlawful activities. Headed up by Spiers Wilson and Tom Patterson, by April 1977 the discos were being held each Saturday night in Caproni's Ballroom on Seacliff Road. The venue was lent by Mr Orlando Caproni. It's interesting to note that, when it appears that fun can now only be had if accompanied by alcohol, in the hey-day of Caproni's Ballroom alcohol was forbidden and those "under the influence" were not admitted!

Many hundreds of young people attended the discos and the police were very helpful in providing transport to bring them from and return them to the various estates and other parts of the town so they could travel in safety.

Christmas Carols on Main Street, Midnight Rambles to raise funds for good causes, under 14s discos in the Borough Gymnasium and the Bangor Maid Swimming Gala were but some of the activities added to the list as we went along. The purchase and delivery of coal to those in need was another Christmas feature.

A film on 'Leadership in Organisations' was used to introduce young people to the value of leadership in their group or organisation.

Committee member Sam Wilson, who emigrated to America some years earlier, had recently returned to the area. He suggested we run a big event each year so participating groups could prepare for it during the long winter months. He said it would be what was known in the States as a T.I. (Total Involvement) Programme. Sam chaired the organising group and I was tasked as promoter. It would be held on a Saturday in June and it was decided to call it Youth Expo – a grand name for a grand event! It would run from 10am until midnight, finishing with a fireworks display and would cater for all ages, including activities from pop concerts to old tyme dancing.

Saturday 11 June 1977 was the date of the first Expo. It seemed a good idea to do something special for the Queen's Jubilee Year. What a show was planned – all six platforms around the town were ready for the host of bands and pop groups. Acrow lent us scaffolding while Harland and Wolff made planks available for the staging.

Demonstrations of art, clothesline art, fencing, judo and boxing, along with a host of other demonstrations and activities were ready to go, bean eating and custard pie fights were prepared, market stalls were laid out in lower Main Street – this was closed for security purposes but that suited us just fine – youth groups could sell goods to raise funds, all the church halls were booked and all was ready – or was it?

The raw egg throwing competition held during 1978's Youth Expo

We awoke to the worst June day in history. It rained non-stop for almost 15 hours and high winds buffeted the town centre. The waves breaking over the Queen's Parade wall put paid to any band performances and a host of other activities planned to take place there. Poor Maurice Henry had spent days collecting generators and lights from hire companies and now had to remove them from under the waves to prevent damage. We had worked until

2am the previous night to erect the platforms, tie up the promotional placards and generally to ensure that all was ready for a good start.

Despite this, the Parade of Floats did take place and most of the youth groups braved the elements so that visitors were able to see something of the work going on in the town. Some of the activities were switched to halls but all in all it really was disastrous.

But the intrepid Youth Council was not to be put off by weather. Thus in 1978 we decided to hire seven very large marquees so that, regardless of the weather, we would have a show. The hire firm provided one man to direct the work but 120ft by 40ft marquees are not the easiest things to erect. However, with

Prizewinners and participants in the Easter egg hunt at the 1978 Youth Expo, along with Sam Wilson (left), Donald Hayes (at rear) and Mrs Wilson (with trophy).

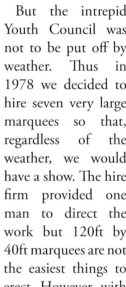

good will and help from a number of young enthusiasts we succeeded. This decision proved to be an enormous success. The marquees were positioned on the grass area fronting the Town Hall. Permission was granted to erect them on Friday on the understanding they would be removed before Sunday and the area would be left clean. We didn't appreciate the work involved in cleaning such an enormous site when some 10,000 people had milled around it all day and dropped papers and rubbish of every description. All the same, the task was completed by a great team of helpers and we were ready for the evening's activities at the seafront.

A jazz band led by trumpeter Robert Dawson was always a huge success and indeed it was almost impossible to get them off the platform to allow the fireworks display to proceed. It was also part of the deal that the North Pier was cleared of all debris after the fireworks. This was completed as dawn appeared on the horizon and Expo was over for another year.

Expo was funded by donations from local businesses. It was extremely helpful at a time when trading conditions were difficult. Grants from the Borough Council and the Education Board covered the £12,000 costs in staging the events, which were all free to the public. Paul Clark, of radio and television fame, provided continuity for our events and did so on a voluntary basis. It was encouraging for us that so many were prepared to give of their time for the young people of Bangor.

In the 70s it was necessary to get police clearance for a fireworks display. This was somewhat onerous, for obvious reasons. However, we finally received the fireworks and, to save money, decided to set them off ourselves. Little did we

Finalists in the 'Miss Bangor' competition – organised in May 1978 by Bangor Youth Council and judged by Radio Ulster's Paul Clark – with winner Isobel Bradford (extreme right). The others are (back, from left): Lorette Robinson, Karen Caskey, Charmaine Finnegan, Alison Hill, Andrea Lindsay. Front: Lorraine Rutherford and Rosemary Craig. 164/14a-2

know what was involved in such a task! Mortar casings were propped up with rocks and rockets were tied to any fence we could find on the North Pier. However, all went off without anyone getting injured. Oh and by the way we were insured. It cost but £50 to insure the entire day's events. Under present legislation, it would not now be possible to run such an event – a pity really – have we destroyed all the fun?

When the new breakwater was being built (now known as Eisenhower Pier), the contractors used very large barges for part of the works. Knowing one of the firm's directors, I asked if we could have access to the pier for the fireworks display, and this was willingly granted. We thought it would be easier to use one of the barges to set up the mortars and rockets and, indeed, it worked well. I spoke to my contact on the Monday morning to thank him for

Tommy Boal in his familiar modern-day role as 'The Mad Monk' at the North Down Museum. *Picture courtesy of the North Down Museum.*

his help and explained what we had done. He put his hands on his head and looked skyward. Not much wonder! Unknown to us, that barge was the one used to transfer diesel fuel to the piling rigs and there was some 10,000 gallons of fuel in it ready for the following week's work. Enough said!

Much was learnt about human relations from all these events. Why is it that, when there is a national security situation, people come together, work together, plan together and pull together for the general good?

A Community Seminar was held for leaders of all organisations in the Borough – sports clubs, churches, youth and adult groups and those who were just simply interested in the welfare of the people of the Borough. As well, a Seminar on the Needs of Disabled People resulted in many young people being brought to realise the difficulties of those unable to be as active as themselves. In many ways Bangor Youth Council provided a lead in voluntary co-operation.

Yes, it was hard work in the 70s, but with it came a great deal of satisfaction and the development of good relations. Under the same circumstances would we do it again – of course we would!! Wouldn't we?

1977
IN THE SPECTATOR

Free Presbyterians gathered outside Wesley Centenary Methodist Church on 19 January to protest over a series of vigils and services being organised by the Bangor Council of Churches during the annual Week of Prayer for Christian Unity. The church events coincided with a newly-issued joint Anglican/ Roman Catholic document aimed at providing further scope for discussion by bishops, theologians and church members on both sides.

Mayor Bertie McConnell officially opened the Abbeyfield Bangor Society's new house at 63 Ballyholme Road on 29 January. The premises, previously Coombehurst School and the Kimberley Guest House, replaced the former Abbeyfield premises at 92 Hamilton Road.

James Wightman, a member of the Bangor branch of the Royal British Legion, was presented with the Legion Gold Badge in recognition of his long and outstanding service. A Dunkirk veteran, Mr Wightman had joined the Bangor branch after being demobilised in 1945.

Prince Charming (Judith McIlroy) goes fishing during the Kilmaine Primary School pantomime in January 1977, with Buttons (Lesley Wilson) ready to bait her hook. *49/18-22*

George Bleakley, who retired on 25 February as a coachbuilder at the Ulsterbus depot in Bangor, received a farewell gift of Waterford crystal from his colleagues, including garage foreman Billy Gordon and depot manager Harry Willis.

The IRA murdered Bangor resident Rory O'Kelly in his native Coalisland on 4 March. Father-of-five Mr O'Kelly (59) was assistant public prosecutor for County Down in the office of the Director of Public Prosecutions. He had moved to Pickie Terrace in 1974 and was based at the DPP's Newtownards offices.

In his spare time he had become a popular member of Bangor Drama Club, with his artistic talents finding an outlet in scenic design.

The largely attended funeral service was held in St Comgall's Church, Brunswick Road, with interment following at Clandeboye Cemetery.

The Queen's Court Hotel closed on 5 March after losing both its entertainments and liquor licences, the latter following a lengthy court hearing. Police had objected to the liquor licence, claiming the premises were not being run in an orderly and peaceful manner. The Council also refused to renew the entertainments licence.

The premises partially reopened in July with a games room, featuring 10 pool tables, and only soft drinks available.

Liam Neeson in the *Spectator!* 9/3/26

A *Spectator* photographer visited the Lyric Theatre in March 1977 to see the final performance of Edna O'Brien's acclaimed play *The Gathering* and the opening of *The Street* by John Boyd. The cast included Bangor actress Linda Wray, but this picture (left) shows three of the male cast members from both plays.

From left: Joe McPartland, Liam Neeson and Louis Rolston.

Country and Western dances at Caproni's ended on 2 April and were replaced by the Blue Lamp Disco. The deal, struck between the Bangor Youth Council and Orlando Caproni, was for an experimental three-month period.

In an echo of events in May 1974, Northern Ireland was gripped by a second loyalist strike, this time largely organised by the United Unionist Action Council.

It began on Monday night 2 May and was called off on 13 May, again with conflicting reports of both support for the strike and allegations of intimidation.

North Down Trades Council opposed the strike and urged Secretary of State Roy Mason to ensure all workers could get to their workplaces.

Senior police officers and detectives examine the Cortina used in the car bomb incident at Abbey Street on 11 May. *72/4a-30*

The second week was marked by an escalation in violence, with the Coachman Roadhouse being set on fire – after a substantial sum of money was removed from the safe – and police officers being shot at while diverting traffic. A bus driver was struck by a brick at the Whitehill Estate, and a car bomb exploded in Abbey Street. No one was injured and damage was slight.

Thirty-five candidates sought the 20 seats on North Down Borough Council in the May local government elections. There were 12 Official Unionists, 11 Alliance, three UPNI, three DUP, two Vanguard, two Progressive Unionists, one Unionist and one United Unionist, UUUC.

Ultimately successful were the following: Area A – Cllr Bertie McConnell (Alliance), Bill Bailie (UPNI), Cllr Eddie Mills (Unionist), Alderman James Hamilton (Alliance), Tommy Barkley (Official Unionist); Area B – Cllr George Green (Vanguard), Cllr Albert Magee (Alliance), Bruce Mulligan (Official Unionist), James Boyle (DUP), Cllr John Shields (Official Unionist); Area C – Hazel Bradford (Official Unionist), Terence Morrow (Alliance), Alderman Mary O'Fee (Vanguard), Cllr

Oscar Rollins (Alliance), Maisie McMullan (Official Unionist); Area D – Cllr the Rev. J. McConnell Auld (Official Unionist), Alderman Keith Jones (Alliance), Ken Kennedy (Alliance), William Bussell (Official Unionist) and Fred White (United Unionist, UUUC).

The final state of the parties was seven Alliance, seven Official Unionists, two Vanguard, one DUP, one Unionist, one United Unionist, UUUC, and one UPNI. At the first meeting of the new authority, held on 19 May, Alderman O'Fee was elected Mayor, with Cllr Shields as Deputy Mayor.

Despite receiving the fourth highest number of votes in Area A, the defeated candidates included future Stormont Minister Sammy Wilson, who lived at Clifton Road and was both a member of the DUP's Bangor branch and party spokesman on economic affairs. By 1979 he was press officer for the North Down Imperial Association.

The Silver Jubilee Honours List included an OBE for former Mayor (by then Alderman) Bertie McConnell for his services to local government and towards the promotion of good community relations. He is pictured at Hillsborough Castle in August 1977 with his wife Olive (right) and cousin Maureen Cameron. *28/13-40*

A civic service was held in First Bangor Presbyterian Church on 12 June to mark the Silver Jubilee of the Queen's accession. Other events in Bangor and district included street parties, a fireworks display from the North Pier, Bangor Youth Council's Expo 77 festivities, and a jubilee drumhead service in Castle Park, hosted by Bangor District LOL No 18.

Herbie Smylie 9/14-35

June 1977 saw the retirement of 80-year-old Bangor blacksmith Herbie Smylie. The smithy at 45 Beatrice Road had been built for his father in 1906 and Herbie took up work there six years later, after leaving school. The premises were taken over by Bangor man Terry Magowan who converted them into a wood turnery, while retaining much of the original interior.

Lollipop man Gilbert Hill, of 63 Innisfayle Drive, was placed third in Northern Ireland in the 'Ladybird Lollipop Man of the Year' competition. He was nominated by children from Grange Park Primary School for the service he provided at the busy Bryansburn Road roundabout. A year later there was a similar accolade for Fred Yates, of 7 Greenmount Avenue, who was runner-up in the national final. He was nominated by the pupils of St Comgall's Primary School, Brunswick Road.

In early September North Down Borough Council vetoed a proposed multi-million pound dual carriageway from Abbey Street to Hamilton Road. The scheme – part of the North Down Area Plan – had been the subject of a public enquiry. Property had been acquired and a start date set for 1980/81.

Councillors objected on a number of grounds, not least the loss of the area of Ward Park that included the bandstand. Cllr Hazel Bradford branded the proposed road "a Berlin Wall" and suggested the money would be better spent on the seafront.

GEA Air Exchangers, based in the Balloo Industrial Estate, won an order worth £3.4m to supply equipment to the Sullum Voe oil terminal in the Shetlands. The deal promised a boost to the already 140-strong workforce.

Firebombers returned with a vengeance on Saturday 17 September, when they planted more than 20 incendiaries in a number of businesses around the town. Almost half of the devices failed to ignite and in most cases only minimal damage was caused.

Four furniture stores – Cavendish Woodhouse in lower Main Street, McCrea's (upper Main Street), Bel-1 (Belfast Road), and Cowan Burnside (Seacliff Road) – the Cavern bar (High Street), Briterome (Market Street), and Barry's on the seafront were targeted, while another device was discovered in a chair that had

Seventeen-year-old Susan Milliken, from 5 Silverstream Road, presented a special posy to the Queen when she visited the New University of Ulster at Coleraine during her Silver Jubilee visit to Northern Ireland. *6116139*

Firemen inside the Bel-1 store at Belfast Road. *31/1a-43*

been delivered to an address in Osborne Drive.

Bangor firemen were supported by colleagues from Newtownards and Donaghadee in tackling the resulting fires. The greatest amount of damage was sustained by the Bel-1 store.

Despite the incendiary attacks, the security barriers, which had closed lower Main Street, Bridge Street and High Street to all but authorised traffic since 1972's car bombs, were raised during daylight hours. Police warned that unattended parking laws would be rigorously enforced.

Former Bangor Grammar School student Tom Trouton, from Donaghadee Road, pulled off a notable double by being top in Northern Ireland in both chemistry and physics in 1977's GCE A-Level examinations. He went on to study medicine at Queen's University.

Cinemas in three local towns were targeted by fire-bombers early on Sunday 9 October, with minor damage being caused to both the Queen's in Bangor and the Comber Cinema, but the Regent in Newtownards was gutted.

Lisnabreen Presbyterian Church was packed on 23 October for a visit by the Moderator, the Rt. Rev. Thomas Patterson, to officially open the enlarged church buildings and the new Cromie Hall. Also participating were founder minister the Rev. Alexander Cromie and Mrs Cromie.

A cassette-type incendiary device was found down the back of a seat on a train at Bangor station on the evening of 4 November. Firemen stood by as Army bomb disposal experts carried out a controlled explosion.

A five-bedroom house at the corner of Manse Road and Greenmount Avenue, bought just months earlier by Dr Barnardo's Homes, was destroyed by vandals who set fire to it on 14 November. The charity had planned to reopen the former Trinity Manse in March 1978 as accommodation for mentally handicapped residents.

Bangor Lions' fundraising efforts fell foul of the law in December at the Disneyland exhibition in the King's Hall at Balmoral. Club officials had offered a Volkswagen Beetle in a ballot but had to withdraw the prize after a week due to the Lotteries Act 1957 (Amended), which stated that no ballot prize could be worth more than £1,000 and no ballot ticket could cost more than 25p.

Dr David Burke, minister of Hamilton Road Presbyterian Church since 1955, was elected the new Moderator of the Presbyterian Church in Ireland, succeeding Dr. Tom Patterson of Portaferry. It was the first time two ministers from the Ards Presbytery had held the top church position in successive years.

It was also announced that another Bangor minister, the Rev. John Turner, of Wesley Centenary Methodist Church, would become President of the Methodist Church in Ireland the following summer.

Ballyholme Parish curate the Rev. Raymond Devenney got more than he bargained for when he opened a tin of biscuits at his Kilmaine Avenue home on 23 December. Hidden among the biscuits, purchased in Belfast two days earlier, was an unexploded incendiary. He immediately carried the tin to his front garden, where it was subsequently dealt with by the Army.

Lyn Orr (left) and Claire Rogers, both of 12th Bangor (St Gall's) Girl Guide Company with the Queen's Badges they received in October 1977. *18/5/46*

Bangor Lions Club Youth Award winner Stuart Elborn receives his trophy and cheque from president Peter Watson in January 1977. Included are Stuart's parents, Mr and Mrs D. Elborn, and Youth Award officer Alf Eddy. 89/11-22

Pupils of St Columbanus Secondary School performed Rutherford Mayne's one-act play Thompson in Tir na nOg in February 1977. Back (from left): Gerard Delaney, Thomas Flanagan, Richard Kelly, Ronald McAteer. Front: Catherine Anyon, David Troupe, Ann Murphy, Martin Morgan and Anthony Irwin. 71/20-24

Male principals from Bangor Amateur Operatic Society's production of My Fair Lady in March 1977. From left: Peter Radcliffe, Winston Johnston, Paul Kerr, Terry Elwood, John McBurney and (at back) George Smyth. Terry Elwood played Professor Henry Higgins. 65/6-26

Geoffrey Miller (right), leader of the Bangor Grammar School Community Service Group, presents a special hand-operated 'Scamp' car to children at Clifton Special Care School in April 1977. The group, who frequently helped out at the adjoining school, obtained the car from Vauxhall Motors. *73/6-27*

Ernie Downing (right), from Rosemary Park, receives a retirement gift from colleagues at the Bangor Co-op Milk Depot, where he had worked for 33 years. Included are Jimmy Apperson, depot manager, Mr H. Moffett, distribution manager, and Mr L. Brennan, union chairman. *3/13a-29*

Sixth (Bangor Abbey) Brownies were on an observation trip in May 1977, when they met re-elected Councillors Mary O'Fee and George Green. Accompanying the group was Brown Owl Sheila Oliver. *43/9-31*

Retirement gifts were presented to two senior teachers at Bangor Grammar School, whose careers stretched back to the 1940s. Picture shows (from left): Bertie Styles, senior vice-principal, George Heuston, retiring head of the English Department, Henry Rea, retiring head of the Modern Languages Department, head boy Brian Speers, headmaster Dr Robert Rodgers, and Joe McKeown, vice-principal. Mr McKeown would retire the following June. *33/4a-36*

Ava Street residents who turned out in force for the Queen's Silver Jubilee street party in June 1977. *62/16a-33*

The Silver Jubilee celebrations at Lismore Avenue and Lisnabreen Crescent attracted many local children. *84/3-33*

Girl Guides from the 4th and 5th Bangor Companies enjoyed a visit to the Ulster Folk and Transport Museum in July 1977. Included are Joan Douglas, District Commissioner, Barbara Minnis, Janice Bradshaw and Betty Blundell (4th) and Senior Guide Hazel Curry. *30/4-37*

Steeplejack John McQuillan (second left) with three of his employees involved in the repairs to St Comgall's Parish Church in July 1977. From left: George Ackerman, Freddy Anderson and Michael Caproni. A successful appeal raised £12,000 within just three weeks. *49/13/39*

Pride of Whitehill Flute Band, the town's largest band, on parade in Bangor on 12 July 1977. *76/4-37*

Skipperstone Youth Club members enjoyed a trip to the Scottish Highlands in July 1977. 32/14-37

Bangor Sea Cadets Corps, TS Decoy, based at Castle Street, returned home from Plymouth with the Ridgwell Cup – a national award – for junior boat pulling. From left: David Cosh, Frank Mills, Colin McAvoy, David Powell, Simon Reardon and Michael Kernaghan, all from the town. 56/18a-42

Members of Bangor band Soundtrack had been together for a year, played contemporary rock and pop and were open to bookings. From left: Anthony Young, drums, Damian Jackson, lead guitar, Martin Morgan, rhythm guitar, and Sean McGivern, bass. 91/1a-47

Sammy Wilson
remembers...

Looking back on the 1977 local Council elections, I certainly never dreamt then that those first tentative steps towards the public arena would bring me to the position I am in today.

I always had an interest in politics, from the time I was at school, and I suppose anyone who became politically aware towards the end of the 1960s couldn't but help be dragged into the political turmoil which developed around that time.

I studied A-Level Politics at Methodist College and gained an A grade in the subject and then went on to study Economics at Queen's University where I was briefly involved in politics. However, during university I joined the Police Reserve and that probably limited my political involvement in the 1970s until the North Down Borough Council elections in 1977.

The election as I remember it was particularly difficult for the DUP because first of all we didn't have any significant base in North Down, which was really regarded at that stage as a traditional Ulster Unionist/ Alliance area.

Secondly, there had been a strike which was organised to highlight the disquiet the Democratic Unionists and others felt about the security policies which were clearly failing in Northern Ireland at that stage and, given the high

The young Sammy Wilson, DUP election candidate for Ballyholme and Groomsport in 1977

Sammy Wilson MP MLA was born in Belfast in April 1953 and is now one of Northern Ireland's best known politicians. Educated at Methodist College Belfast, he went on to graduate in Economics and Politics from Queen's University and then from Stranmillis College.

Mr Wilson took up a teaching post at Grosvenor Grammar School after graduation, going on to

Sammy Wilson's late father, Pastor Alexander Wilson

become head of Economics and assistant chief examiner for A-Level Economics in Northern Ireland.

In 1981 he was elected as a DUP Councillor to Belfast City Council, a position he held until 2010. Mr Wilson became the first person from the party to serve as Lord Mayor in 1986/1987 and again in 2000/2001.

Mr Wilson was elected to the Northern Ireland Forum to represent East Belfast (1996-98) and went on to represent the same area in the Northern Ireland Assembly (June 1998).

In the Assembly election of 2003 Mr Wilson was re-elected as an East Antrim representative. This momentum was carried through to the Westminster election on 5 May 2005, when he was elected as MP for East Antrim with 49.6% of the vote.

Mr Wilson is the DUP spokesperson for Education and Policing, and has a special interest in socio-economic issues. At Westminster he is the party spokesperson on

number of people who were killed in 1974, 1975 and 1976, it is understandable there was major concern.

The DUP opted to contest every area in North Down and I was selected for Area A (Groomsport, Churchill, Ballyholme, Ballymagee and Bangor Harbour). I had been involved up to that date as Press Officer for the DUP and I think I was probably chosen because my father was the minister of the Elim Pentecostal Church in Bangor. He was quite well known and it was hoped some of his reputation might reflect on my vote. The campaign itself was very difficult for us as North Down people had not been very supportive of the strike action which we had backed and we were regarded very much as the outsiders in the political arena.

Canvassing doors in Bangor at that stage was not for the faint-hearted and indeed as a first experience of fighting an election it was quite daunting, given the responses from the people – many slammed their doors in our faces and others, putting it mildly, were less than pleasant in their responses.

I didn't actually go to the count but after the first one was over my election agent phoned me and told me I was fourth with over 600 votes and it was looking good for us to win a seat in the five-seat constituency. However, when all the counts were completed I think I gained about three transfers over the rest of the day and finished up not as a Councillor but as a runner-up.

It was a disappointing result personally but in a way it was probably fortuitous as I then moved away from Bangor to Belfast, stood for election in Belfast and was elected onto Belfast City Council which, of course, was a much higher profile Council and probably gave me opportunities to gain a political foothold I would never have had in North Down.

Looking back more than three decades I don't think at that stage I would ever have envisaged the DUP becoming the biggest party in North Down or gaining the control or progressing to the position it holds today. I don't regret taking the initial plunge but in a way I am glad my political involvement developed in Belfast where, quite frankly, I felt more at home as it was where I taught, secondly, it was where I was brought up and, thirdly, it was where I chose to live.

I still have very fond memories of my involvement in North Down. There are still some of the stalwarts who were there when I first stood for election, members of the party, and when I go to speak at dinners, branch meetings, etc., it is nice to meet up with them again.

When I was Environment Minister one of the Chief Planning Officers I would meet for regular updates on a Monday morning used to make me smile. I can remember canvassing his door one evening during the 1977 elections, just off the Groomsport Road. He interrogated me on the party's policy on planning and in my foolishness I stood and talked to him for half an hour, wasting valuable canvassing time and not even getting his vote at the end of the day.

I don't know if he remembered the incident but every Monday morning when I looked at him I used to think: "You led me a merry dance 40 years ago," which made my interrogation of him as Minister in 2008 all the sweeter.

If he did remember the incident he was never crass enough to mention it, but every time I looked at him I recalled the day when I was standing wasting my time on his doorstep, never thinking that 40 years later I would be his Minister!

Education and Skills, as well as Housing.

In June 2008 Mr Wilson was appointed Minister of the Environment by party leader Peter Robinson, and in June 2009 he took on the role of Minister of Finance and Personnel.

Away from politics Sammy Wilson is a keen gardener and motorbike enthusiast, as well as taking a keen interest in animals and birds.

Sammy Wilson MP MLA today

1978
IN THE SPECTATOR

Vivienne McMaster (14), from Maxwell Road, was selected to represent Northern Ireland in Young Entertainer of the Year, a weekly feature on the BBC's weekly *Crackerjack* programme for children. She was looking forward to her television debut in February, highlighting her tap-dancing and singing skills.

Nineteen-year-old Rose Neill, from Raglan Road, was making her television debut in the same month, co-presenting the UTV schools series *Hop, Skip and Jump* with John O'Hara. It encouraged young children to achieve greater vocabulary and self-expression through songs and stories.

Major General Peter Shapland, director of Volunteer Territorials and Cadets, opened the new TAVR Centre at Balloo Avenue – replacing the huts on the Newtownards Road that had previously served as a base. Two years earlier 74 Engineer Regiment had decided to recruit in Bangor, in addition to 5th Battalion Royal Irish Rangers, raising a total of 150 Territorials.

The Rev. William Erskine preached his farewell address at Ballyholme Presbyterian Church on 22 January, marking the end of his 37 years of active ministry

Bangor couple Ian and Elizabeth McCracken, aged 24 and 25 respectively, were among the 12 victims of the IRA incendiary bomb attack on the La Mon House Restaurant at Gransha on 17 February 1978.

The atrocity – involving a blast bomb attached to two large petrol canisters, each filled with a napalm-like substance of petrol and sugar – occurred as members of the Northern Ireland Junior Motorcycle Club and the Irish Collie Club were attending two separate dinners.

First Bangor Presbyterian Church was filled to capacity four days later for the funeral service for the young couple, from Rutherglen Park, who had married just 18 months earlier.

Businesses throughout the town closed their doors and the community gathered to pay their respects to the dead and to sympathise with the bereaved. The Rev. W. J. McKinstry Wallace returned from retirement to conduct the service.

The funeral cortege for La Mon victims Ian and Elizabeth McCracken moves from First Bangor Presbyterian Church to Clandeboye Cemetery on 21 February 1978. *103/5-1*

He declared: "Ian and Elizabeth were in the company of those who innocently enjoyed and shared their interest in their Collie pets. In a moment the men of hate laid their terrible toll of death and destruction.

"History will record these events and wonder if they were human beings or brute beasts who perpetrated them."

Ian was a native of Bangor, having attended Clandeboye Road Primary School and the former Bangor Intermediate School, while his wife was from Belfast. They had met while both were working for the Northern Ireland Electricity Board at Malone. Elizabeth's mother was secretary of the Irish Collie Club.

in the congregation. The church had also been filled the previous day for the opening of the new £30,000 hall, named the William Erskine Hall in his honour.

Bangor Post Office introduced a single queueing system from the beginning of March. Postmaster Albert Compton explained that the new system, which offered greater privacy, would ensure all customers were dealt with in the order they entered the Post Office.

THERE'S A BIGGER AND BETTER CHOICE AT THE NEW WELLWORTHS

Wellworths new improved store opens Friday April 14th in Main Street, Bangor. There are two sales floors of shopping pleasure offering the finest service, quality and choice. Wellworths have a fine tradition throughout Northern Ireland for quality products at the most competitive prices.

See the bigger and better choice in our Food Hall and General Store
A wider choice of the freshest and finest cuts of meat
A better choice of the freshest and most seasonable vegetables
A bigger choice of frozen and prepacked food products
A greater choice of tinned and bottled goods

THE NEW WELLWORTHS IN BANGOR FOR A BIGGER AND BETTER CHOICE

Bangor man Doug Crowe won a colour television set when he appeared on Anglia Television's *Sale of the Century*, hosted by Nicholas Parsons.

North Down Borough Council agreed in April to change the Tonic's permitted opening time on Sundays from 8.30pm to 6.15pm – but restricted the approval to just 15 days in the year. Members heard from new owners the Scott brothers that extra shows might create the profit margin needed to keep the cinema open.

An £84,000 flats complex at Greenmount Avenue, officially opened on 2 May by Environment Minister Ray Carter, was the first new-build scheme to be completed anywhere following the introduction of the Housing (NI) Order 1976, which aimed to expand the voluntary housing movement. The eight dwellings were built by the Presbyterian Housing Association.

Bangor postmaster Albert Compton presents a retirement gift to Ernie Glithero, who, following Army service, spent more than 31 years as a postman. 176/14a-3

Bangor-born actor Colin Blakely was awarded a prestigious Community Award, presented to Irish men and women for noteworthy community effort or individual achievement in Britain. The former Bangor Drama Club member was honoured for his outstanding contribution to British theatre.

Mr and Mrs Ross Boyd, of 25 Fairfield Park, celebrated their 50th wedding anniversary on 4 June, but the celebration was delayed by a couple of months because Mr Boyd – greenkeeper for some 46 years at Bangor Golf Club – was in hospital. Ross (73) and his wife Florence (68) had six children, 10 grandchildren and two great-grandchildren. Their children were Martha (Parker), Sylvia (Cooling) and Iris (Sterritt), John, Claney and Albert.

SHARON MOURNED IN BANGOR AND BULAWAYO

Tribute to Sharon Faith Swindells

From Bangor Salvation Army Corps

Sharon

Sharon Swindells, from Caroline Gardens – a former pupil of Glenlola Collegiate and a member of the Bangor Citadel of The Salvation Army – was killed while on missionary service in Rhodesia [now Zimbabwe] on 7 June 1978.

She and a fellow member of The Salvation Army were shot in a terrorist attack on the institute near the city of Bulawayo where she worked.

A largely attended memorial service took place at the Bangor Citadel five days later, to coincide with the funeral in Bulawayo, which was attended by her parents, Mr and Mrs William Swindells.

Sharon is remembered to this day by The Salvation Army, with the Bangor Citadel at 7-11 Crosby Street being dedicated to her memory. In addition, the Swindells family has been publicly recognised for their tireless work to raise over £70,000 for the work of The Salvation Army's Usher Institute and the Howard Mission Hospital in Zimbabwe.

Dr Robert Nixon retired on 9 June after a medical career that stretched back 42 years, to 1936, when he joined Dr Bob Bowman's practice on Hamilton Road as his assistant. Dr Bowman was also Mayor of Bangor and this likely influenced Dr Nixon, who went on to serve on the same Council and to represent North Down at Stormont.

North Down Borough Council tackled the thorny issue of 12th July bonfires, voting unanimously in favour of adequate safety measures being required where bonfires were likely to create problems.

Live family entertainment in Bangor was given a big boost when Frankie Vaughan gave three concerts at the Tonic on Saturday 17 and Sunday 18 June, featuring entertainers from his London Palladium shows.

Four local teenagers were among a party of 30 who set off on 30 July for a month's voluntary work in Kenya under the auspices of the Church Missionary Society. They were Helga Cairns (17), from 25 Sandringham Drive, Ian McDonald (18), from 7 Caroline Gardens, Julian Pentland (18), from 10 Farnham Road, and David Rhodes (19), from 19 Morningside. Their destination was Kajiado, south of Nairobi, where they helped to build a church.

One Bangorian followed another as the BBC's National Governor in August, when Lady Lucy Faulkner, widow of the former Prime Minister, succeeded hotelier Bill O'Hara.

A High Court injunction taken out in Belfast prevented an illegal video cassette version of *Saturday Night Fever* from being shown in the Helmsman in August. The action was taken by Cinema International Corporation (UK), a joint subsidiary of Paramount and Universal Pictures. The court heard film piracy was extremely common and was proving very costly to the industry. Although the film had been released in the USA the previous December, it was not screened in Northern Ireland until October 1978.

Following a successful summer season at Eastbourne and the Isle of Wight, Bangor-born comedian Adrian Walsh appeared at the London Palladium in September with top American group Gladys Knight and the Pips.

The opening and dedication of Ballycrochan Presbyterian Church at Silverbirch Road on 23 September marked a milestone for the rapidly expanding east end of Bangor. Fittingly, the event took place during the Moderatorial year of Dr David Burke, minister of Hamilton Road Presbyterian Church.

The following day saw the minor hall – provided by the congregation at a cost of £23,000 – being renamed 'The Beattie Hall' in appreciation of the work under-

Dr David Burke unveils a memorial plaque as minister the Rev. Alex Beattie and clerk of interim session George Henderson look on.
119/113-4

taken by the minister, the Rev. Alex Beattie, and his wife.

Glen Electric, which employed 70 people in Bangor and over 400 in Newry, announced expansion plans at the beginning of October which offered the hope of 30 new jobs at the company's Balloo Industrial Estate factory.

As the queue for the X-rated *Saturday Night Fever* stretched deep into the car park of the Tonic for the film's first screening on 9 October, a smaller group – of objectors – was forming outside the Queen's Cinema, which was showing *Jesus Christ Superstar*. The protest was organised by Bangor Free Presbyterian Church, with support from Bangor Independent Methodist Church, the Elim Pentecostal Church and Newtownards Free Presbyterian Church. They left after handing over a letter which condemned the film as "offensive, blasphemous and injurious to the name of Jesus Christ."

North Down Model Railway Club's inaugural meeting was held on 6 November in Hamilton House with over 40 enthusiasts attending. The meeting was chaired by the Rev. John McKegney who was elected as founding chairman, with Tony Ragg as secretary and Peter Lynch as treasurer. Tasked with seeking out appropriate premises for club meetings were Roy Neill and Peter McVicar.

There was a broad welcome for a feasibility study on the future of Bangor seafront, which supported a 650-boat marina. Borough Councillors, who welcomed the recommendations in late November, hoped the project, if it won government backing, could become a reality by 1984. They also intended to pursue grant support of at least 75% towards the estimated £3.6m cost.

Prison clerk John McTier, who lived off Gransha Road in Bangor, was just 33 when he was shot by the IRA as he drove home on 11 December with colleagues after completing a day's work in the pay office at Crumlin Road Prison in Belfast.

Dinner had been prepared by wife Angeline and John's sons, Cameron (4), Ryan (2) and 14-month-old David, were waiting for their customary hug and bed-time story from Dad. Life, however, ended for John three days later, and in truth, it was never the same for his young family – the gunman robbed them of a loving husband, a doting father and a true gentleman who loved his country with a passion that had brought him home from Canada in the early 1970s.

John's mother and father, both residing in Belfast, never recovered from the news of their son's death and both suffered strokes. His only brother's health also suffered.

Rather than dwell on events back in 1978, his family prefer to remember John for the person he was. He had a great love of writing and reading from his store of books. He also had a great love of birds, nature as a whole, and, of course, he had a great love of Ireland.

The funeral service was held at Roselawn and a tree was erected in John's memory.

A neighbour wrote this poem on the night of John's death, 14 December:

There was a man who worked hard to provide for all the things he loved –
His wife, his children, his dog, his home.
And in return he was loved.
A man like thousands of ordinary men,
But because of his kindness, his compassion, his good humour,
He was more – he was a man in a thousand.
Now he lies in a Belfast hospital,
Shot in the head by a gunman as he drove home from work.
Oh stupid, stupid country,
Shooting the flower of your manhood.
This innocent man with no blood on his hands lies broken –
What a terrible waste.
I know not of right or wrong
To me there are no sides.
Just the innocent and the guilty
And the thoughts of that man
And the man who fired.

Organisers of Sam's Soul Club at the Royal Hotel are pictured after the successful opening of the new disco in January 1978. From left: Peter Burrowes, Wilma Courtney and Mrs and Mrs Bill Moore at the turntables. *22/15-1*

Jeanne Cree and Derek Andrews with other dancers from the Bangor Amateur Operatic Society's production of *King's Rhapsody* in April 1978. *265/8-1*

Grange Park Primary School entered a choir in the Belfast Music Festival for the first time in March 1978. The juniors enjoyed success, winning two trophies. The choir was conducted by John Ekin and accompanied by Ann Murphy. They are included with principal Frank R. Martin (left). *154/16-1*

Bangor Grammar School won both the team and individual awards in the Northern Ireland Schools Debating competition, hosted in April 1978 by the Junior Chamber of Commerce. From left: Cameron Woodrow, David Rhodes, Ian McDonald and Geoffrey Miller (who also won the individual speaker award). The school retained the team trophy in 1979, when those taking part were Patrick McCutcheon, Stephen Rea, Mark Redford and Nigel Pentland. *270/1-1*

Members of the Towerview Primary School choir, with a repertoire of both sacred and secular music, were kept busy in May 1978 visiting senior citizens and attending church services. *102/15-2*

St Columbanus High School student Brenda Dunleavy (centre) received the Youth in Community Award from the Soroptimist Club of Bangor in May 1978. She won the award for her work with the mentally handicapped through Ards Gateway Club. Pictured (from left): Sharon Kent (nominated by Glenlola Collegiate), Lynn Rutherford (1977 winner), Jean Haslett, Soroptimist president, and Dorothy Heuston (nominated by Bangor Girls' High School). *84/0-2*

Prizewinning boys from Kilmaine Primary School at the end of the school year. Back (from left): Mark Taylor, badminton; Jonathan Edgar, football; Richard Jenkins, athletics; Stuart Graham, Junior Club Cup; Daron Richmond, cycling. Front: Neil Evans, Boy of the Year, and Mark McCluskie, music. 7/9-3

Prizewinners at Newtownards Irish Dancing Festival included (from left): Noelene McClenahan, Bangor (Intermediate title); Clare McCann, Bangor (Junior); Diane McCaw, Bangor (Senior); and Colleen Coey, Groomsport (Juvenile). 88/3A-3

Children from the Ballyholme area who raised £40 for Bangor's Save the Children Fund branch in August 1978. Back (from left): Alyson Jamison, Chris, Mark and Shane Ritchie, Alison Balmer. Front: Catherine McQuitty, Lynda James, Sandra Whyte, Joanne Dowey, Lesley Dowey and Lisa Whyte. Not included: Gillian Robinson. 273/18-3

Permission was granted in August for a major shopping complex at the Main Street/ Castle Street junction (Warden's Corner), with a large department store and three small two-storey shop units being included in the proposal lodged by Hampden Developments Ltd. *313/5-3*

The Bangor Abbey choir pictured at their harvest praise service on 8 October in new robes of imperial purple. Included are Canon James Hamilton (left), rector, guest preacher the Rev. Gordon McMullan and organist/ choirmaster Cecil Thompson. *255/17-4*

Bangor Girls' High School won the area final of the 6th annual public speaking competition organised by Bangor Business and Professional Women in November 1978. Pictured with guest judge (and Bangorian) Paul McDowell from the BBC are (from left): Dawn Jolley, Deborah Cannell and Sharon Agnew. *375/14-4*

The first regular meeting of Bangor West Probus Club, organised by Bangor Rotary Club, was held in The Old Inn, Crawfordsburn, on 3 November 1978. Pictured in the front row are (from left): Rotarian Fred Wilson; Fred Owens, secretary; Chambers Marshall, vice-president; John Rea, president; Rotarian Jack Small, president of Bangor Rotary Club; Bill May, treasurer; Billy Campton and Rotarian Edwin Dunlop. *370/7-4*

Christmas arrived early with the second act of Bangor Scouts' *Gang Show '78*, staged in the Little Theatre from 14-17 November 1978, including Sandra Finch's rendition of *You'll be a Santa Claus*. *442/14-4*

Models in a 'Pink Panther' fashion show organised by Bangor's Combat Cancer branch at the local Girls' High School on 28 November 1978. Back (from left): Adrienne Stewart, Brenda Lindsay. Front: Rosemary Palmer, Jo Anne Miller, Shirley McFettridge, Lynda Miller and Julie Mullan. *56/36a-5*

Student of the Year at Bangor Girls' High School in December 1978 was Irene Brown, who received the award from guest speaker Claire MacMahon, vice-principal of Stranmillis College. Looking on is headmistress Marie Brownlee. *36/4a-5**

Austin McGirr

remembers...

I was delighted to be appointed curate of Bangor Parish in 1976. As a child I was always excited to get the train and then the bus to Ballyholme where endless discoveries with sand and water awaited me. When I was old enough I often cycled from home in east Belfast with my friends and could spend as long as I liked in Barry's Amusements.

Rev. Fr Austin McGirr, then Bangor's new curate, sang to his own musical accompaniment at the St Vincent de Paul Christmas dinner in the dining room of St Columbanus Secondary School in December 1976. Looking on is nine-year-old Jane Mulvenna, whose big sister Christina also sang at the function. *36/19-20*

The same sense of fun and excitement was with me, a priest of five years standing, as I moved into the parochial house with the PP, Father Gerry Brady. There were five Mercy Sisters living nearby in St Comgall's Convent, on the Brunswick Road, who were involved with the parish primary school and St Columbanus Secondary School, as it was called then. A long-serving and talented Fr Brendan Murray lived opposite the Convent and Fr Danny Cannon lived in Ballyholme.

The clerical company was rich in wit and varied in per-

Very Rev Austin McGirr was baptised in St Matthew's, Newtownards Road, Belfast, in 1947. Ordained to the priesthood in Belfast in June 1971, he was appointed as Reader to St James' Parish, Whiteabbey (July 1971 – November 1971).

Subsequent appointments as Curate were to Saintfield Parish (November 1971 – August 1976); Bangor Parish (August 1976 – August

1983); St Mary's on the Hill Parish, Glengormley (August 1983–August 1987) and Ballycastle Parish (August 1987–August 1996).

He was appointed Parish Priest to Nativity Parish, Poleglass (August 1996–2006) and then Parish Priest to Portstewart Parish (August 2006 – present).

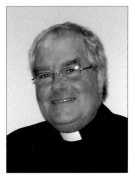

Very Rev. Austin McGirr today

sonality. The Troubles were blowing a gale then. Nightly news of shootings and bombings tested our powers of reaction as we met together for the midday meal. Our parish had a number of police officers among the congregation and their vulnerability was very clear to us. In the seven years I spent in the parish we were spared any paramilitary attacks on our people. However, the church doors in Bangor were daubed with paint a couple of times and an attempt was made to burn Christ the Redeemer Church in Ballyholme. The Oratory in Donaghadee (a former shop) was burnt and later replaced with a new church in its own grounds.

Keeping ecumenical relations alive and vibrant was an important priority at this time when the community was being increasingly polarised by nightly tragedies and fiery politics. There were sensitive issues which could be clarified in a friendly and open way at meetings of all the clergy such as the Clergy Fraternal. Fr Brendan Murray and I attended most meetings of the Fraternal, which were held in a Ballyholme boarding house.

One of the issues we discussed was the prevalence of outdoor drinkers in Ward Park. It was agreed there would be a fully ecumenical, cross-community tour of the park late on a Friday night with Sgt Spiers Wilson to see for ourselves how bad the problem was. However, when we cruised the area there was none to be seen. After almost an hour of searching for these lost sheep in the wilderness, someone in the car suggested the reason for their absence was a prominent article in that week's *Spectator*, describing how the clergy would be out in the park having a late Friday night with the drinkers. Could it be that those absent young people could read as well as drink? Who had leaked the story to the press? Investigations, like the search for the lost drinkers, proved inconclusive.

The Week of Prayer for Church Unity each January was the biggest event of the church year, with services being held in one of each of the four main denominations. I remember welcoming bemused visitors to the not-yet-completely refurbished and extended St Comgall's and leading them in a hymn with my acoustic guitar because the organ was not yet re-installed. It was all very Glastonbury. Relations with the congregations and the ministers of the various churches were warm, friendly and creative.

That creativity spread to our prayers. A Charismatic Prayer Group was started in 1977 with early instructions being given by an American Methodist, Presbyterian lay people and leaders in the movement from the Catholic Church, including our own Mercy Sisters. The spontaneity and joy of those meetings was something I'll always treasure. People's faith grew and with it developed small and big initiatives which brought hope to people in very dark times.

A youth group called NIPPY (New Ideas in Progress by Parish Youth) grew out of efforts by several married couples in our parish to welcome young people. The married couples had benefited from a weekend of renewal called Marriage Encounter. They in turn generously offered their home over 14 weeks to a group of 16-year-olds who would follow a programme of discussions on relationships and faith. The teenagers then gathered as a group and came up with the name and a programme for action.

One idea was to plant potatoes and sell the produce for a give-away price to pensioners. A plot of land behind the parish house was prepared, planted and produced a great harvest. The NIPPY group also grew quite a few romances and marriages which still grace the community 30 years on. To this day I treasure a scrapbook of photographs and hand-written stories from that period. The hairstyles are interesting; the heads and hearts underneath the hair are even more interesting.

The seafront of Bangor and the walks around the coast were always an attraction to any visitors to the parish house. Lairds Boats were available for hire beside Pickie Pool. There was a wee sandy beach there too when the tide was out. The businesses along Queen's Parade were still doing a turn; Ken was selling the only American-style burgers in town until the clubs and pubs got out in the wee small hours. There was hard rock and cafes and the only computer game in Barry's Amusements was Space Invaders. Barry's then traded with the old penny – you con-

Peace worker [and future Nobel Prize winner] Mairead Corrigan was the guest at a meeting of the Bangor Clergy Fraternal in the Ballyholme Hotel on 20 April 1977. She is pictured with (back, from left): Philip Woods, a student from London; Rev. Fr. Kevin Mortimer, Bristol; Rev. J. Robinson, Conlig Presbyterian Church; Captain G. Kent, Salvation Army; Rev. Sidney Frame, Queen's Parade Methodist Church; Rev. Fr. Brendan Murray, St Comgall's, Brunswick Road; Rev. Neil Cameron, Millisle and Ballycopeland Presbyterian Church; Rev. Canon Jack Mercer, St. Columbanus Parish Church; Rev. Dr Michael Dewar, Helen's Bay Parish Church; Rev. Derek Tyney, Groomsport Parish Church; Rev. John Turner, Wesley Centenary Methodist Church. Front: Rev. Fr. Austin McGirr, St Comgall's, Brunswick Road; Rev. R. S. G. Gilmore, Helen's Bay Presbyterian Church, and Rev. John McKegney, St Comgall's Church of Ireland. 18/10-29

Barry's Amusements in the late 1970s. 121-14-6

verted your "new pence" for a stack of old pennies.

In the early Eighties Bangor kept its exciting appeal for me – but only just. A combination of the growing popularity of foreign holidays and the slow strangulation of social life due to legitimate fears for your personal safety meant the attractions were fading, rusting and closing down. The people I knew from the various churches and parishes were, on the contrary, creative, inventive and full of hope. They remain for me now the happy memories of a place that used to be the pleasure ground of ice-cream and sandcastles.

1979

IN THE SPECTATOR

A New Year storm left the Ballyholme promenade seriously undermined, with three large craters appearing where it fronted the park. The ticket booth beside the bathing boxes sustained severe damage.

Drew Davidson (35), of 2 Seacliff Road, won the 35 and over category in the Mr Northern Ireland competition in January. He trained at Mike Bull's health studio on Dufferin Avenue.

Edna Rennie, from Crawfordsburn Road, won a national competition organised by Revlon, with the main prize of a one-week trip to New York. Mrs Rennie also received £1,000 spending money – half of which she gave to the NSPCC – and clothes by Italian designer Fiorucci to the value of £500.

The demise of the Queen's Cinema went largely unnoticed, with an advert in the *Spectator* announcing that, following the screening of *Justine the Virtuous* and *Sex with a Smile* on 27 January, the cinema would be "closed until further notice." Although the owners later claimed the premises were to be redecorated, the cinema never reopened.

QUEEN'S PARADE, BANGOR   Phone 68519

Now showing until Saturday, 27th January
Doors open 7 p.m.
JUSTINE THE VIRTUOUS (X), 8.50; plus
SEX WITH A SMILE (X), 7.10

CINEMA CLOSED UNTIL FURTHER NOTICE
after Last Performance on
Saturday, 27th January

Canadian Technical Tape announced an expansion programme in March that promised 82 new jobs over the following three years. The company, which manu-factured a range of pressure sensitive adhesive tapes, already employed 194 people in the town.

Mayor Mary O'Fee hosted a civic reception on 6 April to mark the golden jubilee of the 1st Bangor Boys' Brigade Company. District chairman George McNeilly and secretary George Preston joined the officers of 1st Bangor for the memorable occasion.

The anniversary was also marked by a series of displays, an Old Boys reunion and a service of thanksgiving at 1st Bangor Presbyterian Church. Inspecting officer for the displays was former member Terry Neill.

343/3-6

Warden's Corner (at the Castle Street/ Main Street junction), was demolished on 22 April 1979 to make way for the new Boots store. The corner got its name from Warden's newsagents, which was located there for generations. It subsequently became home to the Northern Bank before serving as temporary premises for Stewart Miller's newsagents after the 1972 bombing of lower Main Street.

The final Westminster election of the decade, held on 3 May, saw MP Jim Kilfed-der taking on another 'Official" party candidate – Belfast teacher Clifford Smyth, who had topped the poll at a selection meeting in Newtownards a month earlier. The Alliance Party was represented by North Down Deputy Mayor Keith Jones.

Kilfedder was re-elected with a 23,625-vote majority – receiving 36,989 votes compared to the 13,364 and 11,728 cast for Jones and Smyth respectively. He also unsuccessfully sought election to the European Parlia-ment on 7 June, gaining 38,198 first preference votes (the fifth highest total among the 13 candidates).

Clifford Smyth
Probably the most outstanding candidate ever to stand for
North Down
You owe it to yourself to hear Clifford Smyth. He's coming your way, so come along and judge for yourself. Attend one of his meetings. We'll be surprised if you don't agree that he's the man to speak for North Down in Parliament.

Thursday, 19 April ..... Queen's Hall, Holywood, 8 p.m., with Rev. Martin Smyth
Friday, 20 April ..... The Square, Newtownards, 10 a.m., with Rt. Hon. John Taylor
Saturday, 21 April ..... McKee Clock, Bangor, 3 p.m.
Monday, 23 April ..... The Square, Newtownards, 10 a.m., with Rev. Martin Smyth
..... Groomsport Harbour, 8 p.m., with Rev. Martin Smyth
..... Donaghadee Orange Hall, 8 p.m., with Harold McCusker, M.P.
Tuesday, 24 April ..... The Square, Comber, 8 p.m., with Harold McCusker, M.P.
..... Newtownards Orange Hall, 9 p.m., with Harold McCusker, M.P.
Wednesday, 25 April ..... Bangor Market Walkabout, 10 a.m., with Rt. Hon. John Taylor

Vote for the right man
Clifford Smyth
OFFICIAL UNIONIST

Bangor resident David Bleakley, standing as a United Community candidate, received 9,383 votes (seventh highest).

Bangor-born Rev. Gerry Murphy was appointed Rector of Sandringham in May, following an hour-long interview with the Queen. Born in 1926, he was the elder son of Captain and Mrs W. S. Murphy, of Mayfield, Princetown Road. His maternal grandfather was Sir Thomas Wilson, Bangor's first Mayor. The new Rector of Sandringham had won six rugby caps for Ireland in the immediate post-war years.

The Young Men's Christian Association (YMCA) announced it would shortly have a new base in Bangor, following a £100,000 redevelopment scheme at former three-storey pharmacy premises on Queen's Parade.

The new Mayor of North Down Borough was Alderman George Green, who took over from Alderman Mary O'Fee on 8 June. His Deputy Mayor was Cllr Albert Magee.

The highlight of Bangor Youth Council's annual Youth Expo was a free 11-hour live music show entitled 'Rock Generation '79' at Castle Park in June.

When Clifford Rosbotham, of Westburn Crescent, was fishing off the old pier close to Brompton Road at the end of July he landed more than he had bargained for, hauling in a canvas bag containing a considerable quantity of jewellery. The police needed two sheets of paper to list all the items – believed to be the proceeds of a burglary.

Claire Wilson, youngest daughter of Anne Roulston's managing director David Wilson, is pictured with Gloria Hunniford after the TV personality opened the company's new store in Main Street. 105/9a-6

David Bleakley was appointed General Secretary of the Irish Council of Churches in succession to Canon William Arlow. Mr Bleakley was a former Stormont MP and Minister of Community Relations.

North Down Borough Councillors agreed in August to increase the cost of gas supplied through its loss-making Bangor undertaking by 20% in an effort to reduce the existing deficit before a final decision was taken on the future of the local gas industry.

The Department of the Environment revealed in September its intention to

introduce an 80p a day charge for its car parks at Abbey Street and Bingham Street/Hamilton Road. The sliding scale of charges applied on five days of the week, with Thursdays and Sundays excluded. Parking was free for under one hour and 10p for between one and two hours.

Following cutbacks announced by the new Conservative Government at Westminster, the Bangor Marina project was shelved in early October. A delegation from North Down Borough Council was advised that none of the promised funding was available for the scheme.

Aggrieved Councillors said they would still proceed with the demolition of the wooden section of the North Pier and its replacement with a concrete structure, and that they would seek European Community funding towards the overall marina development.

Julie McVea (13), from 71 Kearney Gardens, found this small pot, dated 1777, in August 1979 while using a metal detector in the wood running down to the sea beside Carnalea Golf Club. *350/12-7*

Newly-appointed RUC Chief Constable Jack Hermon had served as a sergeant in Bangor during the early 1960s. He and his family were the first occupants of one of the houses built adjacent to the new police station.

Florence Loudon was named best comedienne at the International Festival of Light Opera at Waterford in early October for her portrayal of Gladys in Bangor Amateur Operatic Society's production of *The Pajama Game*.

A major extension to the Northern Ireland Housing Executive's house sales policy meant 3,900 homes in the North Down area were available for sale to their tenants. Previously, houses were only offered for sale in areas where housing need had been met.

Oneida Silversmiths announced a reduction of between 20 and 25 in its workforce, leaving some 200 employees at its Bloomfield Road factory. The cuts were blamed on the impact of imports from the Far East.

Just 18 months after being formed the St Columba's Parish Church (Kilcooley) Church Lads' Brigade received their colours. Company Colours were presented by the Church Ladies Guild, represented by Lillian Henderson (third left), while Queen's Colours were presented by Alfred Henderson (third right) and his wife. The flags were dedicated during the Harvest Sunday service in November 1979 by Canon Hamilton Leckey. Included in the picture are captain Andrew Dickson (left) and chaplain the Rev. W. A. McMonagle, with Brigade members (from left): Nigel Keogh, Mark Angus, Frank Brown, Ian Magee, Tony Millgate, David Dickson and Stephen Strain.

375/4a-8

Val Doonican topped the bill before capacity audiences in the Tonic on 22 and 23 November – but perched on a stool instead of his familiar rocking chair! Also included on the bill was Bangor-born comedian Adrian Walsh.

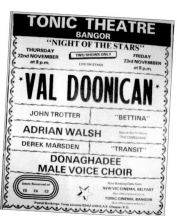

The final *Spectator* editorial of 1979 read: "It has been a long, hard decade – the worst in the history of our Province. We have become so accustomed to atrocity that in a short time we forget about the young women who have been widowed and left with fatherless children. In our home town of Bangor, young children were left without their mother, a Reserve Constable killed by shrapnel from a bomb.

"Can we make Leap Year 1980 one of special significance by leaping over the boundaries of bigotry and ignorance, to show tolerance and neighbourliness to those of different political or religious outlooks? Only then can we claim to have spent Christmas well."

Cast members from Glenlola Collegiate's production of *Finian's Rainbow* in February 1979. Back (from left): Tracy Hanna, Lisa Brennan, Katie Connolly, Rosemary Sheldon, Elizabeth Frazer, with Diane Tregaskis (centre) and Carla Houston (front). *336/a-5*

Joanne Coulter (16), of Ballyholme Parish, was placed first in the Bishop's Medal Examination – a scripture examination run in the Diocese of Down and Dromore. She is pictured with Bishop George A. Quin. *204/16a-6*

Canon James Hamilton (left) retired on 23 March 1979, having served as rector of Bangor Abbey since it became a parish in its own right in 1941. He receives a farewell presentation from people's churchwarden Alan Barton. Also included are Mr E. C. Hennessey, treasurer, John Kane, secretary, Rev. W. A. McMonagle, curate, Tom McMurray, Ellie Henderson, Andy Dickson, Rev. Alwyn Maconaghie, rural dean, and Bob McKillop, rector's churchwarden. The new rector was Canon Hamilton Leckey. *208/17-6*

Kilcooley Primary School's version of *The Pied Piper of Hamelin* included John Travolta and Olivia Newton-John look-alikes Gary Briggs and Esler Reid who sang *Summer Nights*. Included are *Grease* dancers (from left): Kim Scourance, William Anderson, Sandra Edgar, George Emerson and Lynn Dickson. *251/10-6*

7th Bangor (West Church) Scouts won the County Flag after competing for the first time in a decade. The team comprised (from left): Ian Legg (Patrol Leader), Ian Adair, Jess Morrow, Colin Robinson, Alan Browne and Peter Coburn. *675/4-6*

Maureen Fetherstonhaugh retired in June 1979 after serving as P2 teacher at Connor House for 18 years. She is pictured with her last class at the end of the summer term. *199/16-7*

Members of Brunswick Road Youth Club held a 12-hour disco in June 1979 to raise funds towards adding a second storey to their premises (the former St Comgall's School). DJ Kevin McKeown and youth leader Paddy Fox are pictured with some of the young enthusiasts. *220/11-7*

Enjoying the Spacehoppers at a gala and sports day organised by Glenlola Collegiate in July 1979 are (from left): Donna Creighton, Shirley Martin, Jane Pritchard, Sophie Cooke, Debbie McKane and Judith McIlroy. *215/11a-7*

Receiving their prizes after the Bangor area final of the EMI World Disco Dancing Championships in August 1979 are runner-up David Niblock (left), from Bangor, and winner Stephen Connolly, from Belfast. Doing the honours is Coachman owner Trevor Kane. *392/19-7*

These Bangor children set aside time during their school holidays to raise money for the Corrymeela Youth Centre at Ballycastle. From left: Michelle Rainey (10), from 19 Ardmillan Gardens, Patricia Barry (11), 18 Ardmillan Gardens, Sonya Laird (12), 30 Ballymaconnell Road, and (at front) Michelle's brother Richard (8). The children held a sale in the Rainey family's garden and raised £33.50. *113/5a-8*

John Ryan, creator, writer and illustrator of the *Captain Pugwash* stories, visited Bangor Library in October 1979 and met a number of local schoolchildren. He was promoting National Children's Book Week for the South Eastern Education and Library Board. *265/5a-8*

Jean Barton (right), from 57 Silverstream Crescent, met her American penpal of 32 years, Betty Cregin, for the first time in October 1979. Both were members of the International Friendship League when they first corresponded and they maintained regular contact over the years. *318/6-8*

Bangor Gateway Club members and helpers during an open night at Clifton Special Care School in November 1979. The costumes worn by some of the members featured in the play *The Good Ship Lollipop*. 272/2-8

Bangor Ladies Choir members with the trophies they won at Bangor Music Festival in November 1979. Included is conductor Isobel Reid. *421/15-8*

Bangor Amateur Operatic Society's Christmas and New Year pantomime *Mother Goose* starred principal boy Angela O'Hara (left) as Colin. She is joined by Robbie Lightbody (Jack) and Laura Carr (Wilhelmina). *34/13a-9*

Sheevaun McAlister
(née White-Overton) remembers...

Looking back more than 30 years I still find it hard to believe I was at the centre of a story which hit the headlines in a number of local and national newspapers, as well as being featured on the television news.

I was 26 at the time, living at Fifth Avenue and a few years into my career as a hairdresser working for Rottgers in one of those shops at the front of the Tonic Cinema. In the days leading up to Christmas 1978, Fossetts Circus placed an advertisement in the *Spectator*, stating they were looking for a young girl who would be willing to take the risk of spending a minute in the cage with five lions.

I went along to the Tonic – venue for the indoor circus – on a very icy New Year's Day and found the interview involved walking slowly around the outside of the lions' cage without flinching whenever they moved or roared. I'll have to admit this was actually rather easy for me as I'd been to a New Year's Eve party the night before and at that point hadn't woken up properly; all I can remember of the interview is how much those lions stank!

A total of 15 of us auditioned for a chance to take part in the circus and that number was then reduced to five

Sheevaun in the lions' den for a very long 60 seconds. *230/5a-5*

Sheevaun White-Overton was born in Londonderry in 1951 and moved to Bangor with her family in the late 1950s. She attended Avoca House and Glenlola Collegiate.

After a succession of summer jobs she commenced work as a hairdresser with Rottgers on the Hamilton Road. In the mid-1970s Sheevaun moved to Rhodesia, where she also worked as a hairdresser. She returned to Bangor, and Rottgers, two years later.

Sheevaun, who has two sons, Tristan and Conor Aiken, is now married to Charlie McAlister and lives in "blissful" retirement.

Sheevaun White-Overton with lion trainer Mike Sheedy after she ventured in the lions' cage at the International Circus. 231/11a-5

Sheevaun McAlister today

before I was told it was going to be me. On the big night the Tonic was packed. My special appearance had been announced in advance on the BBC and they also sent along a camera crew to capture all the action for the next day's news!

My task was to enter the cage and then walk backwards as lion tamer Mike Sheedy called out his instructions. To be honest Mike, who I learned ran a furniture warehouse in his spare time, had a broad Limerick accent and I couldn't understand him most of the time. I just knew I had to kneel down under a pyramid of five lions – the middle one was called Monarch and he was the one giving the most trouble.

My family and friends looking on in the audience seemed to be more frightened than I was and the circus people did have a man standing in the wings with a gun in case anything went wrong. Quite how he could have shot all those lions at the same time if they had pounced was beyond me!

Tonic manager Charles Carter hosted a drinks reception for everyone afterwards. My brother Jimmy asked one of the circus people if the lions were well fed before the show started, only to be told: "Oh no, we don't feed them until afterwards because if we did they would just lie down and sleep!"

Looking back it was an amazing experience and despite all the other things that were going on in my life I managed to keep in touch with many of the circus folk for quite a while afterwards.

As for that newspaper coverage, perhaps it was just a quiet time for the papers at New Year or maybe they were keen to run a story that would bring a smile to readers' faces in those darker days of the Troubles; either way, it made the front page of the *News Letter* and the *Irish Press*, as well as the *Daily Mirror* and the *Daily Express* (Bangor man John Ley, who worked for the *Express*, made that one possible).

I was paid £50 for spending just 60 seconds in the lions' den – but to this day it remains the longest minute of my life!

Entertainment
in Bangor in the Seventies

Gavin Martin
remembers...

In the 60s I could not grow up quickly enough. Bangor, or more specifically Ballyholme, was a dream wonderland of sun, sea and sand, complemented by the music that poured out of the Dansette in our lounge room at 47 Windmill Road.

My sister, Sharon, had ferociously good taste: Otis, Fabs, Stones, Kinks, Dylan. I wanted to dive in and experience it all. Aged four, I'd rush into my Mum's front-of-house rose garden at around 3pm. The kids were coming out of school and it was my sworn duty to perform, on my Beatles guitar, *She Loves You, I Wanna Hold Your Hand.* Barely grasping the libidinous undertow in the music, I was already swept up in its giddy, transformative power.

But in pre-teen years the hunger to participate was informed by a feeling of being outside looking in. However, the 70s and teen years offered the opportunity to get closer to the pulsebeat. There were obvious obstacles put in the way, though. All those deaths, one by one, had not boded well. I cried with Sharon when Otis died. Jimi, Janis, Jim… and The Fabs were no more.

Then there was the look on my Dad's face when he arrived

A young Gavin Martin pictured by Kurt Savage

Born in Belfast in December 1961, Gavin Martin moved to Bangor in 1963. He recalls that an early attempt to break into showbiz was thwarted when Miss Adrienne (of UTV fame) failed to act on his request to join the cast of *Romper Room*. A lucky escape for all concerned!

Educated at Ballyholme Primary School and, he says, happy to leave Bangor Grammar School at the earliest opportunity, Gavin finished his Bangor 'tour of duty' on a part-time course at Bangor Technical College.

Employed as a Northern Irish stringer for the *New Musical Express* from 1978, Gavin moved to London in 1980, where he has lived ever since. He spent an extended period at *NME* as Staff Writer and Film/ TV Editor, interviewing Madonna, Willie Dixon, Nina Simone, Neil Young and future Northern Ireland First Minister Peter Robinson, among many others.

He also hosted and curated the annual *NME Rock 'n' Reel* film events at the National Film Theatre with Matt Lucas, Noddy Holder, Jarvis Cocker and Mike Leigh amongst the guests. For the past 10 years Gavin has been Music Critic at the *Daily Mirror,* also freelancing for a wide range of publications and occasional host/ curator of the live music, spoken word, video and DJ'd event *Talking Musical Revolutions.* He is, of course, available for hire.

back home the night the first troops arrived in Belfast. I'd never seen him look so shocked, very much a warning sign for the incoming decade. Still, even under siege from the Bangor small town mentality, sheltering from the clouds of conflict, the music could not die; no matter what Don McLean told us.

It had to thrive, as an alternative to corruption in the town. In the years ahead, all that teeming activity on the beach and the aquatic life in the rock pools, round by the yacht club, would die out. That was symbolic. Preferring hippy idealism to entrenched local tribal and political traditions, I felt Bangor was a missed opportunity. As the Troubles progressed, it was relatively unscathed, a perfect setting. I daydreamed of a venue or arts centre where creative potential might grow, a place where the bands from across the Irish Sea, scared off by violence, might feel more at ease: Slade, Sweet, Wizzard, T. Rex... Bowie. Bowie? In Bangor? More chance of Life On Mars.

I expect the Council, already working on selling off the seafront, the town's biggest asset, would have pointed to the Little Theatre or Hamilton House as places where all cultural requirements were being met. The fare on offer at Milanos and Caproni's, those fine but out of bounds alcohol-serving ballrooms, seemed a poor substitute for the real thing (anyone for Chips?).

Living in Ballyholme, searching for the sound around town in Bangor as a pre-legal age teen, you had to take what you could find. The promise was tantalising, though unmistakable. Was there ever such elation, such an intimation of glorious freedom as on that Saturday morning in summer '73, running in the sun, on the sand, with the girl from up the road, past the raft and diving boards at Ballyholme? Laughing and splashing and kicking the water in the air so it fell on our swimming suit-clad bodies like salty glitter and singing *Honaloochie Boogie, Yeah,* the stand-out song from that week's *Top of the Pops?*

No, there was not, but the intimation was fleeting. For just at the point when interest in 'girls up the road' came fully into bloom, the draconian horror of same sex secondary education came calling. In my case, that meant five miserable years at Bangor Grammar School. Music proved a loving bulwark, an escape valve and… a weapon. The radio, weekly magazines such as *New Musical Express,* and local record shops would be vital channels in transmitting it.

There was the Co-Op's record section on the ground floor at the bottom of Main Street. Norman Keenan, the manager, was a family friend and in a showband, and he ensured there were bargains to be had. Then came Aquarius at the corner of Queen's Parade (flamboyant DJ Jon Antony would flounce in and say or do something outrageous, the nearest we had to a local celebrity clown prince). Smyths, between the Belfast/ Ulster Savings Bank and Tylers shoe shop in upper Main Street, would eventually prove a great source of three-for-£1 US jazz and soul import albums.

There was even a bloke who had a cassette rental kiosk at Bangor railway station, just opposite where there had once been a record-yourself booth that dispensed 5-inch singles (that's right, I still have mine). The push button £12 cassette recorder, gifted to me by my parents for passing the 11+, made the music portable. I affixed it to the rack of my bike and blasted Bob Dylan's *Highway 61 Revisited* as a special, no extra cost service to the neighbourhood.

I knew the pop charts by heart – far better than I knew any school work – so I wrote off to Emperor Rosko's Saturday morning Radio 1 show to enter his Hotline Goldmine competition. Weeks went by and I forgot about the entry. One Saturday I came back home after a listless afternoon mooching around Bangor. My Mum was mildly aghast as she told me how "THE BBC!!!" had called and would call again during the week to arrange for me to compete on the Rosko Show live on the air the following Saturday. It gave me time to revise, ensuring the following week that I had named, before the countdown ("TEN, NINE….") began, the Bay City Rollers' just released *Remember.* The excitable Rosko almost exploded into his mic: "My producer's standing here... and he's shaking. He can't believe you got it."

I won 10 singles, which in those days meant a record token for a fiver. I bought two albums, Wings' *Band On*

The Run and Joni Mitchell's *Court and Spark* in Aquarius (sorry, Norman), but told Rosko I'd be buying Paul Simon's *American Tune* single (which I did later in the Aquarius cut-out box for 20p, the same price I paid for Marvin's *Let's Get It On*).

Those early/ mid-70s years were great for music. Songs, like Neil Young's *Ambulance Blues* and the roaring invective of Steely Dan's *My Old School,* connected for deeply personal reasons: the first, for the sadness that came with my older brother Paul's short life and death, the second because it was the definitive word on Bangor Grammar. There were many more songs that could be applied to personal circumstance – the hipster cool putdown of the Dan's *Barrytown* seemed like an Exocet aimed right at Bangor's conformity.

Real live music wasn't much of an option locally. Three years after they'd helped me snare the Wings and Joni Mitchell albums, the Rollers were hanging out in the dressing room, several floors up at the back of the Tonic, one afternoon. The idea of going to see them, or wanting to go to see them, was already laughable. They were friendly enough, though, joked a bit and asked could we get them any drink. Us? Bangor Grammar School boys? I very much doubt it! The teenybop kings seemed kind of trapped up there and there were much more exciting rumblings afoot.

An older pal had turned me on to the mind-altering power of The Who. He explained that, without drink or drugs, but with The Who turned up REALLY LOUD on the stereo, you could actually get further out of your head than with anything else. Indeed I'd already had an intimation of that on the Howell family's fine, big stereo down on Ballyholme Esplanade, with the *Who's Next* track *Won't Get Fooled Again* rattling the double glazing.

When The Who announced they were to play a football stadium in Scotland I bought a ticket, planning to travel with my older pal, but at the last minute my Mum withdrew her carelessly given permission to travel. It proved an intuitive withdrawal, as my pal returned home with stab wounds after being attacked during the trip. My

Mum more than compensated, surprising me, on several occasions, with great vinyl purchases made at church jumble sales.

Apart from a never fully explained but pretty cool short set from Brit soul champs The Foundations in the Grammar assembly hall one afternoon, the first real live band I recall seeing was Irish Prog Rock conceptualists Fruuup. It was Friday night at a very sparsely attended Tonic. Perhaps, if

The Foundations paid several visits to Bangor during the decade – this one occurring in the summer of 1976 when they attended a children's party in the town. *59/3-11*

the concession stall had switched from Kia-Ora orange (yeeeuch) to Olde English cider, a bigger crowd might have made it. The Fruuup show was a decidedly odd, theatrical rock production with a wizened, whiskery, lank-haired narrator, stage right on a rocking chair. What I recall most about the evening was the scary-looking dude, with a First World War tin Army helmet, swigging from a smuggled-in bottle of fortified wine (Mundies) and regularly heckling the narrator in choice Anglo-Saxon.

Friday nights at the Queen's fleapit cinema saw screenings of *That'll Be The Day* and *Stardust*. Afterwards David, brother of the more famous Colin, Bateman, teetering on his orange and brown platforms, treated me and anyone else in the vicinity to impromptu, traffic-stopping performances of latest favourites from Slade (hooray) and Queen (boo!).

I remember my Dad taking me to see Chuck Berry, in Belfast's ABC Cinema, during a curfew.

The curfew, and the steep (£2.75) ticket

Chuck Berry in Belfast in 1976.
Picture: Terence Bowman

price, ensured only the first few rows of the cinema were occupied; but this was a real live rock 'n' roll legend, and when he called for requests I leapt up and asked for *Maybellene.*

He singled me out. "That's amazing. There's a young man who can't have been born when this song was released. We're going to play *Maybellene* for him." Years later, when his autobiography was published, I interviewed Chuck and told him about this. "Oh yes I remember you, you were just in the third row,' he lied, marvellously.

The rumblings, already apparent when the Rollers hung out of the Tonic dressing room, weren't going to fade away. Boosted by John Peel radio play and clarion call features in the *NME,* punk came in, right on time for me. The war on Bangor drudgery now began in earnest, and it was time to make a mark or two. To disguise the palsied dog doo colour of the brown leather jacket, which had been bought via the *Spectator's* classified ad section, I'd taken to covering it with paint-on, black shoe dye. This soon proved ineffectual – the dye rubbed off from the sleeves and gave me a premature 5 o'clock shadow around the jowls.

But the walls of the white shelters on the promenade above Ballyholme Beach presented the perfect white board for the black dye to be used on. It seemed so obvious, it seemed so right. Long since landscaped out of existence, in 1977 The Whites were adjacent to the formerly thriving beachside facilities and Ballyholme bathing boxes. The Whites were cold and unforgiving and permeated with the unspeakable stench of cider-addled urine from underage drinking sessions.

The Whites were the perfect place for words, adapted from The Clash's debut album, to be written. *Bangor's Burning With Boredom* it said and somehow, retaining my anonymity, I even drew attention to the graffiti in a letter to the *Spectator.* I got a kick out of hearing others talking about it, as it was perfectly placed to be viewed from cars and buses travelling along the road above.

Punk was just what I wanted from music in my teens: a weapon to be wielded. I knew its power when I got beaten up for pogo-ing, alone, to *God Save The Queen* at the police-run Blue Lamp Disco on the Hamilton Road. Or when I came down to find my loyalist aunt, visiting from Belfast, in tears after seeing Jamie Reid's safety pin poster of Her Maj given pride of place on my bedroom wall. "When I saw what you had done to our Queen…"

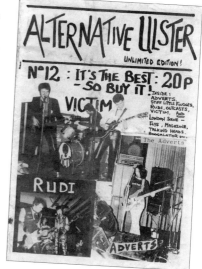

Back at the Grammar School, graffiti-ing punk names on the desk brought me face to face with prefect Dave McCullough, who came not to punish, but praise my scribbles. Together we started the fanzine *Alternative Ulster* – AU as it became known – absolutely no relation to the current bearer of that name. Jake Burns was so taken with the fanzine that, when he changed his band's name from Highway Star to Stiff Little Fingers, he wrote a song named after it.

I was such a bolshie little Martin(et), that when they played it for me live at the Trident, the Bangor venue name-checked in the song, I turned down the opportunity to have it released as a flexi-disc on the cover of the fanzine. Still, no matter, punk was off and running, fuelled latterly by the discovery of magic mushrooms (then still legal and in bountiful supply at the Valentine Playing Fields).

Music discoveries continuing apace... eventually The Doubt would kick some action up, locally, but for live music Bangor was still no epicentre. In the attic bedroom of 47 Windmill Road, I'd put together copies of AU. Then it was up to Belfast to get it printed at Just Books and check out the music of Rudi, Ask Mother, Ruefrex and so on.

The Doubt (from left): Stephen Clarke (drums), Hugh 'Chad' Cairns (vocals), Robert Scott (bass) and Paul 'Corky' Corken (guitar).

By 1978 I was freelancing on the local scene for the London-based *NME*. By the first year of the new decade I was at Aldergrove, ready to leave home for a shoebox in Golders Green with the promise of enough work at the *NME* to sustain me in the smoke. I arrived at the airport with a suitcase full of vinyl singles and albums, from church jumble sales, from the Co-op, Smyths, Aquarius and my sister's family collection. It was bloody heavy.

When I got to the security desk, the lady asked me to lift it up so it could be opened for full further scrutiny. Not wanting to break my back I asked if someone could help me lift the hefty case. The security lady looked at me, mildly horrified. "Why," she demanded, "is there something in it?"

I looked at her, puzzled, and thought... naw, nothing much, love. Just my life...

Gavin Martin today, wielding Rory Gallagher's guitar

Ken Gillen
remembers...

"You are cordially invited to the end of the world".

So ran the advertising slogan for *Eternity Junction*, probably the biggest event in Bangor in the 1970s. It was a show that sold out the 1,300-seat Tonic Cinema at each performance – two on its initial run in September 1975 and again, when it returned by public demand for a second run in December.

Before the world ended in December "the 100-piece Rock Musical" also ran for three packed performances in the McMordie Hall in Belfast during the Queen's University Festival.

It was original, contemporary musical theatre, capturing the mood of the times like counterparts *Joseph* and *Godspell*. It showcased fresh raw new talent and launched a number of diverse careers in the entertainment industry.

Inspired by the New Testament Book of Revelation, *Eternity Junction* depicted the struggle between good and evil, culminating in the Second Coming with the good all going to Heaven and evil going to Hell!

The early Seventies in Bangor was a time when churches were attracting a growing number of young people, both through youth groups and the efforts of ministers like Jack Robinson at Queen's Parade Methodist Church. It was there I became involved as pianist for the monthly service led by the youth fellowship.

Ken Gillen was born in Belfast in 1951. His family moved to Bangor in 1963, having holidayed in the town throughout the 1950s. He attended Regent House Grammar School where he was a sergeant in the Air Training Corps. Ken was awarded a 'flying scholarship' at RAF Biggin Hill and represented Northern Ireland on exercises in Britain and Germany. He also obtained a glider pilot's licence.

Ken joined Bangor Borough Council in 1969 and at the time of writing *Eternity Junction* was Deputy Registrar of

The main cast members (from left): Good Time, Jim Mitchell; Nefarious Sinn, Duncan McClean; Starship Captain, David Miller; Constance, Heather Reid, and Chris, Colin Miller. *90/5a-116.*

Births, Deaths and Marriages. He retired from the Council after 35 years' service and now lives with his wife Colette near Randalstown.

With David Cardwell he wrote the musicals *Eternity Junction* and *Dream World* and in 1988 he wrote a further musical, *Aurora,* with Chaela White from Holywood.

Ken Gillen today

Being young, naive and believing nothing was impossible, I thought Bangor deserved its own rock opera. I had the nucleus of a cast from the church group and an advert in the *Spectator* produced a co-writer, David Cardwell. As I had been a founder member of local bands City Sound and Paul and the Revolution there was the basis of a potential 20-piece 'big band' as an orchestra. So a year and 27 songs later we were ready. The cast had come from churches on Queen's Parade and Hamilton Road with the exception of the bad guy – Duncan McClean, lead singer with City Sound. The band had rehearsed, in sections, in my living room at Crosby Street, as had the principals. The sets (minimal) had been produced by my younger brother Rodney in our parents' garage!

It was time to "see the show before you go!"

What was needed now was a venue so off I went to see Mr Carter, manager of the Tonic, and negotiated the use of the cinema for the show. I had no idea at the time how we would pay the rental or fill more than 2,500 seats! Sound was the next consideration, but it did not pose a problem as the Tonic's acoustics were excellent and only needed the

addition of City Sound's PA to assist in projecting the vocals.

Lighting was another matter. Obtaining theatre lighting in Northern Ireland at that time was almost impossible. Some equipment was kindly loaned by Bangor Amateur Operatic Society and also by Bangor Drama Club. The big difficulty, however, was 'follow spots'. No one

Musical collaborators David Cardwell (left) and Ken Gillen. *74/7-109*

in the province had anything to cope with the length of throw required in the Tonic. After much searching I managed to obtain two from Scotland, which had to be air-freighted to Aldergrove.

Significant advertising and promotion are always required to sell any new venture and such was the case with *Eternity Junction*. However, what sold the show was the attention given by the press. Michael Megarry of the

Spectator ran stories of the production for some two months before curtain up. This in turn generated much broader coverage – even going as far as the *Ulster Tatler* and Ireland's *Spotlight* magazine.

A local travel agency was coerced into selling tickets for the show. This led to my favourite piece of advertising in the form of one of the cast parading around Main Street wearing a sandwich board

Dancers who took part in *Eternity Junction*

carrying the wording: *The end of the world is coming – book now at McClures.*

The early Seventies was still a time of enthusiasm, and it was certainly the enthusiasm of all those involved in *Eternity Junction* that made it such a success. It was a time when people and organisations went out of their way to achieve things; to make things happen by acting sensibly and responsibly without the stifling, curtailing constraints with which modern society and 'Health and Safety' manacles us.

We were all a lot more innocent then – it often feels now as if the end of the world *has* come.

Keith Nicol

remembers...

For over 20 years I was lucky enough to sing and play with a variety of bands in Northern Ireland, Canada and on over 40 cruise ships around the world. My first introduction to horn sections and the live sound of the big bands came as a teenager in the Seventies, an era also known for the 'bubblegum' pop sound made popular by artistes such as The New Seekers, Tony Orlando and Middle of the Road.

The mid-Seventies marked an era of change in the UK music scene. Gone but not forgotten were The Beatles, Elvis was clad in rhinestones in Vegas, Glam Rock had arrived in the shape of David Bowie, T. Rex, The Sweet, Slade, Gary Glitter, Wizzard and Mud, and we had home-grown favourites in Thin Lizzy. Disco was just about to rear its ugly head and teenage girls went all goo-goo over the likes of Donny Osmond, David Cassidy, David Essex and, of course, the Bay City Rollers.

With separate sex schools all the rage in Bangor, one of the most popular evening hangouts was the Epworth Youth Club, hidden behind the Wesley Methodist Church, which attracted teenagers from all of Bangor's schools to a fun social meeting point on Saturday and Wednesday. Romance, friendships and more than a couple of pop bands evolved out of the Epworth, along with one of the club's more defining moments, its involvement in Bangor's

Keith Nicol attended Connor House/ Bangor Grammar School and took night classes at Bangor Tech before heading off to Toronto in 1977 to study Applied Communications, Radio, Television, Film and Journalism at Seneca College of Applied Arts and Technology plus York University before Media Studies existed in the UK.

He was admitted to IATSE when only 21 and worked on a number of Canadian feature films while freelancing with Scarborough Cable Television and CFTO-TV.

He returned to Ireland to briefly join RTE2 and provided freelance photography work for *New Musical Express, Melody Maker, Point North* and *Northern Woman* magazines plus Jim Aiken Promotions and as an audio visual technician at Somerdale Boys' Secondary School. Seeking more variety, glamour and sunshine, he made a major career change and became a cruise ship photographer, which ultimately led to him moving into the entertainment department and becoming one of Northern Ireland's youngest Cruise Directors.

Keith worked in the cruising, entertainment, media and travel industries for 25 years, on 47 ships for 11 companies, while between contracts also finding time to sing and dance with the Bangor, Belfast and Ulster Operatic Societies, appearing as an extra in dozens of local TV productions and commercials, teaching scuba diving in Japan and coaching football in the USA and Bermuda.

Keith married Eva, a former distinguished teacher, choreographer and dancer of Ballet Español and settled in Miami Beach, working with the Casino Training Academy, Image Photo Services and as a TV presenter for Worldwide Collectibles Network and GEM TV.

They now live in Torrevieja, Alicante, Spain with their son Brandon. Keith is editor of *The Associate* business magazine, a photojournalist for *The Leader* and *Euro Weekly News*, a TV and radio presenter, photographer and video producer plus a tennis and football coach – for his son!

original rock musical *Eternity Junction*.

The year was 1975 and the cast of teenagers, fronted by City Sound's lead vocalist Duncan McClean, accompanied by top young musicians from around Co. Down, performed the original rock musical to two packed houses at the Tonic on 19 and 20 September 1975. It was the first time on stage for most of the performers and for some it was the last, but it was a catalyst for new friendships and opportunities that would last for decades, indeed to this very day.

Having put together a talented group of musicians for the show, complete with tight rhythm and top-notch horn sections, it seemed a shame not to try to keep the band together and take it on the road. Thus the Ken Gillen Band, or KGB, was formed and off they went, playing at such venues as the Coachman, Queen's University and Milanos, which was Bangor's number one dance floor, apart from Caproni's.

At any one time the band had up to 20 members on stage and apart from Dave Glover and John Anderson, there were few other local bands playing a mix of big band swing numbers, soul and blues, plus a little rock 'n' roll and pop music for the younger crowd.

The line-up was as follows: Ken Gillen – bass; Nicky Davidson – lead guitar; Roy French – rhythm guitar; Mark Coyle – drums; David Millar – vocals and percussion; Eddie Hill – keyboards; Robert Dawson – first trumpet; Nigel Donald – second trumpet; Roy Davis – first tenor trombone; Ian Simpson – bass trombone; Eric Robinson – first tenor saxophone; Robert McCune – second tenor trombone; George Powell – alto sax; and Malcolm McBratney – tuba.

The average age was around 19 and such was the calibre of the band that many KGB members went on to professional music careers, teaching, recording, playing for shows in all of Ulster's major theatres and performing in bands and groups around the province.

Indeed, even though now in their 50s, a few are still out there on the road and can often be spotted in old reruns of BBC and UTV variety shows from yesteryear. You know who you are!

One group that evolved out of the Epworth Hall was Waveband. Headed by Nicky Davidson on lead guitar and Roy French on bass, it also featured Clive Briggs on rhythm, the late David Reid on guitar and vocals and Rodney Archer on drums.

Audiences were introduced to new bands with fantastic country rock sounds such as The Eagles, Ozark Mountain Daredevils and Joe Walsh as well as the top hits of the day from the likes of Slade, Status Quo, Free, Bad Company, Rod Stewart, David Bowie, Wings, Thin Lizzy, Led Zeppelin, Van the Man and T. Rex, plus classics of rock 'n' roll and the Sixties from the Beach Boys, Elvis, Buddy Holly and The Beatles.

A later version of Waveband (from left): Nicky Davidson, Rodney Archer, Roy French, Clive Briggs and Eddie Hill. *Picture courtesy of Rodney Archer.*

When the opportunity to perform in *Eternity Junction* came along, Nicky was drafted in as lead guitarist while Davy Reid, Roy French and I joined the chorus and had our moment of glory as the team of newsreaders! As Ken Gillen played bass, Roy was out of a job but the three of us had fun learning our steps and the vocals to accompany Ken and David Cardwell's original songs.

Eternity Junction was also performed as a Christmas special on 22 December 1975, as coincidence would have it the same night the Bay City Rollers were on stage in the ABC Theatre, Belfast.

With 'Roller Mania' still very much in evidence during the fantastic summer of 1976, the KGB was booked to play at Milanos. At 17, I was a guest singer more than a regular member of the band and we somehow managed to squeeze ourselves onto a stage that was not built for almost 20 performers! Milanos was more used to hosting such bands as Sunset, Sunshine and City Sound, rather than a group featuring a full brass section, although previously the Christian rock group Liberty Suite had received rapturous reviews there.

My task was easy – sing a few numbers with just the rhythm section to give the brass section a break. Chuck Berry's *Johnny B. Goode,* Elvis' *Blue Suede Shoes* and Buddy Holly's *That'll Be The Day* made up the start of my first set. As Nicky then hit the first five chords of *Shang-A-Lang,* 20 or more teenage girls made their way to the stage and started a mock scream for their favourite band.

Keith Nicol with his wife Eva and son Brandon

As I started singing and moved to the front of the stage, pairs of hands grabbed my outrageously wide, white hipsters and suddenly, still singing, I was being pulled off the stage, much to the amusement of the entire band. Now sitting on the edge of the stage, I was surrounded by these girls, who were just having a bit of fun at my expense.

Red-faced but smiling, I returned to stage centre to finish the song before going back to singing back-up vocals with the band. This was to be my one and only taste of what it might be like to be a real pop star. The Bay City Rollers then followed in the footsteps of *Eternity Junction* by performing at the Tonic in September 1976. It was also my first taste of working with a big band but, thankfully, not my last.

The next year I auditioned for Bay City Rollers manager Tam Paton, as he wanted to start an Irish version of the band. I decided to go to college in Canada instead of joining the group and little was heard of Tam or the Bay City Rollers again. However, every time I hear BCR on the radio, it takes me back to Milanos and KGB!

Barbara Falloon
remembers...

It was Tuesday 28 September 1976. Northern Ireland was in the grip of sectarian violence with Army patrols a common sight, but along the North Down coast another Army was making its presence felt – a Tartan Army! The Bay City Rollers were in town – the Tonic Cinema, to be precise, and my cousin Celine McArdle (now Duffy) and I were part of this unforgettable experience.

Except for going to our local youth club, Celine and I had really never been out unsupervised. This, coupled with the fact we were about to witness Britain's Number One boy band, ensured we would have a fantastic evening.

The band had recently replaced one of its long-serving members, Alan Longmuir, with Downpatrick-born Ian Mitchell. I can remember my older sister, Stella, asking passers-by on the Springfield Road to sign a petition imploring Alan not to leave but alas our pleas had gone unnoticed!

Back in Bangor we were safely deposited at the Tonic, where we joined the ecstatic sea of tartans that had claimed the car park. Over 30 years later I can still recall the butterflies I felt in my stomach. We knew we had no chance of hearing a word they would sing and even less chance of actually seeing them, as this was way before the big screen era, but even now I'm convinced Eric Faulkner waved especially at me! The chants of "B-A-Y, B-A-Y" reverberated

Barbara (left) with cousin Celine

Barbara Falloon (née Magee) grew up on the Springfield Road in Belfast and attended St. Dominic's High School. She was employed by Northern Ireland Electricity for a number of years and it was there she met her husband George – they have two teenage daughters, Emma (b. March 1993) and Lisa (b. May 1995).

During her summer holidays in the Seventies Barbara often stayed with cousin Mary Russell and her husband Jimmy in their Bangor West home. A visit to the Springhill Shopping Centre, the recently opened Bangor Leisure Centre and, of course, a bag of chips swimming in salt and vinegar while walking alongside Pickie Pool are all vivid memories.

"Oh, and it is true – summers were so much nicer years ago!" she adds.

around the town as Celine and I waved our MacDonald clan tartan scarves, along with our new-found Bangor friends.

Soon we were being filtered through the cordons by policemen who gave that 'you'll look back and cringe at this' smile. Here we were on a Tuesday night in Bangor – sorry Miss McCann, Hitler's Foreign Policy would have to wait – pleading with the Rollers to get to the stage and do their stuff.

The lights went out and there they were – it was unreal – these guys who featured on the cover of *Jackie* every week were only yards from us. The Tonic heaved – no one sat as Les McKeown, wearing a skinny rib jumper and white calf-length trousers trimmed in his trademark white tartan, told us: *All Of Me Loves All Of You.* And, of course, who among us would not believe him?

St. John Ambulance personnel ferried those who even after the first song had fallen to their knees hyperventilating, but Celine and I knew this was sometimes a ploy to get carried across the front of the stage and then, miraculously, to leap up and actually touch some of the boys – so sorry, no sympathy.

Bay City Rollers fans are treated by St. John Ambulance personnel 22/8-15

Summer Love Sensation – who could fail to imagine walking hand and hand along Helen's Bay beach with your favourite Roller? We really didn't talk or comment, probably because we would not have heard a word, but how uncool would idle chit-chat have been when everyone around us was screaming, crying or just holding on to every note and every move our Scottish heroes made.

Shang-A-Lang – I can still see Eric strumming out those first notes on his guitar and we all chanted the chorus and clapped at the same time. Eric was my favourite; he always wore the red tartan and had dark shoulder length hair which was spiked on top. Woody and Ian strummed feverishly – they didn't dance across the stage but who

The Bay City Rollers on stage at the Tonic Cinema *21/5-15*

TICKETS FOR ROLLER CONCERT ON SALE IN BANGOR By Michael Megarry

could blame them in their platform soles. Derek played the drums – I always felt he didn't have just as popular a fan club as the others but tonight his name was loud and clear on the roll of honour.

The Tonic seemed to ripple with throngs of young people trying to surge forward to get as close as possible to the stage. "It's a teenage dream to be 17 and to find you're all wrapped up in love" – at 15 never were truer words spoken and at this point the lights dimmed and the screams actually subsided momentarily. Les dedicated this to everyone who was in love – he was so thoughtful!

Keep on Dancing, Give a Little Love, I Only Want To Be With You – all those songs I'd waited patiently to see if they would feature on *Top of the Pops* were blasted out and then to my horror they started to lift off their guitars and wave. We looked in astonishment, although that might have been at the sight of each other with bright pink cheeks and Miners (supposedly waterproof) mascara trickling down our faces. The crowds screamed louder than before and we weren't let down, soon the five were

Fans scream for the Bay City Rollers at the Tonic in September 1976.
25-1-76

back on stage with their pièce de résistance, *Bye Bye Baby* – my heart still flutters at the memory. Heart-stopping, spell-binding and magical, but soon the lights were turned on and the boys were really gone.

Our heart rates had to readjust to normality as we headed outside to be collected. "Was it a good night girls?" asked Jimmy Russell, but how could you really put into words what we had just been a part of? "It was fantastic," we answered. Soon we were heading home with both of us vowing to start saving for a holiday in Edinburgh where we might bump into the lads!

Barbara Falloon and husband George with their daughters Lisa and Emma

The next morning brought with it the awful realisation that Miss McCann might not fully appreciate my reason for not completing my history homework, but who cared – the Bay City Rollers concert would remain with me longer than the Third Reich – and so it did!!

Sport
in Bangor in the Seventies

1970

Bangor reached the County Antrim Shield final with a 1-0 victory over Larne, following an earlier 1-1 draw. Jim Herron headed Brian Morrison's cross home in the 46th minute.

The final, against neighbours Ards, resulted in a 1-1 draw on Saturday 9 May and two more 1-1 draws after extra time on Tuesday 12 May and Monday 18 May, before, at last, a 3-2 win for Bangor on 22 May. It was the club's first senior trophy in its 43-year history. Goalscorers in the fourth game were Jim Herron, Brian Mulgrew and Ivan McAllister.

It was a case of third time lucky in the Senior Cup for Clandeboye Golf Club, when they became All-Ireland champions by defeating Malahide by 3½ to 1½ in August.

Six-year-old Stephen Conn, from Lisnabreen Walk, was the envy of his friends at Bloomfield Road Primary School after he visited Manchester during his summer holidays. During a trip to Old Trafford, home ground of Manchester United, he met Bobby Charlton, Denis Law and George Best.

The foundation stone for Bangor's new heated indoor pool at Castle Park was officially laid by former Mayor Bertie Campbell on Thursday 1 October. It was hoped the pool would be open by summer 1971, offering separate facilities for learners, divers and ordinary swimming in the three-pool complex.

Derby County manager Brian Clough offered Bangor FC £4,000 for their 17-year-old reserve centre-half Peter Dornan. The Bangor Grammar student, who had dropped himself from the school's hockey first XI to concentrate on soccer, wanted to continue his education and complete his A-Levels.

Bangor FC secured their second senior trophy in six months with a 4-3 victory over Derry City in the City Cup on 5 December. It was run as a league with the 12 Irish League clubs playing each other once. Bangor's unbeaten run included wins against Glenavon, Cliftonville, Ballymena United, Coleraine, Distillery, Portadown and Derry City, and draws against Linfield, Ards, Glentoran and Crusaders. In the final game Bangor were being beaten 3-2 with 15 minutes left on the clock, but goals from Tommy Craig and Jim Graham secured the win which put Bangor a single point ahead of Distillery.

The victorious Bangor team pictured before beating Derry City 4-3 to win the City Cup. Back (from left): Ronnie Morrison, Jim Graham, Billy Finlay, Billy Irwin, John Kennedy, Paul Murphy, Brian Morrison. Front: Johnny Cochrane, Jackie McManus, Harry Creighton (captain), Tommy Craig and George Matchett. *234/74/2*

Ballyholme Presbyterian Church won the 5th division of the Ulster Badminton League. Back (from left): H. Kerr, E. Whiteside, the Rev. W. Erskine, P. Escott, B. Blaikie. Front: A. M. Davidson, M. Doran, J. Bowman and B. Jamieson. *224/17/1*

First Bangor Cubs won the Bangor and District Cub Scout Soccer League. Back (from left): Stuart Boyd, Gavin Logan, Michael Dixon, Michael Johnston, Drew Henderson, Alastair Webb. Front: Brian Shaw, Kingsmore Corbett, Alistair Reid (captain), Charles Macrory, Gabriel McDowell and Paul Moore. *225/22/1*

Members who took part in Clandeboye Golf Club Lady Captain's Day in June 1970. Lady Captain Mrs J. Mawhinney is seated (centre). *227/72/1*

The Ulster Arms Supporters Club darts team, winners of the Carling Black Label Perpetual Trophy in September 1970. Back (from left): W. Caruth (president), W. Crone, R. Montgomery, D. Blair, J. Dempster, M. Watterson, M. Murnin (chairman). Front: N. Pickard, W. McCormick, T. McBurney (captain), R. Russell and R. Rutherford. Missing: T. Emerson and J. Cruise. *230/94/3*

Mayor Robert Topping wishes Stephen Burnison and other participants, numbering 350 in total, well before the start of a well-supported sponsored walk organised by Bangor's BB Companies. The event raised money towards a major sports complex at Belvoir Park in Belfast. *231/30/3*

1971

Dick Milliken, captain of Bangor Grammar School's victorious Schools Cup team in 1969, was selected as a travelling reserve for the Irish rugby team against France at Lansdowne Road, Dublin. He had become a regular for Ulster as well as the Irish Universities side.

Bangor FC relinquished their hold on the County Antrim Shield in the most humiliating of circumstances. On a decidedly off day at Clandeboye Park on 27 February, they were defeated 2-1 by amateur side Islandmagee, with the home side's goal being scored early on by George Matchett.

Bangor Grammar School had two representatives on the Ulster Schools rugby team which defeated Leinster Schools at Lansdowne Road in dramatic fashion. The side was captained by 18-year-old Robert Hamilton, who played for most of the second half with a dislocated finger. Propping for the team was John Thompson (17). Ulster won 24-23, scoring in the final minute.

Charlie Tully, who had just signed a new three-year deal with Bangor FC, died suddenly on 27 July at his home in Belfast. He was 47. Having achieved great success as a player with Glasgow Celtic and as an Irish international in the 1950s, he moved into management, initially with Cork Hibernians. Two spells with Bangor, the first in the mid-1960s, led to the club winning its first senior trophies. Tully was succeeded by Alfie McMichael, who in his earlier days had played for Newcastle United.

Bangor's John Pringle, who had made quite a name for himself in the world of motor racing during the 1950s and 1960s, had one of the corners for the 1971 Craigantlet Hill Climb named in his honour.
'Pringle Corner' celebrated his achievement in becoming the first Ulsterman to set the hill record in nearly half-a-century. He achieved the feat in both 1961 and 1962 in his 2.5 litre Cooper Climax.

Garth McGimpsey (16) was defeated in the final of the Ulster Boys Championship at Warrenpoint, but in the same week was selected for Irish Boys to play in a quadrangular competition against England, Scotland and Wales.

Terry Neill, who had been transferred from Bangor FC to Arsenal in 1959 for

£2,500, succeeded Billy Bingham as player/ manager of Northern Ireland. He was a constant figure in the national team – which he had captained before he was 21 – winning 45 caps by August 1971.

Despite existing liabilities totalling £25,000, as well as a looming £32,000 bill for nine more holes by 1973 (bringing the total to 36), Clandeboye Golf Club had its sights set firmly on a secure future.

As well as expecting to have all its debts cleared within six years, the annual general meeting heard calls from some members for the development of an indoor pool and sauna baths at the clubhouse.

With Bangor's new indoor heated swimming pool nearing completion, the local Council turned its attention to the future of Pickie Pool, which had last been modernised around 1929. Members were told that changed times meant they should consider providing a leisure or fun pool, which would involve demolishing the outdoor pool.

Pickie, they heard, cost £2,500 a year to maintain. Recreations manager Jock Affleck was instructed to prepare an outline modernisation scheme.

Members of the Kilcooley Primary School soccer team wearing one of two new strips purchased for 1971. At the time they were joint first in the Bangor and District Primary Schools League. Back (from left): Mr R. J. Besant, sports master, J. Eggleston, P. McVea, T. Dalzell, B. Sloan, Mr A. Glenn, principal. Second row: S. Braund, J. Watton, S. Courtney (captain), P. McGrath, J. Andrews, R. Chapman. Front: M. Montgomery and B. Hagan. *236/47/1*

Bangor Swimming Club members suffered a narrow defeat against their Ards counterparts in a gala at the Newtownards Pool in October 1971. *246/78/1*

Members of the BETS Bowling Club at their annual dinner in the Savoy Hotel in October 1971: G. Jackson, T. McFall, J. McWhirter, W. Cardy, J. Brown (vice-president), J. Pollock (secretary), J. Crawford and J. Lyall. Not in picture: C. Innis. *247/63/2*

1972

Bangor Rugby Club won the Towns' Cup in April, beating neighbours Ards 3-0 at Ravenhill. Conn McCall's penalty secured the club's 11th cup since 1882 and their first since 1969.

Bangor's new indoor heated pool finally opened – initially to schools – in April. The pool, which was available to the public from 24 May, had cost £400,000. Early attendances averaged 1,000 each day. The official opening, performed by Mayor Robert Topping, followed in March 1973.

Terry Neill scored the winner in Northern Ireland's famous 1-0 victory over England at Wembley on 25 May. The game marked his 50th international appearance and made a mockery of suggestions Neill was only in the team because he was also the manager.

Members of the St Columbanus Secondary School basketball team who won the North Down League in June 1972. 2571/9-1

Twelve-year-old Wendy Archer, a member of 4th Bangor Girl Guide Company, won the Portaferry to Strangford swim in August 1972. She is pictured with Helen Gordon (holding flag), Elizabeth McCabe, Frances Brownlee and Jackie Stone. *63/11a-57*

Cubs and leaders from Bangor District who took part in an inter-Company sports day at the Bloomfield Road playing fields in October 1972. *259/16-1*

Rathgael Rangers FC received a new skip in November 1972 from Abbey Street businessman John Kelly (front, second left). Included with team members and supporters are captain Dessie Hanna (with shirt) and joint managers Dessie Keenan (third left) and Maurice Purvis (with socks). *74/3-59*

Fourteen-year-old Vincent Bedford, of 1 James Mount, signed for Nottingham Forest in November 1972. The Bangor Grammar pupil, who played at right-half for Ards III, was spotted by Forest scout Bill Oakes while playing in the Downpatrick Youth League for Kerry United. *22/14-60*

1973

Dick Milliken became the first member of Bangor Rugby Club to be capped for Ireland when he played against England at Lansdowne Road on 10 February. Roger Clegg quickly followed in Dick's footsteps when he too was selected to play against France in Dublin on 14 April.

Irish Internationals Roger Clegg (left) and Dick Milliken (right) receive presentations from Bangor RFC president George Lightbody in August 1973. *18/14a-68*

At the age of 23 John Elder became Bangor's first home-produced Irish cricket international when he played against Wales in June. He would win 37 caps for Ireland, his last game also being against Wales, in August 1987.

Bangor's Liz Gadsby captained the Northern Ireland women's soccer team which was beaten 4-1 by the Republic in Dublin on 30 June. Substitutes included Doreen Lyttle, who played for a brief spell, and Liz McNamara, a member of the *Spectator* office staff.

Bangor Golf Club's Billy Pope became Ulster Boys Champion at Royal Belfast in August. He beat Jimmy Heggarty (Masserene) in the semi-final and Hugh Boyd (Royal Portrush) in the final.

The first schools rugby match under floodlights in Northern Ireland took place at Upritchard Park on 12 October. The encounter involved U-13 teams from Bangor Secondary School and Bangor Grammar School, with the latter winning 20-4. Coaches were Derek Nash and Jimmy Welsh respectively.

Pupils of Bloomfield Road Primary School enjoy newly-installed climbing equipment in the assembly hall. Looking on are (from left): Mr E. Webb, PTA chairman, Mrs S. Segasby, treasurer, Mr J. A. Magee, principal, and Mr W. J. B. Thompson, vice-principal and PTA secretary. *78/10-62*

Members of the Bangor Boys' Secondary School swimming team who represented the school in March 1973. Included are Phillip Edmunds, Alan Hall, Clifford Wilson, Peter McMackin, David McCullough, Niall Wallace, Bryan Hopley, Noel Munnis and Timothy Smith. *263/54/1*

Canon James Hamilton, rector of Bangor Abbey, receives part of a new skip from Michael Murnin, vice-president of the South End Social Club. The full skip was presented through Canon Hamilton to the Abbey's football team – one of a number of clubs and charities to benefit from the newly-formed social club. *54/14-66*

Bangor Young Men FC at Castlereagh Park, Newtownards, prior to their Junior Shield success over Dunmurry Young Men. Back (from left): D. Smyth, F. Craig, E. Moore, N. Henderson, J. McManus, J. Duff, M. McCullagh. Front: W. Friar, P. Vaughan, A. Moore, W. Crothers and V. Hyvart. *87/7a-66*

Eric Halliday from the Blue and Gold Supporters Club presents the 5th Bangor Old Boys 'Player of the Year' award to Billy Larmour. The second team award was shared by Gerry Nelson and Tony Thompson. *19/20a-68*

Members of the Heller Ladies Darts Club who received three trophies at the Bangor and District Darts League presentations. Included are Ruth Cranston (individual champion) and John Burns (captain). *100/3a-68*

Sixth Bangor Cubs defeated 12th Down CBSI 3-1 in the Bangor and District Cubs Knock-Out Cup at Clandeboye Park. Back (from left): Patrick Leeke, Peter Bell, Michael Fegan, Paul Holmes, Tom Gibson, Colin Pyper, Robert McKee. Front: Stephen Gibson, Francis Duff, Martin Burch, Gary Pagels, Gerald Troupe, Scott Fulton and Philip Thomas. *26/10a-68*

Bangor Swifts at the Valentine Playing Fields with the Wilson Shield they received in September 1973 for being runners-up in the Bangor Summer League. *50/3a-74*

Members of the Pickie Veterans bowling team at their annual meeting in October 1973, including trophy winners. Seated (from left): C. Allen, Veterans League runner-up; J. Nicholson, pairs runner-up; J. Bell, chairman, Rinks Cup; and W. J. Allen, McMurtry Rose Bowl. *88/10-75*

Bangor Archery Club committee members at their first dinner in the Dunallen Hotel, Donaghadee, in December 1973. *49/3/77*

1974

Norrth Down Council congratulated Dick Milliken on being selected for the British Lions' South African tour between May and June (the team would win 21 of their 22 games, drawing the last).

Bangor were defeated 16-6 by CIYMS in the club's first Senior Cup final, held at Ravenhill on 20 April. Bangor's try by Kenny Young was converted by Billy Mc-Combe.

In early August Shrewsbury Town FC expressed an interest in signing two young Bangor players after their impressive performances against the English club during a short pre-season tour. Centre-half Ian Jaffrey (19) was the tallest player in the Irish League, while 20-year-old striker Gerry Armstrong was also a leading Antrim GAA player.

Bangor boy Chris Barbour broke the school record at Campbell College's swimming championships in October when he recorded a time of 1min. 26.6secs. in the 100m breaststroke.

Ian Robertson, Mark McConville and Kyle Christie compete in the youth section at an Easter Monday meeting organised by Bangor Archery Club in April 1974. *77/22a-81*

Members of Ballyholme Primary School football team in May 1974 with (back, from left): teacher Mr G. Whittle, the Rev. Raymond Mason and headmaster Mr D. Cummings. Their success in various competitions earned the boys a letter of congratulations from Fulham captain Alan Mullery. *64/4-82*

Heather Stewart, captain of the Whitehill Boys team – that's not an error – receives the Duke Orr Memorial Shield in the North Down Junior League from Mrs Orr in June 1974. Back (from left): Gerry Thompson, Don Craig, Ian Stewart, team trainer and Heather's brother, and Sgt. Spiers Wilson, RUC Community Relations Officer. Middle: Kevin McAuley, Eddie Thompson, Brian Magee, Jim Andrews, Dessie Hill, Graham McAteer, Jim Maitland, Alan Hopley, J. Davidson. Front: Colin Brown, Bobby Malcolm, Colin Bennett, John Drennan, Johnny McCamley, John Armit, Martin Thompson and Stephen McCamley. *6/4-86*

Bangor Bowling Club won the NIBA Senior Challenge Cup at the end of July 1974, beating Musgrave by a single shot. Back (from left): Billy Hanna, Austin Fulton, Alex Hall, Billy Pollock. Middle: Martin Graham, Willie McClelland, Hugh Hayes, Billy Kirkwood, Sam Shaw, Morris McKeown, Victor McKeown. Front: Billy Hardy, Dick Snoddy, Gerry Sloan, George Martin (president), Eddie McMaster, Eddie Gaw, George Selman and Alfie Thomas. *82/8-89*

Glenlola Collegiate's hockey team took part in a tournament at Upritchard Park in August 1974. From left: Marietta Halsall, Gail Holland, Barbara Firth, Rosemary Lightbody, Valerie Cromwell, Joy Redman, Susan Jones and Rosemary Brookes. *55/6a-89*

1975

A third Bangor player, Billy McCombe, joined Dick Milliken and Roger Clegg on the Ireland side for Five Nations fixtures against England and Scotland during January. Ireland won the first game 12-9 but lost the second 20-13.

Bangor Rugby Club followed up their Easter Monday Towns Cup victory by being proclaimed Senior League champions – regaining a title last won 45 years earlier. Victory over Civil Service by 35-7, along with a crucial win by CIYMS over Instonians, ensured Bangor's title success.

Bangor FC won the County Antrim Shield with a 2-1 victory over Glentoran at The Oval on Tuesday 13 May. On the way to the final the team beat Linfield 3-2 at Windsor Park, Ards 4-2 at Clandeboye Park and Distillery 4-1, also at home. Among the scorers was Gerry Armstrong, including a winning header against Glentoran.

Gerry Armstrong, pictured with Clandeboye Park groundsman John Heyburn. 22/2-32

Bangor forward Gerry Armstrong quit the Northern Ireland Housing Executive in November to join Tottenham Hotspur as a professional – just days after the Irish League club rejected a bid from Arsenal. Although Bangor had a long-standing link with 'The Gunners' following Terry Neill's transfer in 1959, by November 1975 Neill was manager of rivals Spurs – although he would return to Arsenal, as manager, the following summer.

Bangor FC won their second trophy of the year, adding the City Cup to the County Antrim Shield after a penalty shoot-out victory over Distillery at Seaview on 10 December. Scorers were Jim Thompson, Stephen Feeney and Ronnie McCullough. The club had won the same two trophies in 1970.

Bangor builder John McAlorum, driving a lightweight BMW, clinched the Northern Ireland Rally Championship in mid-December after finishing second in the Queen's University Motor Club winter rally with co-driver Paul Phelan (Dublin).

Boys who took part in a sponsored five-a-side match at Bangor Boys' Secondary School in February 1975 to raise money towards a new minibus. They played for 18 hours with each pupil being sponsored at 2p per hour. *5/32-101*

Bangor 2As defeated Dungannon 3-0 at Ravenhill on Easter Monday, 31 March 1975, to regain the Towns Cup. The only score came midway through the second half when Mike Wilson dropped a goal from 50 yards. Back (from left): Brian McDowell, James O'Fee, Neil Grainger, Gary Swenarton, Mike Wilson, Billy Kirk, Brian Crawford, Adrian Mencarelli. Front: James Conn, Edwin Conn (club president), Tim McMillan, David Carson (captain), Ken Finlay, Lyn McCallum, Randall Herron, Jimmy McAllister and Conn McCall (coach). *57/13-104*

Carolyn Brown, of 40 Abbey Park, with the two cups she won in the Irish Badminton Championships in April 1975 – under 12 girls doubles and mixed doubles. *108/8-104*

The victorious Bangor football team with the County Antrim Shield in May 1975. The trophy is held by Ronnie McCullough and groundsman John Heyburn. *40/15-107*

Holding the City Cup are (from left): Jimmy Apperson, vice-chairman of Bangor FC, players Ian Jaffrey, Selby Addis and Gordon Stewart, and club treasurer Bob Montgomery. *2a/122*

Bangor student Kenny Hooks (15) became All-Ireland Junior Boys 100m champion in a time of 11.5 seconds at Belfield, Dublin, on 8 June 1975. *73/2-109*

Rathmore Primary School netball team shared the Bangor and District Cup with Bloomfield Road Primary School in June 1975. Among those pictured are: Mrs M. McCormick, Kathy McCreanor, Mr A. Boyd (principal), Carolyn Quee, Joanne McBlain, Karen Cochrane, Elaine Ruston, Gillian Bogey, Anne Powell and Denise Weatherup. *98/5-109*

World professional snooker champion Alex 'Hurricane' Higgins gave the opening display at the new pool table in the Queen's Court Hotel in September 1975. *76/13a-116*

Bangor's Sam McClements (29) returned home from the Isle of Man where – riding a Yamaha – he won the Senior 500 Manx Grand Prix on 4 September, setting a record for the fastest lap. Sam's best lap was his third, at 103.10mph, while his average for the full six laps was 101.04mph, also a record. Sam is pictured with wife Ann and the trophy he brought back from the Isle of Man. *5/8-116*

Ward Park Afternoon Bowlers (over-65s) concluded their season in late September 1975 with a membership in excess of 90. Chairman was Alfie Donald, secretary was John Marshall and treasurer was Bob Graham. *19/5-117*

Bangor Archery Club member Alan Bates performed the once-in-a-lifetime 'Robin Hood shot' during a club night at Bangor Boys' Secondary School on 3 December 1975, firing one arrow into another. *66/16-121*

Mark Orr was selected to represent Ireland at the European Chess Championships in Holland. The 20-year-old student had become Ulster Schoolboy Champion while at Bangor Grammar School. *50/8-122*

1976

The 1976 Benson and Hedges Circuit of Ireland Rally, covering 60 special stages over a 1,500-mile route, began at Castle Park on Good Friday, 16 April. The rally finished in Larne on Easter Tuesday with Cork driver Billy Coleman being acclaimed the winner. Bangor's John McAlorum was the highest-placed local driver, finishing 11th overall.

Bangor schoolboy Chris Fleming, of 6 Bloomfield Place, was signed by Wolverhampton Wanderers as an apprentice professional in early June. The teenager, who had played for 1st Bangor BB, was already establishing himself on the Wolves youth team, which had just won the FA Youth League.

North Down Councillors bowed to public pressure at the end of June and agreed to provide the traditional diving boards and bathing raft at Ballyholme Beach, having previously indicated they intended to scrap the facilities to save just £180.

That earlier decision sparked uproar among residents and visitors. However, there were no objections to the closure of the bathing boxes on the promenade.

Eight thousand fans packed Ravenhill to watch Bangor take on Willie John Mc-Bride's International XV in a special match on 1 September to boost the Adrian Mencarelli Appeal Fund. The former Bangor stalwart had suffered a serious spinal injury while playing in a club fixture almost a year earlier. The fundraiser finished 54-10 for the International XV.

Ballyholme Yacht Club members sustained their worst losses for many years after gale force winds and mountainous waves claimed over a dozen vessels on 9 September. Out of a fleet of 78 sitting at anchor in Ballyholme Bay, 19 boats broke their moorings and ran ashore and 20 more were sunk.

Former Bangor FC player Peter Dornan (23) signed for Linfield at the end of September after impressing manager Roy Coyle while playing for Shorts in the Amateur League. He had just completed his legal studies at Queen's but was taking a year off before entering a solicitor's office to concentrate on football and other work.

Peter Dornan in September 1976. 67/2-14

Kenny Strutt, of Orchardville Avenue, made history in October as the first Bangor Boys' Secondary School pupil to be selected for an Ulster Schools Rugby trial. The school had taken up rugby just four years earlier, becoming affiliated to the Ulster branch of the Rugby Football Union in 1976.

Kenny Strutt in action against Sullivan Upper at Upritchard Park. *97/18-14*

Peter Dornan was joined on 20 November by Linfield first team debutant Glenn Thompson, also from Bangor. He had played a number of times for Linfield Swifts that season before moving up to the senior team. Dornan signed for Sheffield United towards the end of the year but returned to Linfield after four weeks.

Hamilton Road Junior 'A' badminton team won the Ulster Plate in March 1976. Back (from left): Ian Mackie, Peter Minnis, Mervyn Mooney, Harry Adair. Front: Doone McFadden, Marion Lavelle, Gillian Nesbitt and Carolyn Brown. *90/3-128*

Bangor Ladies took part in a charity match against a Bangor FC select XI at Clandeboye Park on 18 May 1976 to raise money for Glencraig Curative Schools. The final score was 3-3. Back (from left): Glenda Graham, Marian McGrattan, Patricia Mallinson, Jenny Ayre, Julie Wilson, Lillian McCaw. Front: Roberta Houston, Margaret Bickerstaff, Liz McNamara, Marian Bowler, Brenda Mills, Susan Beswick and Jean Cromie. *50/1-4*

Rathmore Primary School won the Bangor Primary Schools Netball Shield in June 1976. Back (from left): Margaret McCormick (teacher), Alexis Scullion, Ann Powell, Julie McCune, Deborah Anderson, Pamela Clifford, Mr H. R. Boyd (principal). Front: Corrine Minnis, Pauline Hickmott, Karen Close, Mandy Wylie and Alison Donnan. *34/9-4*

Whitehill Boys receive the Alderdice Cup for winning the Ards Schoolboy Summer League from Dennis S. Nash (*Spectator* junior soccer columnist), as team manager Ian Stewart looks on. *52/13-9*

Eighteen-year-old David Feherty left the town in mid-July to take up the assistant professional's post at Mid-Herts Golf Club near St Alban's in Hertfordshire. Bangor's David Jones declared the local teenager "has all the attributes to make a good professional." *100/20-9*

Bangor Golf Club beat City of Derry 5-1 in the Carlsberg Trophy final in July 1976. Sponsor Jack Hinds presents the trophy to club captain Sam Hamilton. Included are Jack McCloskey (team captain), Terry Taylor, Ted Guthrie, Brian Boston, Bertie McCartney, Wallace Forde and Tom Herron (Bangor secretary/ manager). *24/6A-10*

Members of Bangor Amateur Swimming Club pictured in 1976. *Spectator picture*

1977

An Enterprise Ulster team started creating an area of parkland beside Bangor FC's ground on the Clandeboye Road. The land in question, which would offer a soccer pitch and kickabout area, had been a dump for old air raid shelters.

Hockey players Stephen Martin and Sean Curran, both pupils at Bangor Grammar School, were selected for the Ulster Schools XI in late March, with a third pupil, Billy Dixon, the travelling reserve. In addition, Stephen and Sean were on the Irish Schoolboys side, with the latter as captain.

David Feherty notched up his first success since turning professional when he won the Hoey Cup at Carnalea on 27 April. One of the oldest competitions in Ulster pro golf, it dated back to 1924 and previous winners included Fred Daly, Ernie Jones and Christy O'Connor.
Later in the year he picked up prize money totalling £430 following a semi-final finish in the Carroll's Irish Match Play Championship.

Bangor Rugby Club's 1st XV became Senior League champions, lifting the Stevenson Shield. They were also runners-up in the Bass Boston Cup and winners of the Carrick Sevens. Under captain Roger Clegg they lost just two games to Ulster sides during the year.

Margaret Dunlop, of Ward Park Ladies Bowling Club, became the new Irish Women's Bowling Association champion after beating Myra Wilson (Holywood) in the final at Belmont in August.

Oarsman David Gray, from Belfast Road, along with Lady Victoria Club team mate Iain Kennedy and cox Noel Graham, travelled to Amsterdam to compete for Ireland in the World Championships, missing a place in the final by just three seconds. The following autumn the trio went to New Zealand for the 1978 championships.

It took extra time and 12 penalty kicks to resolve the Bass Boston Cup final, which had finished in a 13-13 tie between Bangor Rugby Club and Queen's University at Upritchard Park on 20 December. Victory for the home side saw the trophy returning to Bangor for the second time in four years.

Young people competed in an inter-club volleyball tournament at Bangor Technical College in February 1977. Bangor Youth Club came first in both the boys' and girls' events, while Epworth Youth Club won the mixed section. *48/6-23*

2nd Bangor Junior BB won a Bangor District six-a-side soccer tournament in February 1977. With captain Jim Gardener (left) and lieutenant Albert Gardiner are (back, from left): Colin Tenner, Stephen Burns, Neil Kirk, Robert Orr, Stephen Boyd, Julian Maxwell. Front: Gavin Maxwell, Gareth Latimer, Mark Latimer (captain), Ian Weatherup and Brian Tenner. *78/9-24*

Bangor Girls' Secondary School U16 badminton team became All-Ireland champions after, as Ulster representatives, beating the league champions of Leinster, Munster and Connaught in Dublin in April 1977. Back (from left): Roy Beattie, coach, Kim McMonagle, Marie Brownlee (headmistress). Front: Heather Stewart, Marion Lavelle and Carolyn Brown. 411a-27

In hockey, Bangor Ladies earned promotion for the second successive season, winning the Qualifying B League outright in May 1977 after beating Greenisland in a play-off. Back (from left): W. Agnew, M. Stevenson, B. Holland, G. Holland, J. Martin, L. Downie, T. McVicar (chairman). Front: N. Hopkirk, P. Stewart, M. Lilburn, G. Richardson and G. McKee. 3/10a-30

Teams who took part in a netball tournament organised by Bangor Youth Council in May 1977. 89/5-30

Edith Thompson (front, fourth from left) with members of Pickie Ladies Bowling Club at her President's Day in September 1977. 91/7a-42

Skateboard fever hit Bangor in October 1977, with these young enthusiasts displaying their skills at Kearney Gardens. Pictured with some young friends are Clarke Martin (9) and Bobby Coulter (8). *79/8-45*

Members of Joe Scott's weightlifting club at Croft Street are pictured in October 1977 after a successful season. Joe congratulates Eric Dowey, who had just added the Mr Ireland title to his list of achievements. Also included are Moore McConkey, Philip Wilson and Trevor Harvey, winners of their section in the Northern Ireland Power Lifting League; Brian Thompson, winner of the Junior Northern Ireland Even Stone Power Championships, and Michael Legge, winner of the Senior event. *47/5-46*

Stephanie Major, president of the Glenlola Collegiate Former Pupils Association, was given a lift, literally, by guest speaker Mike Bull, who by then was running his own health studio in the town, at the group's annual dinner in November 1977. The top pole vaulter was hoping to increase his tally of two gold and two silver Commonwealth Games medals in Edmonton the following year. *40/5a-47*

Gransha High School's U15 rugby team made their debut in the Medallion Shield in the 1977/78 season, losing narrowly to BRA. Back (from left): Mr H. McClenaghan (coach), H. McKee, J. Webster, N. Rankin, M. Kernoghan, M. McDowell, B. Stronge, Mr D. Bennett (coach), Mr J. McCullough (headmaster). Seated: B. Watson, P. Holmes, S. Cardy, T. Martin, S. Armstrong, R. Fergie, G. Webster. Front: B. Pyper, P. Caughey. *38/3a-49*

1978

North Down Council agreed to investigate a number of sites around Bangor, with a view to designating specific skateboarding areas. The site chosen for a "commercial" skatepark was at the junction of Bloomfield Road with the ring road.

Bangor-born rugby enthusiast Fred Isdell hung up his boots in February at the age of 65, having played the game competitively for 50 years. Although he was on the books at Holywood RFC, he was also a member at Bangor.

Sixteen-year-old Alison Smyth, of 6 Cranley Grove, became Ulster Schoolgirls Chess Champion on 4 February.

A Bryan Law penalty had earned Bangor Grammar School a Schools Cup semi-final replay for Jim Bell's side against Campbell College in 1976, but the Seasiders had to wait until the 1978 side, led by flying winger Kenny Hooks, brought the cup to College Avenue for a second time.

Assisted by jubilant teammates, captain Kenny Hooks – who later won six caps for Ireland – holds the Schools Cup aloft. *Spectator picture*

It was hardly surprising that a team with such a phenomenal record – played 25, won 23, lost 2, with a points-for tally of 475 and conceding only 141 – should win schools rugby's Holy Grail.

BGS had match winners all over the park, not least in the captain who amassed 18 tries in 17 games and was to make his senior international debut against Scotland in 1981. Derek Larmour, the 'baby' of the side, helped himself to 64 points, while John McMaster notched up 131 points and virtually defeated Regent single-handedly in the quarter-final.

Dungannon held them to 3-3 at half-time in the semi-final but were routed by tries from McAuley and Hooks (2), with McMaster slotting over two penalties, two conversions and a drop goal.

Before a record Ravenhill crowd against Annadale GS in the final, Bangor had to come from behind with Larmour finding David Hooks with a beautifully weighted kick to score in the corner, while Kenny Hooks finished off a fine backline movement to score, leaving a Larmour penalty to wrap the game up for a 17-9 victory.

Little wonder coach George Cameron declared: "We are the ones who are privileged to have watched you."

Spare a thought though for Neil Hamilton's very talented 1979 side which came so close to retaining the trophy… only to lose in six minutes of injury time. *Rugby report contributed by Brian Kelly.*

A £76,000 sports pavilion at the Arras Park end of Ward Park was officially opened by Mayor Mary O'Fee on 28 April. She then took off her Mayoral chain, lifted a hockey stick and led a team of Council colleagues in a match against Council officials. The Councillors scored first, through Alderman Bruce Mulligan, but lost 2-1, with the officials' goals being scored by Gary Sloan and Brian Sloan.

Bangor Cricket Club opened the new season with an away fixture against Woodvale. John Elder created a bit of history by not only taking nine wickets for 44 runs, but also ending up on the losing side. Woodvale were dismissed for 105 runs, but Bangor ran out of wickets and overs, being all out for 100.

Bangor's Garth McGimpsey won the North of Ireland Championship at Royal Portrush on 14 July, beating Colm McGuckian, from Rathmines, by a single shot. Described as a "long shot outsider", he had sounded warning bells for opponents by winning the bronze medal for the best qualifying round at Dunluce.

Charlie Hunter, from Raglan Road, a well-known Ulster and Irish diver back in the 1930s, was elected president of Bangor Amateur Swimming Club in October. He was only the fourth president since the club's formation in 1919.

Garth McGimpsey with the North of Ireland Championship Trophy. *108/17a-3*

World 1,500m champion Steve Ovett (second from left) at Castle Park on 14 January 1978 with local athletes and officials, as well as members of North Down Athletic Club. Included (left) is Bangor man Bill Brannigan, manager of the Northern Ireland team. *18/11-1*

Mayor Mary O'Fee in January 1978 with members of the recently established Rathgael Gymnastics and Trampolining Club who had just gained their Grade 1 British Amateur Gymnastics Association badges – the highest award given by the Association. From left: Paula Curran, Donna McVea, Susan James, Caroline McKibbin (Donaghadee), Barbara McCabe and Gillian Weatherup. *47/8-1*

Noel Patterson (12) was the special guest of Bangor FC's new commercial manager Victor Haslett after he wrote to the club offering his services as a player. He is pictured with team members (back, from left): Colin Crawford, Jim McAuley, Eric Magee and (front) Ian Jaffrey, Billy McCoubrey, Richard Porter and Stephen Feeney. *42/15-1*

Bangor Grammar School supporters were out in force when the team regained the Schools Cup on St Patrick's Day 1978, following a 17-9 victory over Annadale GS. *168/20a-1*

The victorious Bangor GS 1st XV pictured with the Schools Cup. Back (from left): John McMaster, Michael Wilson (substitute), Neil Hamilton (substitute), Andrew McAuley, Donald Thompson, John Henderson, Garth Maxwell, Colin Rodgers, Derek Larmour. Front: Richard Blackie, Robert Yourston, Gordon Halliday, Kenny Hooks (captain), David Hooks, Jim Coffey, Mark Nolan and Ronnie McCombe. *Spectator picture*

Glenlola Collegiate 1st XI, winners of the Ulster Schoolgirls Hockey Plate in March 1978. Back (from left): Mrs M. Gibson (coach), B. Webb, J. McDonald, F. Glendenning, J. Millar, L. McDowell, Miss A. Davidson (coach). Front: A. Moore, S. Blundell, M. L. Wilson, L. Bruce, L. Morrison. Not included: M. Gibson. *177/11-1*

Hamilton Road Presbyterian Church juvenile badminton teams in May 1978. The A team won the North Down Cup (First Division) and the Ulster and Presbyterian Cups, while the B team won the North Down League (Second Division). *9/10-2*

Two young Bangor swimmers, Arnold Mahood and Estelle Munnis, both aged 15, were in the eight-strong relay team which knocked 65 minutes off the junior world relay record for swimming the English Channel on 11 August 1978. They are pictured a month later at a reception in their honour hosted by Mayor Mary O'Fee. The Lada Ireland Channel team completed the 20-mile swim in 8hr. 40min, each swimming for an hour. The previous record of 9hr. 45min. had stood for 11 years. *58/7a-4*

Ward Park Junior Tennis Club champions and runners-up in July 1978. At back: boy champion Neil Armstrong and runner-up Ian Boal. Front: Lesley Campton (girl winner) and runner-up Anne Farlow. *258/8-2*

Bangor Grammar School golfers won the Irish Inter-Schools Shield in summer 1978. From left: Mark Robson (captain), Michael O'Donnell, Paul Brunton and Stephen King. Not in picture: Richard Blackie. *174/4-3*

Nancy Anyon, of 2 Oakwood Avenue, won the All-Ireland Women's Sea Angling competition for the fourth time in August 1978. *378/4a-3*

Pictured in new football kits, provided by the PTA, are members of the Grange Park Primary School team with coach Ernie Long. Back (from left): I. Thompson, A. Upton, I. Lavelle, G. Lindsay, J. Bennett, P. Fletcher. Front: I. Lule, S. Walton, K. Woods, M. McCall, C. Innis and I. Tyson. *52/9a-5*

1979

Jonathan Ritchie (left), from 10 Springfield Road, and Allen Robson, 46 Ward Avenue. *253/7a-5*

Richard McWilliams (16), from 2 Greenmount Avenue. *258/8-5*

Peter Barry (16), from 18 Ardmillan Gardens. *258/3-5*

Four members of the Bangor Table Tennis Centre – Richard McWilliams, Peter Barry, Allen Robson and Jonathan Ritchie – played key roles in Ulster's successes in Junior (U-17) and Cadet (U-14) inter-provincial competitions at the Ulster Polytechnic on 6 January.

Richard and Peter, ranked one and two in Ulster, won five and four matches respectively against the other three provinces in the Junior series to enable Ulster to emerge as winners for the first time since 1972. Richard also defeated Peter in the singles final, while the boys combined to take the doubles title and Peter, partnered by Louise Gibson (Lisburn), won the mixed doubles.

In the Cadet inter-provincials Allen (11) and Jonathan (13) brought credit to their town and province as Ulster chalked up their first victory in this event.

Bangor man Bob Coulter, who boxed with the Donaghadee club, won the Ulster Senior Heavyweight title at the first attempt. His victory over E. McCallum (Carrickmore) came at the Ulster Hall on 6 February.

Peter Dornan (24) was signed from Linfield by Third Division Swindon Town on 12 February for a fee believed to be around £30,000.

Bangor captain Ronnie Elliott became the fourth town player to gain a full cap for Ireland, following in the footsteps of Roger Clegg, Billy McCombe and Dick Milliken. He played against Scotland at Murrayfield on 3 March.

Pickie Bowling Club resumed the annual pre-season friendly encounter with their Leinster counterparts in April after a four-year gap. The game proved to be somewhat one-sided, with Pickie winning 95-40, finishing ahead on all four rinks. However, the making and cementing of friendships was deemed more important than the score.

David Feherty won the Irish Assistants Golf Championship at Laytown and Bettystown on 23 May, his best achievement to date as a professional.

Bangor teenager Sean McGivern (17) was offered a two-week trial by Glasgow Celtic, shortly after being signed by Cliftonville from Bryansburn Rangers. He was a member of the Bangor Boys team who played in America during the summer.

Four local boys were selected for the All-Ireland Gymnastics team following trials in Dublin in mid-September. All members of the Rathgael Gymnastics and Trampolining Club, they were Richard (8) and Douglas Skelton (10), from Kilmaine Primary School, Paul Gillespie (11), from Gransha High, and Michael Conlon (10), from Belfast.

Bangor motorcyclist Stephen Cull, riding a Yamaha, secured the Wills Embassy Championship with a win on 15 September at Aghadowey. He then travelled to Dublin for the Irish Motor Racing Club Golden Jubilee two-day meeting at Phoenix Park, where he won the solo race. Fellow Bangor rider Sam McClements was fourth.

Garth McGimpsey was crowned the new long driving champion of the British Isles. He gained the title, his third for long driving, at Stoke Poges on 2 October after hitting the ball 307 yards and 3.2 inches. Remarkably, father Hal won a Volkswagen car by guessing the length of the drive within 0.2 of an inch!

Two hundred members and former members of Bangor Amateur Swimming Club gathered at The George on 5 October to celebrate their diamond jubilee. The 60 candles on a three-tier anniversary cake were blown out by club captains Conrad Simpson and Karen Parkes.

Bangor Abbey withdrew its two teams from competitive soccer at the end of October. The reserves had competed in the Down Area League, while the seniors played in the North Down League.

Former Bangor star Billy Irwin rejoined the club on a three-month deal from the Washington Diplomats and in his first game, on 3 November, played a major part in a 4-2 victory over Linfield at Windsor Park. He was signed after first team 'keeper Terry Nicholson suffered a serious knee injury. Bangor's goals were scored by Billy McCoubrey (penalty), Bryan McLoughlin and Jim Barrett (two).

Nineteen-year-old Kyle Thompson, from 35 Abbey Drive, with the 29 trophies he won during the 1978/79 kart-racing season. He competed in the 250cc National class at races throughout Ireland and England. It was his first full season and his successes included the Northern Ireland Karting Association's Driver of the Year title. *273/3-5*

The five McCann brothers from Prospect Road, all members of the North Down Athletic Club, took part in cross-country running competitions at Castle Park on 17 February 1979. Michael (18) was the first North Down member home in his event, while his 16-year-old brother Jim was another finisher, with Desmond (12), John (11) and Peter (9) all completing their respective races. *14/15-6*

Members of Bangor Boys FC were preparing for a four-week visit to the USA during summer 1979. They were accompanied by coach Herbie Barr (right) and manager Jim Butler (back, third from right). 69/2-6

Three Bangor Netball Club members were selected for the Northern Ireland team to play in Trinidad in August 1979. From left: Valerie Walsh, Barbara Millar and Anne Leggett. 133/4a-6

World darts champion John Lowe (right) visited Bangor on 30 March to open a new dart room at the Ulster Arms in High Street. It was named the "J. Lowe Dart Room" in his honour. He is pictured with the seven local players who qualified to play with him (from left): Bertie Kennedy, Sturgeon Black, Victor McPeake, Colin Cousins, Hugh Long, William Watterson and Chris Tanham. *253/1a-6*

Gifford McConkey, vice-principal of Gransha Boys' High School and secretary of Bangor FC, presents first year pupil Liam Curran with his trophy for winning Gransha High's penalty competition at Clandeboye Park on 7 April 1979. Included are (front, from left): Neville Fleming, runner-up, Neil Morrow and Gary McDowell, joint third, and goalkeeper Mark Gillespie, a fourth year pupil at the school. Back row: Bob Martin (organiser), Walter Wilson (referee) and Michael McLaughlin (organiser). *299/11a-6*

Members of Bangor Liverpool Supporters Club, flanked by secretary Hugh McCauley (left) and recently appointed Bangor FC manager Billy Johnston, before setting off for Liverpool v. Arsenal at Anfield in April 1979. Liverpool won 3-0. *288/10-6*

Cecil Braniff, chairman of the Bangor Youth Football League, presents the Bangor Youth Cup to Malcolm Bartley, captain of Whitehill Youth, after they defeated Donaghadee Boys 4-0 at Clandeboye Park on 15 May. Two of the players, Trevor McBriar and Leonard Breen, were subsequently recruited by Bangor FC. *477/3-6*

Three members of the Bangor Girls soccer team were included on the Northern Ireland panel for a match in Italy in July 1979. Jacquie Higginson (front) is pictured with Fiona Clendenning and Heather Stewart. *75/4a-7*

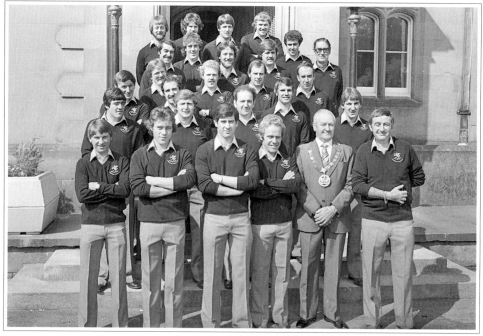

Mayor George Green with the 28-strong party from Bangor Rugby Club who set off in August 1979 on their first major overseas tour, taking in Boston, Portland (Maine) and New York. *45/15a-8*

Brian Kelly
remembers... tennis

When former Irish No 1 Lorna Agnew set up her coaching clinics at Ward Park in 1969, I was one of her first pupils and, I suppose, may have entertained the odd aspiration that this could be a whole new era for tennis in Bangor. After all, I had just lifted the junior singles crown in the Ward Park club's annual tournament, beating a talented young left-hander by the name of Glenn Thompson, I believe.

Little more than a decade later Ward Park had rocked the upper echelons of the sport in the province by claiming all five of the major titles in the Belfast and District League – a feat never before achieved. They remained unbeaten throughout the campaign in lifting the prestigious Division One Mixed League title, while the Division One Men's and Ladies' Singles Leagues and both the Senior Men's and Ladies' Knockout Cups all fell to Ward Park, with their unique blend of experience in Bertie Styles, Francis Boal and Audrey Stephens, ably backed up by the fine crop of youngsters who had progressed through the club over the previous half-dozen years or so.

It was, however, game, set and match for my own tennis aspirations as another of Lorna's young protégés, by the name of Gail Holland, would have a significant role to play over the next decade, not to mention that young left-hander called Thompson.

Born in Belfast in 1955, Brian Kelly and his older sister Joyce moved to Bangor in 1960 after parents Minnie and Hubert purchased a property in Railwayview Street to convert into a small confectionery and grocery store.

In 1964 Kelly's Cash Store opened in larger premises at 30 Dufferin Avenue, just down from the railway station, with Joyce joining the business.

Brian was educated at Trinity Primary School and Central Primary School before attending Bangor Grammar School (1966-74). He was a boy chorister at St Comgall's Parish Church from 1963-1969, at the same time as future golfer David Feherty.

He was a member of 6th Bangor Life Boys when Bertie Thompson, Gifford McConkey

Ward Park junior singles winner Brian Kelly (back, left) and runner-up Glenn Thompson (back right) with (from left): Elizabeth Stephens, Valerie Cromwell, Cathy Stephens and Rosemary Brookes.

I consider myself privileged to have followed the Ward Park entourage around the countryside, both north and south of the border, reporting over the next two decades on all their successes... and the very odd disappointment!

No report of Bangor's growing reputation in Ulster tennis during the Seventies would be complete without identifying the part played by the revival of the North Down Junior Hardcourt Championships after around 15 years. Local businessman Jim Holland, who, along with his wife Edie, was a member of the Ward Park club, was at the helm of this initiative and the young players from North Down certainly brought home the silverware.

In seven years the boys' singles title was to go outside the area on only two occasions and in 1973 Ward Park's Billy Rankin captured both the Under 16 and Under 18 singles titles, overcoming one of the country's most talented young players. Rankin who, like Thompson, lived little more than a stone's throw away from the courts, recalls: "I had won the Under 15 Boys' Singles at the Boat Club the previous year – beating Glenn in the final – and we were therefore relative newcomers to the junior scene, but beating the hugely talented John Biscomb gave me a major boost. That year I was to play him no fewer than eight times, with victories shared at four-all."

It came as no great surprise in 1973 when Billy Rankin and Glenn Thompson made their junior inter-pro debuts after promising performances on the traditional tournament circuit, including Belfast Boat Club, Windsor, CIYMS and Ballycastle.

Thompson, a talented defender in the Beckenbauer-mould for Linfield, Crusaders and in his later years Brantwood, has cause to rue this particular scribe, though

and Jean Moore were leaders and later the Company Section when Eddie Miley was captain.

Brian began reporting on badminton and tennis for the *Spectator* at 16, with the encouragement of editor Annie Roycroft, and recalls the Seventies and Eighties as "an enjoyable time to be doing just that."

He met future wife Sheelagh in 1976 when he started work in the Belfast College of Business Studies, where she was a secretary in the Catering Department. "I was delighted that she was happy to set up home in Bangor West in 1979. And so I would never forget our wedding anniversary she agreed to getting married on 10 March (the day after my birthday!)."

Son Robert was christened in St Gall's Parish Church on 31 December 1983 and after winning a Young Rugby Writer of the Year competition he began to show an interest in journalism. He obtained a BA (Hons) in Journalism at Edgehill College, is now married to Carolyn and works as a senior journalist with the he only voiced it for the first time in preparation for this article: "The *Spectator* carried the headline 'Bill and Glenn the Tennis Men' but I was playing for Linfield against Glentoran at the Oval that weekend. As I ducked to let the ball go over my head and out for a throw-in, one comic from the crowd shouted, 'Why didn't you hit it with your tennis racket?'"

Thompson was also to lift the prestigious Ulster Under 18 Boys' Singles title at Belfast Boat Club, beating Biscomb in the 1975 final. That would have been some achievement beating Biscomb on the lush grasscourts but, typical of Thompson's good fortune, the final had to be transferred to the hardcourts due to rain. He couldn't collect his trophy either as he was heading off immediately with friends for a holiday in Greece, leaving Gail Holland to collect the trophy and make the speech on his behalf!

Thompson and Rankin had been junior inter-pros from 1973 to 1975, establishing themselves as a formidable doubles partnership, being unbeaten in the junior inter-pros, though Rankin adds: "It was a totally different case when we moved up to intermediate inter-pro level!" In mixed doubles they were already hard to beat too, with Glenn partnering Gail Holland and Billy with Joy Redman, who was to win an Irish Ladies' Doubles title.

Rankin and Thompson first broke through into the senior inter-pro side in 1979 at Donnybrook, but they didn't have too far to travel when they retained their places for the 1980 series, hosted by the Ward Park club, which had seen a £50,000 refurbishment.

Joined that same year by the ever present Miss Holland, there was also a debut appearance for the top junior in Ireland, Peter Minnis, son of ILTA coach Bob and Barbara, who was later to take over the reins of the North Down Junior Hardcourt Championships. With former Irish No 1 Sean Sorenson actually flying in on the morning of the Championships from Wimbledon – my wife Sheelagh and I were his chauffeurs that morning – Minnis occupied the No 2 singles slot behind Lyle Carson and Ulster caused the upset by lifting the title too.

Enter Gail Holland onto what was to become something

Chorley & Leyland Guardian in Lancashire.

Brian continued covering badminton and tennis in the local press – becoming the Ulster Council's Press Officer at the beginning of the Eighties. He also had a weekly sports column in the *Sunday News*. He freelanced for the *Irish Printer* and *Bakery World* magazines and was a contributor to both *The Newspaper Book* and *The Advertising Book* by Hugh Oram, which traced the history of newspapers and advertising in Ireland.

Before leaving Bangor for Lisburn in 1987, Brian compiled a brief history of St Gall's Parish Church and had published "The Story So Far", which traced Bangor Grammar School in the Ulster Schools Cup.

Brian keeps up to date with things in Bangor through his sister Joyce and tries to see Bangor Grammar in the Schools Cup at least once in the season.

He worked for over 25 years in education administration at the College of Business Studies, Lisburn College of Further Education, Wallace High School and RBAI and recalls on a few occasions being asked by senior staff which team he was supporting when Wallace or Inst were playing Bangor Grammar in the Schools Cup!

Brian Kelly today

of a production line. She made her junior inter-provincial debut the year after Billy and Glenn (1974) and she was to claim the North Down Senior Girls' Singles title in 1975, with Thompson claiming the Boys' title, while not to be outdone Rankin, the other member of the Ward Park trio, had won his first junior international cap against England in Dublin.

"Although we may have lost 15-1," Rankin reasoned, "England had a very strong team at that level with both Ann Hobbs and Jo Durie – future regulars at Wimbledon – in their side."

Jim Rea, representing the Milk Marketing Board, presented the prizes at the North Down Junior Tennis Championships, held at Ward Park in July 1975. Receiving one of her three trophies is 16-year-old Gail Holland. 67/9a112

Gail's rising reputation, notably as a doubles specialist, saw her follow Ward Park teammate Rankin into the junior international arena in both 1976 and 1977, playing against England and Wales.

She was to be called up to the senior inter-pro squad in 1977 and 1978. "The senior inter-pros remain among my most enjoyable memories of my tennis career," admits the Rockport teacher, who is still enjoying her tennis. She was unbeaten in the Veterans' inter-pros... that is, in the "50+ age group" she hastily reminds me.

For the first couple of years she partnered Helen Pollock, then it was Diane Craig and in 1981 she partnered Jackie Logan to a very fine three set victory over Helen Lennon and Michelle Buckley. She was a fixture on three winning inter-pro sides in Ballycastle, Bangor and Galway and it remains one of the great mysteries of Irish and Ulster tennis of that period how the Bangor player continued to be overlooked, having such a doubles record in the senior inter-pros.

Another highlight and memory of her tennis career was

when she was selected over the Christmas 1977/ New Year 1978 holiday to play in the United States. Peter Little, another of the Ward Park successes – he played junior inter-pro in 1977-1979 and was a North Down champion in 1976 and 1977 – was a member of the team too.

Young tennis players Gail Holland (left) and Julie Hastings were on hand in the late 1970s when Harp marketing manager Michael Cook presented a sponsorship cheque to Gail's father Jim, a Ward Park club stalwart and Ulster Council president.

Gail recalls: "Whilst all the other national teams were kitted out in their tracksuits, we had to wear our own and they all had team managers while we looked after ourselves. Tracy Austin made her name as one of the finest American players of that era and she actually drove us around the place while in the Boys' events they had to contend with Ivan Lendl in the draw."

With the end of the decade rapidly approaching, a whole new group of youngsters were eager to replace Rankin, Thompson and Miss Holland. Alan Ringland, Stephen O'Hara, Brian Law and Moyra Brooks all won junior honours; Susan Blundell and David Cunningham played at intermediate inter-pro level, while the latter was a reserve on the 1981 senior side, but there was one youngster in particular who was making rapid strides to a level not reached by any of his predecessors at Ward Park.

In 1978 Peter Minnis was ranked No 5 in the Ulster junior list, but following wins at Ballycastle, Ward Park, the Boat Club and CIYMS he finished the season as both Under 16 and Under 18 Grand Prix champion. He made his junior international debut (v. Wales) in 1978, missed out on Junior Wimbledon nomination and lifted the Irish Covered Court title and not unexpectedly was ranked No 1 junior in Ulster and No 4 in Ireland.

He was to captain Ulster to victory in the junior inter-pros and in 1979 became the first Ulster player since 1970 to lift the coveted Irish Junior title. When he retained it the following year it was a feat that

Peter Minnis

had not been achieved since the 1960s. The affable young architectural 'fresher' at Queen's University at the time was to make his senior inter-pro debut in Bangor, occupying the No 2 singles slot before making the No 1 slot his own in Galway when Ulster retained the title.

But something which has since become Irish tennis folk-lore among those fortunate to have witnessed it, actually took place in the period 30 September – 2 October 1983, in the RDS in Dublin. My wife Sheelagh was expecting our son Robert in less than six weeks and she wasn't going to miss it either! Peter was in the Irish squad to take on the mighty USA – John McEnroe et al – in a Davis Cup match. The atmosphere at a Cup Final could not have bettered this.

From left: Billy Rankin, Gail Holland and Glenn Thompson today

McEnroe even delighted everyone with the odd tantrum and whilst obviously Ireland would utilise only their top two full-time players, Matt Doyle and Sean Sorenson, in all the matches, to see a Ward Park player involved at such a level was just reward for everyone associated with the club.

Without doubt whilst the club flourished with an influx of youngsters in the 1970s, Ward Park had its stalwarts too and it would be unfair not to mention just a few who had an impact on everyone at the club. The names include the ageless Billy Meharg, Jim and Rosemary Matthews, Audrey and Sam Stephens, Betty and Tom Roycroft, Bertie Styles – 18 times a finalist and 13 times a champion up to 1980 – Francis Boal, whom we lost in early 2011, Norman Holmes, Bob Minnis, who never really forgave me for informing everyone in every report that he was an ILTA coach, Olive Croskery, who was just a wonderful friend to me over many, many years, Jim Holland, who by 1982 was welcoming an English national side to the Province for the first time in nigh on 20 years, and Marsden Fitzsimons.

Julie Brown

(née Parkes) remembers... swimming

I was born to swim. My parents Fred and Elizabeth were both Irish International swimmers and Irish champions. I learnt to swim in the sea, taught by both parents, on my first continental holiday in Spain when I was three. My first race followed when I was five, in the 'under sevens' one width – I swam the doggy paddle and came third.

The spectacular Bangor pool opened in 1972, when I was seven, It had a 25m training/ competition pool, diving pool, 15m learning pool and baby pool (we all jumped into it to play after our swim session was finished). It was a big change from Pickie Pool, where we swam outdoors in sea water. Now the swimmers could swim in the winter and in the evening, in the warmth of the indoor pool.

Maureen Simpson (née Lloyd) was a past Irish champion swimmer and was to become one of the future presidents of Bangor and also the Irish Swimming Association. She was made an Honorary Life Member of Bangor Swimming Club and was club president during the diamond jubilee celebrations in 1979. Her son Conrad and my sister Karen were the club captains that year.

Tuesday night was 'club night'. Karen (three years my senior) loved meeting up with all the other club members. We did our swim session and then played in the other three pools. The highlight on the way home was stopping for sweets in the garage shop. Great contemplation was

Julie (right) and her sister Karen with parents Fred and Elizabeth in 1974

Julie Brown (née Parkes), who was born in 1965, is the daughter of Elizabeth (Armstrong) and Fred Parkes, both Irish champions and Irish International swimmers. She was a pupil at Bloomfield Collegiate, with her final two years of school being spent at Campbell College.

She attended the University of Tennessee, Knoxville, at 18 on a Swimming Scholarship and then went on to do a BA Honours degree in Sports Studies with PGCE

Coach Billy Massey with Bangor Amateur Swimming Club members at the new pool in September 1973. At front (from left): Wendy Archer, Dawn Carter and Jenny Mayne, who won the Gamble Trophy race from Pickie to the pier and back. At rear: Jane Carslake and Sonia Wallace, who were in the runner-up team. The winning team also included Julie Caughey. *28/19a-74*

at the University of Ulster, Jordanstown.

In 1989 Julie married Raymond Brown (a fell runner, who competed for Northern Ireland in 1999 at the World Fell Running Championships in Borneo, Malaysia).

In the intervening years she has raised their three children – Stuart (b.1990), Emma (b. 1992) and Jamie (b. 1999) – whilst also working as a part-time P. E. teacher in Strathearn School and Sullivan Upper Preparatory School.

Her main achievements include – at the age of 11, winning two British Finalist Pennants at the British age-groups; 1978 Commonwealth Games in Edmonton, Canada – aged 13; 'Swimmer of the Meet' on three occasions (Lisbon, Portugal in 1979 and Luxembourg in 1981 and 1983); Junior Europeans in Sweden in 1980; 1982 Commonwealth Games in Brisbane, Australia; 1983 European Championships in Rome, and 1984 Los Angeles Olympics.

had over what to buy with our five pennies!

Although we competed in many galas probably our most enjoyment as a club was at the Provincial Towns Galas. A few Ulster clubs competed in these galas, which were held on Saturday nights. One of our swimmers, Noel Munnis, designed the badge for the league, which was, of course, sewn onto the front of my Bangor tracksuit, along with all the other badges. It was a 'fun gala' – no medals or prizes were given, just points towards a trophy for the best overall club. All events were over 50 metres of the pool and each club put three swimmers in each age-group race.

The club travelled by bus to the away competitions. This was where we sang songs and got to interact with senior members, who always nabbed the back seats! At the end of each gala a generous and appetising 'spread' was always laid on by the host club. However, for some of the boys 'their eyes were just too big for their bellies' and a sick bag was required on the way home. Not too much singing was done by them on the return journey!

Swimmers came from different religious backgrounds; it was never an issue and was never discussed. Our club had a great relationship with the City of Derry Swimming Club and the only time we were aware of the Troubles occurred when we crossed the bridge into the Bogside and our bus was pelted with stones! Even then this didn't stop us going ahead to compete in the pool there. That was the beauty of swimming: it was, and still is, an Ireland sport and fortunately religion takes a back seat.

During the summer, after our early morning swimming session, we all headed down to Pickie Pool, stopping along the way to buy a doughnut for breakfast. Our day was spent playing in the pool and out on the raft in the sea at the back of Pickie. The boys threw lots of white jellyfish to frighten us. We spent endless hours all crowding onto the raft to try to sink it – which, of course, we could never do. In fact, we'd eventually slide off because of the weight of numbers, scratching our skin on the ropes in the process.

I remember a couple of the older swimmers who were good divers (one was Ross Carter), standing at the top corner of the steps overlooking the sea and diving in. Other eejits were brave enough to jump in. Even though the tide was in, it was still extremely risky. What would Health and Safety say today!

Sea swims during the summer months were high on Bangor Swimming Club's itinerary. Pickie to the Pier was based on your speed, so the fastest swimmer had to go last. Times had been taken from the 800m swims we'd previously done in the indoor pool. This was an annual event I always dreaded as I hated touching the pier which was full of barnacles. Also I swam with my eyes closed for most of the race as I didn't like to see the fish beneath me. The older swimmers had told us there were basking sharks and I was terrified. Needless to say, I was in and out of the sea as quickly as possible.

My sister was the sea swimmer with Wendy Archer, both girls completing the five-mile stretch of Belfast Lough from Crawfordsburn to Carrickfergus. Wendy was 15 and Karen was 13 – the youngest girl at the time to complete this swim. Other avid sea swimmers included Neil Cooper, Terry Dillon, Noel Munnis, Arnold Mahood and Sonia Wallace. I only swam in sea races when I really had to. Other sea swims included Pickie Pool to Seacourt, Copelands to Donaghadee, Portaferry to Strangford and Warrenpoint to Omeath.

In early September we all met up at Portstewart Strand for the club's summer outing, where we surfed and had a barbecue. On Christmas Day club stalwarts Barry Lightbody and Eddie Officer led us into the icy sea from the beach at Helen's Bay (without wetsuits I may add!), and piping hot turkey soup was enjoyed afterwards.

In total Julie set 128 Ulster Junior and Senior records and 28 Irish records. She was an Irish Schools Internationalist from the age of 11, every year in succession till she was 18, and was on the Irish Senior International team, winning over 40 caps, from the age of 14 till she retired at 19.

Julie was a reluctant participant in the Pickie to the Pier sea swim

The club entered us into age-group galas. My swimming career started to take off when I remained unbeaten for six years running in the Ulster age-groups in all four swimming strokes. I was awarded the *Belfast Telegraph* Swimmer of the Year Award on a few occasions. My desire to compete could be seen when I travelled to Leeds at 11 and won two British Finalist Pennants for the 100m butterfly and freestyle.

Members of the Bangor relay team who were second in the Irish Championships in June 1976. From left: Margaret Mayne, Julie Parkes, Karen Parkes and Julie Caughey.

History was made in 1976 at the annual Sir Dawson Bates War Memorial Gala, when the Bangor girls won the cup for the fourth time in succession – Julie Caughey, Jenny Mayne, Margaret Mayne and me. I remember being so nervous that I would leave the block before Jenny touched the wall. It was called 'doing a flyer'. I was on the senior team for the first time with my hero, Julie Caughey, who was the golden girl of Bangor and Ulster in the early 70s. I really admired her, setting my own goals on her many achievements. She had won 15 (junior and senior) gold medals at the Ulster Championships.

I decided at the age of 12, when I won my first Ulster Senior title in the 100m backstroke, I would go for gold in every future event I swam in. I achieved this dream at 15 when I won 28 gold medals (junior and senior), picking up 14 trophies in the process. Julie Caughey unfortunately retired from swimming at 17, without fulfilling her full potential of making the Commonwealth or Olympic Games.

Julie travelled to Leeds at 11 in 1976 and won two British Finalist Pennants for the 100m butterfly and freestyle

Life saving was revived in the 1970s and members entered the Royal Life Saving Society Gala on an annual basis. Jim Macintyre, father of twins Jacqui and Caroline, took classes which enabled us to obtain awards, eventually achieving the Bronze Medallion.

One of the biggest and most successful galas staged at

the new Bangor pool was the Ormo Gala. Pioneered by my father Fred (past Ulster and Irish president), it was the first to hold 25m races for children aged up to 11 from all over Ulster in the one venue! One thousand competitors showed up in 1976 and the seemingly massive gallery was full to capacity with spectators.

It was a day-long affair, with the boys' events starting at one end and the girls' at the other. Ormo bread sponsored the event and it was the first time every child who made the final of their event received a pennant.

Another aspect of Bangor Swimming Club was the diving section, where Hazel Spratt (first in the Irish Springboard Championships) and Ann Munnis (fourth in the same event), along with 14-year-old Mark Miller (bronze medal), followed in the footsteps of former Ulster and Irish champions Kevin Carter and Dr Vivien O'Neill. Kevin's children Ross and Dawn were prominent swimmers in the early Seventies, along with Jane Carslake, Mitch Colville and Paul and Michael Moore – who organised club discos in the Dufferin Hall.

Bangor swimmers with awards they won during the 1979 season, including the Provincial Towns League Cup, the *Belfast Telegraph* mixed relay squads trophies and the Londonderry Civic Trophy. Back: Eddie Skelly (coach) and Simon Magowan. Middle: Julie Parkes, Julie Packenham, Gay McKillop, Niall Murphy, Paddy Crothers. Front: Karen Parkes, Conrad Simpson and Lindsay Harron. *208/4-7*

The late Eddie Skelly was our swimming coach and he is fondly remembered for his famous instructions to us as we stood on the blocks ready to dive in – "Let it all hang out" and "Take it out hard and hold it." We were all so embarrassed but, to tell you the truth, I reckon it helped to psych out competitors in the lanes beside us! During our swim, Eddie's famous whistle, using thumb and finger, could be heard throughout the pool. People would sit with their hands over their ears!

Each Christmas we got together to sing carols in Abbey Park and district. Back in 1975 the *Spectator* recorded: "The splendid sum of £15 was raised and the children themselves have decided this year to donate the sum raised to the Gateway Club – a very worthy cause."

Julie Parkes then aged 14 and swimming for Ireland in July 1979, won the individual medley relay in an international triangular match against Iceland and Israel, setting a new Irish Junior record in the 100m. fly. 208/6-7

In 1978 my very close friend Moya Sloan came to prominence by winning the Elizabeth Long Trophy for Ulster Junior Swimmer of the Year. At the War Memorial Gala our under-14 team of Kathy McCreanor, Gay McKillop, Julie Packenham and me secured gold. Julie Packenham and I were great friends, becoming known as 'The Two Julies' around the club. Unfortunately Julie died on a skiing holiday in 1990.

In 1979 Lyndsay Harron and I were selected for an Ulster Junior team to go to Philadelphia, Washington and New York on a two-week glamour tour. This was the second America-bound trip for Ulster swimmers in the Seventies. Earlier in the decade Bangor had a magnificent seven swimmers on that trip.

Towards the end of the Seventies Bangor continued to dominate Ulster swimming, with Simon Magowan and me swimming in the 1978 Commonwealth Games in Canada. As I was only 13 at the time (the youngest competitor there) the organisers had to bring along an official (Maureen Cowdy) to act as chaperone and to supervise me! However, there was no similar need in 1984 when I was 19 and swam at the Los Angeles Olympics. This successful trend had continued into the Eighties with Simon and me, joined by Moya Sloan, at the 1982 Commonwealth Games in Australia.

Bangor Swimming Club was where I established many lasting friendships and to this day I greatly value the friendship of Moya Sloan, Jacqui and Caroline Macintyre and Barbara Fair, who all swam on Bangor teams with me. I will always have strong links with the club as I was made an Honorary Life Member, a position I treasure to this day.

Julie and husband Raymond with children Emma, Jamie and Stuart.

Cecil Worthington
remembers... bowling

At the beginning of the 1970s Ward Park's bowling greens were home to a thriving bowling community, with no fewer than four men's clubs: North Down, Bangor, Castle and BETS (Bangor Engineering and Trades Society). Add to that the two ladies clubs, Ward Park and Ballyholme.

At the tender age of 16 back in 1971 I joined North Down, which was a friendly if somewhat unfashionable club full of retired teachers, bank managers and clergymen. It was just surviving near the bottom of division two of the Parks League with no great ambition or competitive edge. Bangor Bowling Club was clearly the 'top dog' of the park with all the best players and regular trophy winners. In truth, bowls was still regarded as an old man's game and a teenager playing bowls was extremely rare.

I remember my first game for the North Down 'B' team which, strangely enough, was known as the junior team although it was full of men who were aged 70 or more. Indeed, one of my teammates, a lively 80-year-old, was five times my age!

In 1972, my second year at North Down, and with the Troubles raging in Northern Ireland, bowling leagues were zoned to reduce unnecessary travel. We were playing local teams within the Co. Down area and as usual we finished near the bottom of the league. However, by the following

Cecil Worthington moved to Bangor in 1968 when his parents opened Worthington's Bakery on Queen's Parade. He continues to live in Bangor with his wife Anne and four grown-up children.

Cecil trained as a social worker and currently is Director of Children's Services in the Northern Trust, based in Ballymena.

After bowling in Ward Park throughout the Seventies he then played at the Knock Club becoming a British Isles Champion in 1981 and an international bowler representing Ireland in 1995 and 1996. He has not played bowls since 1998.

North Down's bowlers were division two champions in 1974. Back (from left): Alec Oliver, Bert Mawhinney, Sam Ferguson, Cecil Worthington, Dougie Farthing, Sandy Todd, Jimmy Boyd, Jim Waugh, Davy Steele. Front: Walter Friar, Ernie Magee, Walter Guy, Floyd McMullan (president), Carl McGimpsey, Davy Martin, Billy Loudon and Stanley Hazlett. *Spectator picture*

year, with the divisions thankfully restored, we finished mid-table and, thanks to an influx of some experienced players from Belfast, North Down was definitely on the up.

Members of North Down Bowling Club at their annual dinner in November 1976 at the New Savoy Hotel, following a highly successful season during which one of their rinks won the NIBA Championships, while another secured the Ward Park Rinks Cup. Seated are club president Jim Gildea and Mrs Gildea with (from left): Carl McGimpsey, Jim Heatley, Cecil Worthington, David Steele, Joe Compton, Walter Friar, David Henry, Sandy Dalzell and club secretary Stanley Hazlett. *54/3-17*

In 1974 the club were division two champions, winning promotion after losing only one league game out of 16. That game was against Bangor who for some reason always seemed to have the psychological edge with international and Commonwealth Games players like Gerry Sloan in their ranks.

All the same, being in division one in 1975 was quite an achievement for little North Down. However, relegation followed and a further division two title in 1977 was also followed by the drop in 1978. By the end of the Seventies the club's brief flirtation with success had passed.

Looking back, I learned a lot from the "old boys" and I reckon my youthful competitiveness might well have rubbed off on them. As a teenager it was an interesting experience in the changing rooms with long johns everywhere I looked! I remember on one occasion we had to change into our whites behind trees at Woodvale Park in Belfast because the pavilion there had been burnt down and I am sure it was quite a sight.

My desire for the North Down team to be competitive was only surpassed when I represented the club in individual competitions. In 1973, to recognise there was a steady increase in younger men playing the game, the Parks Association introduced an under-35 competition. Maurice McKeown from the Bangor club, who was next youngest to me in the park, being about five years my senior, won the Parks title in its first year. I went one better and won the Irish under-35 title in 1974 but not to be outdone Maurice matched this in 1975.

That same year I won the open park singles. While the rivalry was fierce we respected each other's ability and were on friendly terms (off the green!). To complete a hat-trick of titles in 1976, Jimmy Gildea, Walter Friar, Carl McGimpsey and I won the fours parks title. This was the first time in 47 years that a North Down four had won the title. Truly the period 1974 to 1977 represented a purple patch both for me and for the club.

My other big memory of the Seventies was the annual Bangor tournament during the 12th Week. Sponsored each year by Bangor Maid, bowlers from all over Northern Ireland would flock to Ward Park for the week to compete in singles and pairs. It cost just 40p to enter the singles (with a £30 prize voucher to be won) and 70p for each pair (with £20 each as the prize). Hardly the professional era! The tournament was promoted by all the clubs at Ward Park and also Pickie Bowling Club, based in Broadway. There were huge crowds watching all week, with some 250

Club president Martin Whiteside and Mrs Whiteside (seated) are pictured at a dinner in the New Savoy Hotel to mark the club's 60th anniversary in 1979 with (back, from left): Stanley Hazlett, Walter Friar, Jimmy Gildea, Cecil Worthington, Davy Steele, Cecil Walker, Bob Lawson, Sandy Dalzell, Mark Oliver (deputing for his father Alec), Davy Henry, Leslie Mark, Carl McGimpsey and Jim Boden. *Spectator picture*

entries in the singles and 150 for the pairs.

The *County Down Spectator* covered the event and playing bowls all week was great fun. I managed to win the pairs two years running, in 1978 and 1979, partnering my cousin Jim Baker. Jim took a holiday in Bangor to play in the tournament and later went on to become an international and a world champion. I always thought picking a good partner was important.

By the end of the 1970s a sizeable number of young people playing bowls was commonplace at every club and approaching the age of 25 I was regarded as something of an old hand!

David Addy
remembers... table tennis

I still get a bit of a buzz when strangers who hear my name tell me they remember my achievements as a table tennis player in the 1960s and 1970s. It's not a particularly television-friendly game these days and as a result has fallen somewhat out of favour but back then table tennis was very popular, whether you were a participant or a spectator.

Players had their place among the sporting fraternity and we could set our sights high – my own personal "best" came in 1977 when I was on the team selected to represent Northern Ireland at the Commonwealth Games Table Tennis Championships which were held in Guernsey.

Going back to my childhood days in Bangor, I was very keen on all sports. Like most of my contemporaries my mother kept a scrapbook full of cuttings from the *Spectator* which showed my involvement in swimming, soccer, hockey and rugby. You name it, I played it. One of the reports indicated I was captain of the school cricket team ("As usual, Addy led Sullivan Prep with skill and dash"), while another recalled how I'd won the wheelbarrow race with John McClean at the 5th Bangor Scouts sports!

But in the end it was table tennis that won me over. By the age of 14 I had joined the Downshire Tennis Club in Bangor and in between matches I played a lot of table tennis. From that early interest I went on to be selected for

David Addy was born at Cultra in 1951 and moved to Bangor at the age of eight. He attended both Sullivan Upper (Prep. Dept and Senior School) and Cregagh Technical College. His first paid employment was with Lairds Boats and then Barry's, including a stint with the children's amusements on the pier.

Following six months at the Lightship public house at the bottom of High Street, Bangor, David joined the staff of Wardens in Newtownards. It was while working there he met future wife Anne and the couple married in 1973.

After two-and-a-half years with Wardens David was

David wears his first Ulster shirt with pride

Ulster Schoolboys while a pupil at Sullivan Upper and I was ranked at number two in Ulster at that level.

About a year later I left school and soon was playing for the Junior Ulster team. At 18 in November 1969 I was capped for Ulster, playing against English county champions Essex, and was ranked among the top 10 in the Province. By the time I was 19 I was ranked at number two in Ireland and was praised in the papers for giving the Belgian number one, Norbert Van Der Walle, a tough game in a competition at Ballymena. In that match I was 16-14 up in the third and final game but he just pipped me in the end.

Over the next decade I played in a number of tournaments and enjoyed a fair amount of success, winning the Belfast and District Senior League twice with Bangor and a total of four times for two different Ards clubs. During the Bangor Table Tennis Centre Championships I won the men's singles and men's handicap singles, as well as the men's doubles with Peter Mayne.

Pictured early in his career, David Addy receives the trophy for senior individual league champion from Mrs June Best, secretary of the Bangor Table Tennis League. Others pictured at the Bangor Sports Centre social event in the Bryansburn Inn are (front, from left): Tommy Deaney, Rosemary Clegg, Mary Dickson, Mrs R. Patterson, Albert Cumming. Back: Maurice McCullough, Jackie Clegg, Stewart Melville and Davy Scarr. 184/34/1

I played for Ulster over a period of six or seven years, competing in around 50 singles matches. The big matches were the inter-pros involving Munster, Leinster and Connaught. When it came to the Commonwealth Games, that was the Northern Ireland team and my big chance arrived in 1977 when they were held in Guernsey. It was an amazing experience taking part in the opening parade where the players from all the Commonwealth countries marched behind their respective flags.

When I look back that was definitely the peak of my

recruited by the Universities Press in Belfast, where he trained to be a compositor. That was followed by a lengthy period with the Civil Service before David took early retirement due to ill health.

Anne and David have a son, Stephen, and two daughters, Kathryn and Caroline, as well as three grandchildren (two boys and a girl).

playing career. I competed in the singles and although I only made it to the second round it was something I will never forget. Just getting there was an achievement in itself.

I did a lot of travelling with the table tennis back then but I didn't mind; every week there was something different. There was a great sense of camaraderie among the players – there was no place for religion or politics. I remember a time I was asked to do an exhibition game "somewhere in Belfast" in the 1970s. I hadn't a clue where the venue was – all I knew was that a friend

David with his son Stephen, a Bangor Rugby Club player and second team coach

would be picking me up and taking me there. It turned out to be at the Star of the Sea club in Andersonstown and for a boy from Bangor in the middle of the Troubles that was a bit of a worry. But I was treated really well – and that was how it was for anyone involved in table tennis.

It's just a shame the game has lost much of its popularity these days. The table tennis authorities have tried to tackle this by changing the rules. Nowadays it's first to 11 by two clear points, rather than 21, and best of five, with two serves each, rather than five. It was always a very quick game but it's even quicker now. What's important to me is I have my memories of those days in the Sixties and Seventies when table tennis was really special and I wouldn't trade them for anything!

Elaine Taylor

(née Firth) remembers... sailing

Both my parents hailed from Lancashire, pretty far away from the sea; but growing up in Waverley Drive and having my Dad Les sailing and building Enterprise dinghies, I couldn't really get away from it. Dad was keen to get the family into sailing, so he decided it would be a great introduction to take my Mum and me on a picnic.

I was about four years old and there was a 'Picnic Race' to the Copeland Islands. The Copelands are only four miles away, but in a 14ft

Elaine and Les Firth after winning the Gallagher Trophy for Enterprises at Strangford Lough Yacht Club in October 1974. Included is Pat Duddy, wife of Jack Duddy, promotions manager for Gallaghers Ltd. in Northern Ireland.

Enterprise dinghy it was quite a journey past Groomsport through Donaghadee Sound to the Copeland Islands. It was blowing stink, my Mum Barbara was not a 'sailor' and I was seasick. Mum tried to stop me from falling over as I was sick over the side, while Dad yelled through wind and waves to "keep the boat steady". My Mum never set foot in a dinghy again and I was told by Dad that once I was seasick, I was a real sailor. So at the age of four, I became a 'real sailor'.

A few years later, during a coffee morning, my Mum got chatting to a lady who had moved to Bangor with her

Elaine Taylor (née Firth) grew up in Waverley Drive and went to Glenlola Collegiate until fifth form. After a secretarial course at the Tech, she spent a year as a 'Trainee Mountaineering Instructor' at the Tollymore Mountain Centre outside Newcastle. Managing, as she puts it, to blag her way into Stranmillis, Elaine started teaching at Glastry High in 1980 and she is still there.

Her Dad Les inspired her

Allison with Curtis Haire

love of sailing, taking her out in his Enterprise dinghy. In her teens the family moved around the corner to Ballyholme Esplanade, where Elaine spent her O-Level time "gazing out at the racing on Ballyholme Bay instead of revising."

Sailing consisted of crewing for everyone else until she bought her first Laser in 1977 for £466 – that was brand new! She went on to represent Ireland at the Laser Worlds in Canada in 1980.

Lasers turned into fast catamarans in the 90s and in 2006 Elaine and her husband David competed in the ISAF World Sailing Games in Austria. Elaine has crewed on keelboats over the years – big boats always need a lot of crew members, so it was a great, inexpensive way to go big boat racing and cruising.

A few years ago Elaine with husband David went into boat partnership with Tolson Sherwood and they now own a Sigma 33. This they race and cruise with enthusiasm – giving newcomers to the sport a chance to learn to sail.

Elaine has been involved with Ballyholme Yacht Club over the years – organising events, running Cadet classes and she became Commodore in 2007. She followed in her father and

husband who worked for Oneida. She managed to set me up to crew in a 10ft Cadet dinghy with Peter Collins. Of the four Firth girls I was number two so following in my older sister Allison's footsteps – she was already crewing for hot shot Belfast boy Curtis Haire, who, sadly, died at a very young age.

Ballyholme Yacht Club was within easy walking distance and not only provided a safe haven for teenagers, but also introduced me to many great sailing families – the Swanstons, Ritchies, Finlays and Hamiltons. We all raced Cadets in the days when Ballyholme had over 70 boats moored in the Bay. Not only were you battling the elements, you also had to dodge the moored boats whilst surfing along on a reach; accompanied with the booming commands from helm at the back of the boat to "lean out harder".

Both Ballyholme and Royal Ulster Yacht Clubs ran racing on Tuesday and Thursday evenings and Saturday afternoons from May to September. Regattas around the Lough meant travelling to other clubs to race. All the Cadet dinghies were towed by Jimmy Morgan, the Boatman – we were like a family of ducklings being towed to Whitehead, Carrickfergus, Holywood and Royal North of Ireland Yacht Clubs. After a soggy race, tea and buns and a 'stolen' beer if you were old enough, Jimmy towed us in formation back to Bangor.

It was a perfect opportunity to mess about in boats – heading off to the beach for a capsize practice on the way there and then meeting up with chums. We were all pretty safety conscious – we always wore lifejackets, but unfortunately didn't always check out the weather. On one particular occasion a couple of over-confident Cadets – Anne Pope and Julie Hamilton – decided to venture outside the Bay. The wind got up, they got into difficulties and Jimmy the Boatman had to rescue them near Groomsport and tow them back to the Club. Both girls were given a good talking to and then were unceremoniously put up in front of the General Committee of BYC and given a right roasting by Commodore Robin Simms – Anne and Julie will not forget that one.

Racing was competitive in the Cadets and we travelled as far as Cork, Strangford and Cultra to compete in championships. The club and championship racing fuelled us up for more racing in different boats and led some of our more successful members on to European, World and Olympic titles. Bill O'Hara went on to sail in two Olympic Games, coach, then manage the Irish team in two Games and has been on the International Jury at the past two Olympics – a total of six Games! Bill and his family are well known Bangorians and Bill himself quite a character. At the tender age of 10 Bill was protested by another Cadet sailor, John 'Splodge' Cunningham.

husband's footsteps, becoming the first woman Commodore in the club's history.

Commodore and Mrs J. H. Hamilton (centre) with prizewinners at Ballyholme Yacht Club's annual dinner in October 1973. 50/12a-75

Bill was called to give evidence in front of the protest committee in Royal Ulster Yacht Club. He was ushered into the wood-panelled hallway and ascended the wide-carpeted stairs past the silver trophy cabinets up to the 'Thomas Lipton Room'. Bain Dickinson was chairman of the protest committee and asked a knee-trembling Bill: "Are you the protestee or protestant?" Nervously Bill replied: "No – I'm a Roman Catholic!"

Bangor man Bill Whisker, a member of Ballyholme Yacht Club, was acclaimed the new World GP14 yachting champion following his victory, with crew member Jimmy McKee, at Stone Harbor, New Jersey, at the end of July 1975. They won three out of four stages to claim the title. Bill is pictured here with his wife Rosemary and daughter Claire. 81/2-113

As we were growing up in BYC and moving on to bigger and faster boats, we started moving into Fireballs, Scorpions, Enterprises, GP14s and the popular Laser dinghy, which was designed in 1975. Also during that year two young GP14 sailors from BYC won the GP14 World Championships at Stone Harbor, New Jersey – Bill Whisker and Jimmy McKee in their boat *Whiskee Too*.

The idea to go to the Worlds started in 1973 when Jimmy and Bill were chatting in the bar to Jimmy Hamilton of Hamilton Shipping. They explained they were trying to get a 40ft container to the USA with eight boats inside. Jimmy H said: "No bother. Here are two tickets to a reception at the Belfast Harbour Commissioner's offices. I'll introduce you to the right man." Jimmy McKee and another GP sailor, Burton Allen, went along to the reception where Jimmy Hamilton introduced them to a gentleman, and promptly left. He asked them what the problem was and the lads replied that they wanted to get eight boats across the Atlantic to New Jersey. "That's easy – it normally costs £2,000 but I'll do it for free!"

Elaine and David Taylor

The next stroke of good luck was Raymond Coffey from BYC who managed to get free haulage of the container from Ballyholme to Dublin and then they paid $805 for haulage from Montreal to New Jersey return! The 16 crew of the eight boats going to the Worlds only had to pay £15 towards travel as they'd raised so much sponsorship.

When they arrived at Stone Harbor they were put up by Sue and Jim Collins, a couple who knew Molly and Reg Dalzell's daughter. That's the lovely thing about sailing – the world over, you'll find someone who is a friend of a friend who offers hospitality. The boys raced well and had a clean sweep with 1st, 3rd, 1st, 1st and 11th – after the 11th place result the Race Officer thanked them for staying out of the way and letting the other boats race!

These results were more than enough to give them the title of GP14 World Champions. Bill and Jimmy proved that with sheer determination and hard work you could be the best in the World! They led the way for aspiring champions from Ballyholme Yacht Club.

Bangor Cricket Club
in the Seventies

Looking forward to the new decade – the all-conquering 1969 teams pictured in front of the old wooden pavilion on Broadway. Back (from left): Ian Wallace, Derek Balnave, Jimmy Toogood, Brian King, Tom Edgar, William Carlisle, Bob Magee, Philip Pack. Middle: Ian Houston, Jimmy Kirk, Ken Perrott, Billy Heron, Maurice Moore, Conn McCall, Harry Eadie, Roly Agnew, Ray Davison, Roy Dennison, Stanley Glass, Barry Muir, Alec Horsley. Front: Jimmy McGookin, George Murphy, Robin Anderson, Bob Marshall (president), Raymond Christy (captain, 3rd XI), Billy McMillan (captain, 2nd XI), Michael Rea (captain, 1st XI), Robin Dixon (captain, Midweek XI), Ian McCullough, Roy Morrow, Jimmy Glass (scorer) and Ken Boal. *Spectator picture*

The 1970s for Bangor Cricket Club mirrored much of what happened to the town and Province during that often volatile decade (as Michael Rea's recollection of the Coal Lorry Episode appended to this article aptly illustrates!).

Just as Bangor's population mushroomed from (circa) 20,000 to (circa) 50,000, so the club grew from a three-team to a five-team operation and that despite being without its Ward Park home for a full two seasons. The development of the excellent Upritchard Park ground was still well in the future, but the Seventies was also the decade wherein the Bangor Rugby and Bangor Cricket Clubs became the Bangor Rugby Football and Cricket Club which we still see today.

To say the Club entered this period in good health would be something of an understatement as in the 1969 season the 1st XI (captained by Michael Rea) had won Senior League Section 2, the 2nds (captained by Billy McMillan) had won Second Division Section C, and the 3rd XI (captained by Raymond Christy) had won Second Division Section F. Additionally, Robin Dixon had skippered the Midweek XI to Rothman's Shield success.

Bangor Cricket Club's first XI were champions in Section II of the Senior League in 1970, but won the title outright following a deciding match against North Down at Stormont on Saturday 12 September. Back (from left): John Flanagan, Ian Houston, Jimmy Kirk, John Elder, Robin Dixon, Tom Edgar. Front: Brian King, Bob Magee, Conn McCall (captain), Michael Rea and Maurice Moore. *230/44/2*

Play was in the old Ward Park ground which was serviced from the wooden pavilion situated where the line of conifers on the west side of Broadway gives way to the houses. The ground itself undulated somewhat and was rather open with the large trees down near the tennis courts being too far away to offer significant protection.

After the 1974 season stumps were pulled as the Council embarked on a major re-development of the whole site, leaving the three gravel hockey pitches with floodlights, the new cricket ground (both these remain fairly well intact) and a rugby pitch at the Broadway end. There was enough space at the town end for a grass hockey pitch which was rarely used and then a soccer pitch which eventually morphed to its present location.

It must be recorded that the new ground had, and indeed still has, a significant slope across it but that it has excellent drainage and has often defied the heaviest of showers to provide playable conditions in quick time. Its openness has never been conquered but it has always benefited from passing trade in terms of spectators and advertises to one and all that cricket is played in Bangor. Even before the end of the 70s, some memorable matches had taken place there.

In many respects the most noteworthy day of all came at the unveiling of this venue when the future Sir Colin Cowdrey, then arguably still England's best known cricketer, took part in a re-opening match along with John Jameson (also a test player and later an umpire at that level). They bolstered the Bangor team who were opposed by a side containing most of the then current Irish XI and it is estimated that more than a thousand hardy souls braved the blustery conditions.

This match in 1977 was reported in the *Guardian* newspaper and *Country Life* (inter alios) and it is believed it was Frank Keating in the former who referred to Colin Cowdrey as the GLE (Greatest Living Englishman) – a title he claimed Cowdrey had inherited on the death of Sir Winston Churchill?!

Despite having to play 1st XI home matches at various venues during the two season hiatus of Ward Park, Bangor's strength as a club increased throughout the period with many notable players migrating from other clubs. In many cases this was because families had relocated to the expanding and more peaceful borough, having found early 1970s Belfast (at best)

Legendary England captain Colin Cowdrey signs an autograph for Alan Rosbotham at Ward Park before playing for Bangor against an Irish XI in May 1977. 99/15-29

disagreeable. In the late 60s Conn McCall, Ian Houston and Tom Edgar had arrived from Holywood with Brian King (from Civil Service), and in 1972 they were joined by Vinty Fitzimmons (also Holywood). Tim English and John Bell made the journey from Instonians and were joined by the late Billy Thompson, for many years the much loved headmaster of Bloomfield Primary School.

Alastair Borthwick, a Scottish accountant, added class to the batting for several seasons and he achieved selection for Ulster Country. Lowry Cunningham, who had played with English and Bobby Gray at Queen's, and Alan McCully, also from Queen's via Woodvale, all added to the playing resources, as did Chris Harte (who had been teaching at BGS but playing for Downpatrick) and, for one season only, Robert Farmer whose travels had included Queen's, Holywood and CIYMS.

Harte had played for Ireland in 1972 and 1973 but went off the radar only for a maiden Guinness Cup century to catapult him back into the side during his first Bangor year. There he joined club stalwart John Elder (a regular feature on the national side since his 1973 debut), who so often in those pre overs limitations days bowled unchanged or, at least, spells of the length that would have Health and

Safety lawyers licking their lips in the anticipation of a big payout nowadays!

Many of those mentioned contributed to the strong showings of the 1st XI through the latter parts of the decade but without the Bangor core of Michael Rea, Jimmy Kirk, Bobby Magee and Howard Bingham (whose record as an Irish Schools player in 1974 and 1975 was outstanding), the advances would have been much more

A cold-fingered Colin Cowdrey and wicket-keeper Chris Harte look on as Jim Harrison swings the ball away on the leg side during the match to reopen Ward Park in May 1977.

limited. It is also of note that the Bangor Cricket Club habit of producing young cricketers who went on to achieve greater acclaim as rugby players (e.g. Jan and Bryn Cunningham and Mark McCall) had been presaged before the end of this decade by the likes of Davy Morrow and Terry McMaster.

There was also a corresponding increase in numbers at Bangor Grammar School, which continued to be the main nursery for players and wherein the stalwart work of Harry Eadie

Bangor Cricket Club's Boys' XI in 1977, winners of the Graham Cup. Back (from left): Ron Wickens, Peter Barry, Brian Douglas, Peter Cunningham, Antony McClements, Alan Millar, Mark Tinman. Front: Conn McCall (chairman), Alistair Shaw, Gary McGimpsey, Peter Minnis (captain), Stephen Morrow, Jeff McMaster and Chris Harte (coach). *Picture: Malcolm Lee*

was supplemented by Chris Harte and many others. Several sons of both long serving and new members of the club were beginning to make their way as the photographs of the 1977 Graham Cup-winning team and the 1979 5th XI, who won 4th Division Section B show. This Graham Cup

side, our first to win since 1945, produced an international player, albeit that was captain Peter Minnis who went on to represent Ireland in the Davis Cup (tennis)!

Amongst others it included Stephen Morrow, son of Roy and brother of Davy (a 1st XI cricketer at that stage), Jeffrey McMaster, son of Jack and brother of John and Terry, Mark Tinman, son of Lou, Peter Cunningham, son of Billy and brother of David and John, and Alan Millar, brother of Brian (our Club captain in 2011!) and who is currently Club secretary of Bangor RF & CC.

That long term commitment to the Club is even better illustrated by the 5th XI, a seamless blend of stalwarts and rising stars. Captained by the redoubtable Brian Ellis, who was cricket secretary for many years (and had captained the 3rd XI to Cup success in 1976), he was joined by Ronnie Boston, K. W. (Ben) Boal, Jimmy Toogood, Michael Kane and John Doherty. Genial Garth Arnold was an "older youngster", while cricket's future was epitomised by Jackie Erskine, Ron

Bangor Cricket Club's 5th XI, winners of the 4th Division Section B, in 1979. Back row (from left): John Doherty, Ronnie Boston, Jimmy Toogood, Jeff McMaster, K.W. (Ben) Boal, Ron Wickens, Michael Kane. Front: Peter McCall, Jackie Erskine, Garth Arnold, Brian Ellis, Stephen Burns and Michael P. Rea.

Wickens, Stephen Burns (son of Davy), Jeff McMaster (again!), Peter McCall (son of Conn) and Michael P. Rea (son of Michael).

With such family involvement and promise for the seasons ahead, Bangor Cricket left the decade in even better health than it entered it – but that's another story.

With sincere thanks to Chris Harte, Michael Rea and John Elder

The Coal Lorry Episode as recalled by Michael Rea

Travel was often problematical in the Seventies and in 1972 the 1st XI were faced with a fixture at Ballygomartin Road (the ground is situated between the Upper Shankill Road and Twaddell Avenue!) against Woodvale at a time of significant civil unrest.

Much of this disruption was in the part of the city where the ground lies but despite numerous road blocks and car hijackings the intrepid cricketers of Bangor decided that nothing was going to prevent them playing the match.

Some of the team had family connections in Belfast and thereby made arrangements to get to the venue, whilst others travelled by train to the city. After much pleading they prevailed upon a taxi driver to deposit them somewhere in the vicinity of the ground. One player showed further initiative by getting a lift in a coal lorry which was allowed through the barricades on the basis it was delivering to the families of those manning the obstructions!

Bangor Cricket Club stalwarts to this day (from left): Chris Harte, Michael Rea, John Elder. *Picture: Harry Doggart.*

After the match (the fact the result is not recalled seems to suggest it may not have been a successful one!) it was realised the situation on the streets had not improved any and there was no hope of a further taxi being summoned to facilitate return to the railway station. However, it was a case of coal lorry to the rescue because it had been booked on a two-way basis and it emerged the driver was prepared to offer transport to Holywood for a (?) reasonable price!

With one player in the passenger seat (who lived in Holywood incidentally), the others hunkered down as best they could in the back amongst coal bags and coal dust. They were duly waved through the barricades and eventually completed their journey back to Bangor, having maintained the good name of the Club for overcoming minor adversities!

Captains of Bangor Cricket Club
1970 – Michael Rea
1971/2 – Conn McCall
1973/78 – Ian Houston
1979 – Chris Harte

Bangor Hockey Club
in the Seventies

The history of Bangor Hockey Club, as with any sports club, is punctuated with varying stories of success. The list of playing achievements provides one measure of such success and progress. For Bangor, one can point to promotions to the upper tier of hockey and trophies won by teams throughout the club.

John Smyth, Walter Dowdall, Harry Brady and Raymond Parker – the backbone of Bangor Hockey Club.

However, equally as important is the backdrop to off-field achievement – the development of the club itself, the contribution of key personnel and the incidents and events that help to define the character of the club.

One key constant for Bangor, since the club's formation in 1921, has been the lack of a permanent home. Since the time hockey was first played in the town, the hockey club has had many locations. Starting in Church Street, the meandering route around Bangor took members to Godfrey Avenue, Ashley Park, Silverstream, Castle Park (in 1957), Ballymacormick and then to Ward Park in December 1975.

Eight members of the original 1921-22 Bangor Hockey Club XI are pictured at the 50th anniversary dinner in the Savoy Hotel on 30 September 1971. From left: R. M. Connolly, the Rev. R. C. H. Elliott, former Bishop of Connor, H. Russell, C. Cassidy, H. Johnston, F. Stevenson, W. S. Mercer and C. McNeill. Club chairman in 1971 was Walter Dowdall. *246/81-3*

The Bangor Grammar School grounds at Ballymacormick provided a wonderfully picturesque venue into the early 1970s. Initially, there was one gravel pitch at the lower level of the sprawling grounds and one grass pitch at the upper level (latterly there would be two all-weather pitches). An abiding memory is of hurriedly donning gear in the spartan changing facilities and then walking down the slope to the lower pitch, which was surrounded by fields and offered a distant view of the village of Groomsport.

The barn adjoining the rugby and hockey pitches was home not only to the maintenance equipment for the grounds, but also to the goal posts and nets that, on an annual basis, were trundled along the dual carriageway to their temporary home (for one week) at Upritchard Park, where the Bangor six-a-side tournament was hosted.

Both club and school played at Ballymacormick until 1975 when they moved to the facilities at Ward Park, which in fact turned out to be the home venue for some 20 subsequent years. Three all-weather pitches and floodlight provision allowed the Men's and Ladies' clubs to field a total of nine teams between them. The improved facilities also allowed the club to initiate the first ever-floodlit tournament in Ireland (in February 1976). The winners of the tournament in the Seventies were

Bangor Hockey Club's committee in July 1972. Back (from left): D. Ferguson, R. Parker, A. Stewart, A. Coburn, J.V. Smyth, P. Watson, J. Hunter, L. Mulholland. Front: H. Brady (treasurer), D. G. Lamb (president), W. Dowdall (president, Ulster Branch), D. Forshaw (secretary) and G. Stevenson (club captain). *Picture: W.T. Kirk*

Belfast YMCA (1976, 1977, 1978), Lisnagarvey (1979) and QUB (1980).

Another first, albeit an inadvertent one, was Ward Park playing host to the first floodlit cricket match in Ulster. The spread of the floodlight's glare was sufficient to allow a match on the adjacent cricket pitch to progress into the twilight hours when normally play would have been called to a halt!

Ward Park also became a playing base for both Bangor Grammar and Glenlola Collegiate schools. Hockey had been introduced to the Grammar School in the mid-1960s and, under the guidance of J.V. Smyth and Chris Harte, the school progressed to become one of the leading centres in Ulster.

Walter Dowdall and North Down Mayor Jack Preston at the official opening of the all-weather pitches at Ward Park on 5 December 1975.

The school progress, in turn, impacted on the club as it provided a regular drip-feed of players for all teams (with the number of teams fielded fluctuating between five and six throughout the decade). A notable achievement was the 1st XI regaining Senior League One status in 1977, for the first time since the 1961/62 season. Two of the players, Sean Curran and Philip Martin, along with Gary Devon, also from Bangor, were selected for the Ireland under-21 squad for games in Madrid in May.

Indeed, it was the younger Martin brother, Stephen, who also represented the school and club for the first time in this decade, progressing eventually to play for Ireland and Great Britain (in the gold medal-winning Olympic team of 1988).

In 1970 David McManus gained his first international cap against West Germany.

Six-a-side Tournament
Back in 1955, little did the organisers of the club's inaugural six-a-side tournament realise just what they had started. The first of its kind in Irish hockey, the tournament then represented a great act of faith. Billy Addison circulated on the Thursday and Friday evenings, collecting contributions in the 'little green box' and then buying the prizes on the Saturday morning.

The Seventies proved to be a boon time for the event. Over 100 teams congregated at Upritchard Park in mid-August and whilst there was a vibrant social dimension, the tournament was also seen as a vital precursor for the season ahead. Senior League teams provided the event with considerable prestige and profile, with leading clubs such as Cliftonville, YMCA, Cookstown, Banbridge and Annadale all regular attenders.

Fond memories abound. A hardy band of club members mowed the pitches, painted (reasonably accurately) the lines and umpired, sometimes for three hours at a stretch. Spectator numbers were invariably healthy and the tournament provided an excellent forum for promoting the game in the Borough.

The people
The influence of the club extended beyond the boundaries of the Borough. It was in this decade that the legacy of Bangor involvement in Ulster Branch administration began. In 1973, Walter Dowdall was elected as president of the Ulster Branch of the Irish Hockey Union and in 1976 he was afforded the honour of being elected president of the Irish Hockey Union.

Along with Walter, Harry Brady is a club stalwart who, from his first involvement in the late 1940s, was integral to the initiation of club activities and events, which survived healthily into the 1970s and beyond – the Sportsman's Ball and the six-a-side tournament being the most notable.

J.V. Smyth joined the staff of Bangor Grammar School in 1966 and quickly established hockey on the school sporting curriculum. Within five years the school had established a strong reputation. Whilst there was an inevitable time lag between the introduction of the game and subsequent success, by the early 70s the first signs of achievement were very evident. However, equally important as playing prowess was the way in which things were done.

Understated by nature, John brought an incredible enthusiasm to sport in the school. His calmness of approach disguised an astute organisational brain. Indeed, these organisational skills were recognised at Ulster Branch level as John took his first steps on a path which ultimately led him to presidency of the Irish Hockey Union. It was in the early days that John became instrumental in the administration of Ulster Schools hockey, a role which then expanded to incorporate All Ireland Schools hockey as well. Indeed, perhaps one of his proudest achievements was leading Bangor Grammar School to Irish Schools Championship success in 1989.

John continued to play into the late 1970s. He had served the 1st XI with distinction and played for each team in the club. Who can forget his rampaging runs on the right flank, shirt tucked ever so precisely into the fading blue shorts?

However, the legacy is not just that of playing and administrative achievement. John's mantra from the early days was 'think smart, look smart, play smart'. These words were repeated regularly at training sessions on wet, windy Wednesday afternoons at Ballymacormick and on the school bus en route to every away fixture.

His ease of personality endeared him to all and it is rare to have a teacher who is so fondly remembered by so many schoolboys.

From his first appearance for the club in 1968, Raymond Parker demonstrated the competitive edge that came to define his play. A veritable dynamo, his unrelenting stamina and fine stick ability saw him establish a reputation as one of the most effective players in Ulster hockey. One Ulster cap may have been scant return for such a fine player, but for Raymond it was always the club that came first. A tireless organiser, he became synonymous with the Sixes tournament, touring teams and club committee. The constant on-field exhortation of "Come on boys!" no doubt still rings in many a Bangor ear and his modesty of manner has earned him many admirers.

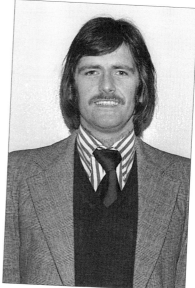

Raymond Parker in 1974. 53/9-95

If success is relative to expectations then promotion to Senior League 1 in 1977 represented a major achievement for Bangor under the captaincy of R. Parker. Even more impressive, some would argue, is that to this day Raymy still takes the field, with distinction, for Bangor.

Forty-three successive years of play, 26 for the 1st XI, 13 as club captain and unbroken service on the club committee. An impressive tally indeed!

Over the years, many things change, but as the history of any club reveals, the one constant is the spirit and commitment of those individuals who, on and off the field, define its personality – across the decades.

With sincere thanks to Walter Dowdall, Raymond Parker, John Smyth, Harry Brady and, especially, George Wilson.

Culture

in Bangor in the Seventies

Bangor Art Club
in the Seventies

The Bangor Art Club plaque was carved by member Reggie Hamilton

Bangor Art Club approached the new decade in great shape, the members having realised, in 1968, their long-cherished ambition of owning their own clubroom. Their new 'Studio' home was (and remains) the former Girl Guide hut in Ward Park, close to the Carnegie Library.

The club had been founded in 1952 by a number of enthusiastic amateur artists, most notably Mr Gordon W. Mulligan, with its inaugural meeting being held on 24 July that year in the Milan Café. With Mr Mulligan taking on the role of secretary, the chairman was Capt [later Major] Jock Affleck and the treasurer was Mr W. Weir.

Over the years the many and various efforts to promote the club and the needs of its membership indicated a disinclination to let the grass grow under their feet. And so it was, with the Ward Park clubhouse a reality, that another major project, with its roots in the early Sixties, came to fruition during the early months of the new decade – the restoration, at no expense to the ratepayers, of the two derelict fishermen's cottages at Cockle Row in Groomsport.

Two pivotal figures among the scheme's many supporters had been Catherine Weir and Bertha McGimpsey, with the latter undertaking a battle with the local Council, during which she petitioned the authority, through a series of letters, not to demolish Cockle Row to make space for a new car park for the village. Instead, she urged the Council to allow the Art Club to take over the cottages with a view to restoring them.

Finally in 1969 the Council relented and agreed not to demolish the buildings. A 20-year lease was subsequently signed by the Council and the club at a peppercorn rent of just £1 a year. Attempts were made to engage the services of various builders but none was willing to take on what even some Art Club members reckoned was an impossible task. However, work did begin, on 16 August 1969, and involved

Alex Minty

two club members, Alex Minty and Lewis Dunn. Within a week they had managed to rebuild a collapsed wall and had fitted a new door frame. A replacement window frame followed and within a short time the building had been made safe.

The roof of the older building was already thatched but this had been covered with sheets of corrugated iron which had become badly rusted. After much discussion it was decided that re-thatching with flax would be the best solution. The club managed to obtain the services of skilled thatcher Bob Douglas, as well as a supply of flax and willow sticks, and the work was done to everyone's satisfaction at a very reasonable cost.

The other building was comparatively modern with a number of tiles missing from the slate roof, but the club was fortunate to have access to a good supply from a house in Cultra. Replacement second-hand window frames and a new door frame and door were eventually added. Perspex, however, had to be used in place of glass for the windows because of repeated attacks by vandals.

The floor of the loft was covered using packing cases bought for 10 shillings (50p) each from a tobacco factory in Belfast's Sandy Row. A modern fireplace in the older building was removed, along with a substantial quantity of bricks, and replaced by a massive Scrabo stone affair made by Mr Dunn to resemble a typical old fireplace, complete with crane crook, period pots and kettle. For the other cottage a fireplace was rescued from the bedroom of a previously demolished house adjacent to the nearby church and fixed into the inner room. Three granite kerbstones, lifted into place by a couple of burly fishermen, were added, one on top and the others on either side. Tiles decorated with the club's logo were added, courtesy of Mrs McGimpsey's art pupils at Bangor Secondary School.

It took a year of hard graft before the buildings were deemed presentable. By then the walls inside and out had been whitewashed and the woodwork painted black. Numerous very welcome donations helped them to complete the interior work. These included a 100-year-old Singer sewing machine, as well as an old mangle, ornaments, cutlery and crockery which gave the place a more domesticated look.

The club also enjoyed considerable support, especially in terms of fundraising, from the Marchioness of Dufferin and Ava, who remains patron to this day.

The official opening ceremony was performed on 31 October 1970 by North Down MP and local Councillor Bertie McConnell. From that day onwards Cockle Row became an important tourist attraction, not only for Groomsport but for the whole of North Down, attracting thousands of visitors from all over the world. Until 1989, when it was taken over by North Down Borough Council [the 20-year lease having expired] and fitted out as a Tourist Information Office and Exhibition Centre, Bangor Art Club maintained the Cockle Row cottages and an exhibition of crafts and paintings was held there during May and September, supervised by a faithful band of female members (Joan Moles, Betty Pentland, Delia (Dee) Rimington, Iris Ritchie and Winnie Thompson).

Paintings by club members were displayed on the walls of the newer cottage and these, along with assorted crafts, were put on sale with a small percentage going towards the general maintenance of the buildings. This again emphasised how the club received no financial support from the Borough Council.

These days Cockle Row continues to draw visitors to the district, but it most likely would not even exist had it not been for the restoration work carried out at the beginning of the Seventies and beyond by Bangor Art Club.

Art Club members during the decade included Jock Affleck, Lolita Alexander, Sarah Baxter, George Bennett, Bea Bridgham, Pat Cooley, Molly Cunningham, George D'Arcy, Lewis Dunn, Janet Emerson, Frank Fitzsimons, Stella Franks, Rosemary Garrett, Pearl Geddis, Claudia Gow, Reggie Hamilton, Maureen Heyn, John Hogg, May Hunter, Jean

Lewis Dunn in familiar pose at Cockle Row

Irvine, Ronnie Irvine, Jack Kane, Muriel Kempson, Bertha McGimpsey, Pad y McIntyre (née Barkley), Pat McManus, Alex Minty, Joan Moles, Betty Pentland, Doris Rainey, Dee Rimington, Sydney Scott, Frank Shannon, Violeta Sheppard, Phoebe Stewart, Ida Teuton, Winnie Thompson and Marjorie Williamson.

This contribution to *Bangor in the Seventies* has been compiled from a series of articles and reports written during the decade and in later years. Special mention goes to Alex Minty, Winnie Thompson, Reggie Hamilton and Yvonne Best. Anyone interested in joining Bangor Art Club can contact Mrs Colette Roberts on 028 9042 2755.

Members of Bangor Arts Club with friends from Lisnagarvey Art Club at Cockle Row in September 1976

Pictured at the winter exhibition in the North Down Museum, held during November 2010, are then president Reggie Hamilton and founder member Major Jacques (Jock) Affleck. The latter passed away in May 2011.

Members of Bangor Art Club during a visit to Silent Valley in 2000

Tony Ablett

remembers... Bangor Drama Club

Bangor Drama Club in the Seventies bore no resemblance to the day in October 1935 when my father, Ronald Ablett, and five others formed the club following a meeting in Main Street's New Downshire Hotel.

The other founder members, for the record, were Edwin Haire, Edgar Goodly, Kitty McKibben, Tommy Johnson and John Rawlings – the latter two being well known teachers at Bangor Grammar School. The club had developed over the post-War years and with the acquisition of the old Home Guard building off Central Avenue, we had the basis of a decent clubhouse.

Weekly play readings have always been the backbone of the club and are an ideal way to be initiated into the world of amateur drama. The reading committee read a great many plays during the summer and arrange an eclectic selection for reading on Thursday nights. They also arrange for guest readings from and to other clubs, plus the occasional solo evening by a club member.

Looking through the list of committee members in the Seventies we come across husbands and wives doing their bit – but not in the same year! Kenneth and Patricia Irvine, Kay and Brian Rothwell, plus many other notables like Gwenyth Bayly, Bill Murphie, Carol Andrews and Terry James. As well as entertaining club members on Thursday nights, the play readings give the incoming production

Bangor native Tony Ablett was born in 1939 in the former and now sadly demolished Westroyd Nursing Home on Clifton Road. He attended Connor House, Bangor Grammar School and Campbell College.

After serving in the Merchant Navy, mainly in the Far East, for about three years Tony developed diabetes, which necessitated a change in career. He worked in England for the tyre division of the Dunlop Rubber Company for nine years, before returning to Bangor where he joined Cyril Lord Carpets. After the company closed down, he moved to Gainsborough, which had taken over the

Cast members from Bangor Drama Club's production of *The Magistrate* in 1971. Included are J. Hogg, A. Best, R. Spence, R. Harwood, H. Morrow, T. Ablett, M. Stewart, H. Stewart, J. Fleetham, H. Williamson, J. Gilmore, S. Pinkerton, D. Anderson, L. Gilbert, E. Jones and R. O'Donoghue.

former Cyril Lord factory at Rathgael.

The final 20 years of Tony's working life were spent in the linen industry as sales manager with Ulster Weavers.

Married to Sandra since 1964, his main hobbies are sailing and cars. He was a member of Ballyholme Yacht Club for many years and pursues an interest in kit cars through membership of the Ulster Kit Car Club. He is a past chairman of Bangor Drama Club and is a trustee of the club.

committee the opportunity to assess a play's potential in the Little Theatre – then a home for Bangor Amateur Operatic Society and also rented out to their fellow thespians across Central Avenue, i.e. Bangor Drama Club.

The production committee has the unenviable task of reading and choosing plays for public productions. Each year the club endeavours to produce four full-length plays for local, festival and, not forgetting, an annual Portrush Summer Theatre appearance. In the Seventies the club achieved this on a regular basis and, with a membership approaching 200, it would necessitate auditions with the producer and production committee in attendance.

The first play in February 1970 was *The Admirable Crichton,* which was described by *County Down Spectator* drama critic Joy Bannister as "a sad comedy." However, she did concede that both the settings and costumes could not be faulted – after all it is not easy for a stage manager to produce a bamboo hut and half a dinghy! The play was produced by Jim McNinch and Mike Conway was the stage manager.

One-act plays have often proved useful vehicles for training producers, stage managers, not to mention actors.

Many leading lights have made their debut on the tiny stage upstairs in what is now the green room of the Studio Theatre. Access backstage was via a vertical ladder from the workshop on the ground floor – certainly not for the faint-hearted with vertigo!

In 1974 the club decided to present a programme of three one-act plays in the Little Theatre – *Spring, Losers* and *Fair Play is Bonnie Play.* Some current members appeared in the cast lists together with two of the club trustees, John Neill and Laura Gilbert. John played a young married man and Laura played 'old' Mrs Wilson. Joy Bannister described her performance as "a startling change from the juvenile leads for which she is better known."

The Bayly family were much in evidence with Gwenyth producing the third play, while husband Charles gave a superb performance as Andy in *Losers* and also stage managed his wife's play. From this, one can gather there has always been a strong family connection in Bangor Drama Club and we now have third generation appearances

Goodnight Mr Puffin was presented by Bangor Drama Club in the Little Theatre in October 1973. Back (from left): John Neill, Jeremy Lewis, Charles Bayly, Norman Ellison, Don Ritchie. Front: Diana Stewart, Rosemary Forrest, Joan Farbus, Patricia Irvine and Helen Mayne. *45/1a-75*

from the same family. Another bonus is the number of marriages (mine included) that have blossomed in the club premises. My wife Sandra (née McCormick) was on the lighting team for many years, learning her 'trade' from Sam Patton and John Lorimer.

Another example of family participation was in February 1974 with *Everybody Loves Opal.* Stage manager was Eric Jones, property mistress was his wife Elsie and their son Chris played a leading role in this very successful comedy, which came first in Ballymoney Drama Festival. The adjudicators' comments stated "this production was as near professional as dammit with this group of very talented people."

In October 1974 the club opened its 40th season with

Principals from *The Wizard of Oz* in December 1979: Bill Murphie (Lion), Billy Rea (Scarecrow), Alison Gordon (Dorothy) and Tony Ablett (Tin Man)

The Prime of Miss Jean Brodie, described as "an outstanding achievement and a great success." As well as club stalwarts like Valerie Burns, Don Ritchie and Ronnie Harwood, there were also 12 teenage girls, some of whom were the daughters of senior members. The part of Jean Brodie was carried admirably by Margaret Barnard and the school principal was well played by Gwenyth Bayly – both incidentally were teachers in real life.

One of the most interesting plays with which I was involved was *The Wizard of Oz.* This was performed in Hamilton House prior to Christmas in 1979, and also went to the Group Theatre in Belfast. The club had received a request from UTV to appear in their early evening programme, hosted by Gloria Hunniford. With the play opening at 7.30pm in Belfast, the three of us appearing on UTV had to change into our costumes and drive up to Havelock House, ready to dash down the road to appear on stage.

Alison Gordon, as Dorothy, appeared fairly normal in pigtails and gingham dress. Bill Murphie, however, was in full costume as the friendly Lion and I was outfitted as the Tin Man with a well-engineered suit made out of surplus aircraft aluminium from a nearby aircraft factory! I was the driver and had visions of being stopped at a police/Army checkpoint (of which there were many in the 1970s) and trying to explain my costume of close-fitting aluminium! Both the play and the TV interview, however, went well and the club gained good publicity, allied to a reasonable profit.

One of the largest – if not the largest – casts to

Tony Coghlan and Carol Andrews, from the May 1976 production of *An Italian Straw Hat*

appear in a BDC play was in May 1976 when we produced *An Italian Straw Hat*. It was a light-hearted period romp set in the 18th Century and had a cast of 42, not all speaking parts but a producer's nightmare nonetheless. The play was produced by Kay Rothwell and her assistant was Heather Cottle. There were some musical items, which was something new, and we were lucky to have Jean Marshall on piano to add the necessary expertise.

Portrush Summer Theatre remained strong during the 1970s, despite the Troubles, and the club sent a play every year to the Town Hall. *Crystal Clear* was chosen for 1970 and Joy Bannister was obviously not very keen on the play itself. She described it as "comparatively short for a three-act play which is the only thing that can be said in its favour." Despite this, she thought the acting was competent and she enjoyed the performances of Laura Gilbert and Dennis Reynolds as the young couple. The play was produced by our future president and bastion of amateur drama, John Knipe MBE. That play, incidentally, ran for eight months with a final performance on 23 April 1971 in the St Columbanus Church hall at Ballyholme.

Another Portrush play which hit the headlines for the wrong reasons was *Fish Out of Water*, produced by Tony Coghlan in July 1976. There was a bomb blitz on the Tuesday night and the cast members were evacuated, not only from the Town Hall but also from their hotel. Joy described the play as "very entertaining", which was the prime motivation for a Portrush play – most of which have been from the pen of Sam Cree.

Among notable plays from the Seventies was *Bequest to the Nation,* a period drama about Lord Nelson, produced by Kenneth Irvine, while *Paddington Bear* was a complete contrast, also successfully produced by Kenneth. One of the many Alan Ayckbourn plays the club

Cast members from the May 1977 production of *Bequest to the Nation,* directed by Kenneth Irvine

Appearing in Alan Ayckbourn's *Table Manners* in October 1978 were (back, from left): Harry Williamson, Di Stewart, Alan Huffington, Tony Ablett and (front) Barbara McLaughan, Carol Adair and June Townsend.

produced was *Table Manners* in October 1978 and I had the pleasure of acting with June Lyness (née Townsend), one of the most talented actresses in Bangor Drama Club.

Talking of June reminds me of my one and only moment of glory, when we won the Northern Ireland section of the UK one-act competition in 1972. The play was *Rise and Shine* and it took place in a graveyard. This had great appeal not only to producer Dennis Reynolds, but also to the stage manager as all he had to supply were a couple of headstones! The UK finals were held in Cardiff's New Theatre and although we did not win, the craic was mighty. June and I were slightly overawed when shown the gigantic stage in a 1,500-seat theatre. Contrast that with our little club theatre which seated 36!

Happy memories and that really is what Bangor Drama Club has meant to me over the years, particularly in the Seventies. The pleasure and satisfaction of working backstage with experienced stage managers such as Robin Jones, Dan Gilbert and John Burns or appearing on stage before an appreciative Bangor audience is very rewarding. With the high standards created, the club has done much to maintain local interest in the general aspect of theatre with a varied vein of entertainment, which will no doubt prevail for many years to come.

Bangor Drama Club chairmen	*Presidents*
1970-72 – Brian Rutherford	1970-77 – Lord Dunleath
1972-73 – Ida Empey	1977-85 – Ron Ablett
1973-75 – John Neill	
1975-77 – Charles Bayly	
1977-79 – Dan Gilbert	

Donna Revie
remembers... dancing and ballet

I was born in Bangor in 1967 so most of my early childhood was spent in the 70s. Growing up in a family of dancers we lived in a little dancing bubble and were to a degree sheltered from the reality of what was happening in parts of our country during the Troubles.

Dancing is in my blood. My mother, Carolyn McMaster, was Northern Ireland Irish Dancing champion, as was my uncle Raymond. Mum also ran an Irish Dancing school in Bangor. My grandmother, Sadie Adams, taught tap classes and performed alongside other members of her family with the Dufferin Players and entertained the troops at the Savoy Hotel during the Second World War. It was inevitable that my sister, brother and I would follow in their footsteps.

I was taught Irish Dancing at the age of three by my Mum and took up ballet when I was five. Our ballet classes were held in the Orange Hall on Hamilton Road and were later moved to the Brookborough Hall, just off the Knock carriageway in Belfast. I don't recall us encountering any problems getting to ballet classes, but when I started Irish Dancing classes with Patricia Mulholland things certainly

Gillian and Donna Revie in the late 1970s after winning their respective age groups in the Northern Ireland Championships. 71/4-10

Born in Bangor, Donna Revie began Irish dancing and ballet at the age of three. She won her first championship when only seven years of age and shortly after became Northern Ireland Champion. As a member of the Patricia Mulholland Irish Ballet Company (a forerunner to the now famous *Riverdance*),

Early success for six-year-old Donna Revie (second from left), pictured in 1973 with (from left): Susan Kelly, Olga Jane Lowe, Rachel Lynas, David Cree and Yvonne Kielty. *30/10a-67*

she performed throughout Ireland.

In 1985 Donna studied Dance and Education at Roehampton, London, where she achieved a B.A. Honours degree and discovered her talent for choreography.

On returning to Northern Ireland she began teaching and choreographing small productions for local theatre, creating, in 1996, *Celtic Images*, followed by *Beyond Reality* and the critically acclaimed *Elementals*.

Donna Revie's other choreographic engagements have included the opening of the Odyssey Arena and, for television, the BBC's *Children in Need*, *Making a Difference* and *The John Daly Show*.

In 2002 Donna was awarded the prestigious Dance Northern Ireland Choreographic Initiative Award.

At this time she opened her own dance school, which now has over 200 pupils. She is assisted by her mother, former Northern Ireland Champion Carolyn McMaster.

became more difficult.

Miss Mulholland lived at Duncairn Gardens in Belfast and almost every week we faced diversions, road blocks and police checkpoints. It was something we became used to and actually didn't really pay much attention to. My sister and I sat in the back of the car and sang songs, waving to the Army Land Rovers as we went by. Mum and Dad were very persevering and I think there was only one occasion when we couldn't get to class. They just kept heading in the right direction and eventually we got there. One week we had to divert to Lisburn and approach Belfast from that side of town. Dancing was our priority and my parents were determined nothing would stop us from pursuing our goals.

I always felt safe in Bangor, that bombs and shootings were things which happened to other people in other places. I remember being in Belfast at a dance competition taking place on Rosemary Street, which at that time was inside the security barriers. Again, I felt safe when I was in that area. At lunchtime we went with a group of other dancers to a restaurant outside the barriers and I was really frightened. I cried the whole time, sure we would all be blown up and I wouldn't get a chance to perform my new set dance. Needless to say we were absolutely fine but Mum was furious with me for making such a fuss.

My sister, Gillian, travelled to London in 1979, successfully auditioning for the Royal Ballet School, which she attended the following year. She remembers finding it strange that in England there were no security guards at shop doors. She says for a long time she used to walk through the door of a shop and hold her arms out and her bag open to be searched, only to find people looking at her strangely.

My brother, Michael, was born in 1975 and so can't remember very much about that time. What he did find, however, was that when he followed in Gillian's footsteps and travelled to London to attend The Royal Ballet School when he was 11, people had a very narrow view about what life in Northern Ireland was really like. They thought we all faced gunmen and bombings on a daily basis and on one occasion Michael was asked if we had a bomb shelter in our garden. This was largely due to the negative media coverage of the situation here at the time.

It took Michael quite some time to convince his friends that life in most parts of Northern Ireland, especially in areas like Bangor, was little different to life in England. In fact they were quite shocked to hear we were able to go out leaving our houses and cars unlocked and that the general rate of crime was lower here than in London.

The diversions and bomb scares we grew up with were just an inconvenience that we became used to and were a part of everyday life. They did not affect our daily routine in a major way. We danced on, regardless of politics and the conflict around us. At this time there seemed to be a determination of spirit to get on and to do well regardless of any obstacles that were put in our way. Out of this came great artistic ability and imagination. Some of the most creative developments in Irish Dancing came in this era.

During the 70s my sister and I took part in festivals throughout Northern Ireland and so had to travel on a regular basis. We met children from other areas, backgrounds and religions. Any differences between us were irrelevant; we were all united in our love of dance. I can't remember even being aware of what religion anyone was. We had fun

Mum Carolyn McMaster in the 1960s

Gillian Revie is a former Principal Character Artist of The Royal Ballet Company at Covent Garden and is now living and teaching in Sydney, Australia.

Michael Revie, following his training at The Royal Ballet School, has danced with Deutsche Oper am Rhine in Dusseldorf, Birmingham Royal Ballet, Zurich Ballet and South African Ballet Theatre. He is now assistant artistic director of Mzansi Dance Productions in Johannesburg.

Celebrating their success at the Belfast Festival of Irish Dancing in 1978 are (back) Robbie Lightbody and Ellen Hosick with (front): Donna and Gillian Revie.

Today Donna runs the Donna Revie School of Dance

and I am still friends with many of the girls I met during that time; some are now teaching dancing, as I myself do. We still meet up at the same festivals with a new generation of children who are mixing and developing friendships through a common interest, just as we did 30 or 40 years ago.

Growing up in the 1970s in Bangor was idyllic in its own way. There was plenty to do and we got out there and did it. During term time we had school and our regular dance classes to occupy ourselves. In the summer holidays we swam at the beach and at Pickie Pool, rowed Lairds Boats in the harbour and played tennis at Kingsland. We fed the ducks in Ward Park and went to the Tonic Cinema at the weekend. The weather always seemed to be better in those days.

I feel very lucky to have spent my childhood at a time when, although we were exposed to conflict, we were encouraged not to let anything stop us from achieving what we wanted. It made us more resolute to grab life with two hands, enjoy it and really live it.

Gillian Revie, former Principal Character Artist with the Royal Ballet Company, dances the role of Carabosse, the wicked fairy in *Sleeping Beauty*, in 2010. *Picture: Johan Perrson*

Michael Revie rehearses for a recent Zurich Ballet production of *Mozartina*

Spectator
Reporters
have their say...

Ian Alexander
remembers...

The accompanying photographs of the *Spectator* being printed on an old Cosser press at 109 Main Street, Bangor, powered by a tractor, bring back memories of an age before the internet and the digital revolution that has transformed the newspaper industry.

The *County Down Spectator,* just to remind readers, was founded by David E. Alexander, a Glasgow journalist who emigrated to Ireland in 1894 (he was 22) to edit the *Leitrim Advertiser* in Mohill, Co. Leitrim. He was to marry a girl from there and that ensured he was never to return to his homeland.

Instead he came to Bangor in 1897 to edit the *North Down Herald.* Clearly an ambitious man (what Scot isn't?), he took a gamble and set up the *County Down Spectator* and its sister publication, the *Newtownards Spectator,* in opposition to the *Herald* in 1904.

While times were difficult he kept the papers going until, in 1933, he made what proved to be one of the shrewdest decisions of his life: he bought a secondhand Cosser press for £3,000. The beauty of it was that it could print 16 broadsheet pages at one pass, putting it on a par with the most advanced dailies in Ireland.

It was the making of the *Spectator* which could now carry more news and appear on the streets earlier (Friday

Ian Alexander in his time as a photographer for the *Spectator*

Ian Alexander is a grandson of D. E. Alexander, founder of the *County Down Spectator.* He attended Bangor Grammar School and Queen's University. After graduating he emigrated to Canada (cost was £15 for an assisted passage) where he enjoyed himself immensely. He was a surface worker at a uranium mine for a time and later worked as a roughneck on oil rigs.

When Ian joined the newspaper he started as a linotype operator before becoming a photographer/reporter. He also worked as a sales representative and edited the *Spectator* for a number of months when Annie Roycroft was on sick leave.

He has been golf correspondent for almost 40 years and has written light-hearted columns for the paper, firstly *Shooting From the Hip* and latterly *Our Grumpy Old Man*.

Ian is a director of Alexander Newspapers.

Ian Alexander today

morning) than ever before. Sales took off. That press continued to work, never missing an edition, until November 1971 when the *Spectator* went web offset and a paper of 24 broadsheet pages could be printed on a brand new Solna press.

It was the start of the technological revolution that now sees the *Spectator* produced by computers and the whole panoply that goes with them. The original Solna was replaced in 1991 (no Cosser-like longevity unfortunately) by a new version that has the capacity to print 64 tabloid pages, 36 in full colour.

But what of our photographs and the tractor-driven Cosser (then almost 50 years old)? It happened like this. It was December 1970 and a power crisis had brought industry to a standstill; weekly newspapers were banned from printing. We were deemed non-essential.

It seemed for the first time there would be no *Spectator* that week. Then someone had the idea, probably chief printer Joe Cairnduff, that the Cosser could be belt driven, just in the way tractors (before the days of combine harvesters) powered threshing machines.

We decided to give it a go. Well, there was little option. A hole was punched in the dividing wall between the works and Bertie Brookes' garage and John Woods (my uncle as it happens), a farmer from Ballygrainey, volunteered his tractor and a belt.

Miracle of miracles, it worked. The Cosser rumbled into life and the *Spectator* was printed without a hitch. The *Spectator*, we like to think, had many good days, but surely that was our finest hour. We had never missed an edition before and we have never missed one since. Long may the presses roll!

John Woods, Joe Cairnduff and John Alexander weighing up the possibilities. *234/95-2*

John Woods and that tractor which kept the *Spectator* presses rolling. *234/97-2*

Job done. John Woods and Joe Cairnduff watch the *Spectator* coming off the press. *234/92-1*

Annie Roycroft, editor of the *Spectator* for almost 30 years, with members of staff as she waits for the first copy off the press. *234/96-1*

Peter Gibson
remembers...

While I understand this is all about Bangor in the Seventies I first need to touch on the Sixties, or at least the last few years of the decade.

At the tender age of 16-plus in 1967 I transferred from Bangor Technical College, then on Hamilton Road, to Avoca House at Princetown Road, which will only mean something to the very few testosterone-driven Co. Down males who had the great pleasure of attending the 'girls' school. It was all part of my master plan to become Northern Ireland's greatest journalist – or to pick up girls.

I had talked to *County Down Spectator* editor Annie Roycroft when my interest in recording the facts became, well, an interest, and was told I would need certain standards of English, typewriting and shorthand. So off I went to Avoca House, which turned into a brilliant almost-two-years. Thank you Linda, Jane, Ann and Yvonne (from Ballyholme, who later became a street walker... she joined the police force). Not to mention the lovely girl from Holywood, whose face I can still see (I think her name was Margaret).

In May 1969, clutching certificates that showed I could do this and that and might be able to do bits of something else, I bravely and confidently set out to find a job. While there were no openings at the *Spectator* at that time, the search ended swiftly and with glorious results – I got a job

Peter Gibson was born in Bangor Hospital, on 10 May 1951, to Nora and William Gibson of Groomsport, and a brother for Maree and Shirley.

He attended Ballyholme Primary School and, he states, managed to scrape through the 11+ to attend Bangor Technical College and then Avoca House to take shorthand and typing classes.

A very brief career with the Civil Service transformed into a life-long career in journalism, starting with the *Co. Down Spectator* in January 1970. He spent one year in the 'subs' room at the *News Letter* before moving to Canada in February 1975. Peter was married to Gerry (née Hilling) shortly before the move to Canada and they have three sons: Kevin, Allen and John. Kevin and wife Karlie have one daughter, the wonderful Emma Rachel Mae, who was born on Christmas Eve 2009.

Peter returned to Bangor in January 1980 and worked (briefly) at the *Belfast Telegraph* before returning to the *Spectator* as sports editor.

He went back to Canada in 1981 and spent several years at the *Calgary Herald* in various capacities, before moving to the *Calgary Sun* and served as Sunday Editor and later Managing Editor.

In 1986 he moved to *The Vancouver Sun* in beautiful British Columbia and works there as a News Editor, residing in North Vancouver with partner Ann, who has two daughters, Kristy and Jennifer.

for the summer in the wonderful 'Port pub, located only the length of about four football fields from my front door in Groomsport.

It was great, simple work. Haul crates of this and that up from the cellar, stock the bar – no fridges or cold shelves in those days – and sell the products to the punters when the doors swung open. The legendary Billy Dunbar was in charge of the pub and would oversee myself and cousin John Watterson doing all the heavy lifting and grunting. The pub employed local people in the 60s and 70s and on a visit in 2010 I was delighted to see the tradition continuing – two of Billy's daughters (Hilary and Alison) are involved in the pub and sister-establishment, The Stables.

Working nights wasn't great for the love life, or getting to go out with my mates, so eventually I applied for a clerical position with the Northern Ireland government. Following an interview at Stormont Castle I ended up with the Ministry of Defence on the Lisburn Road. Usual stuff – type this, file it; pull the file, add this, retype it, refile it.

The daily drudge had begun. Bus from Groomsport at 7.10am, train from Bangor at 7.30am, bus from (the then) Queen's Quay up the Lisburn Road and fire up the trusty typewriter before 8.30! Brilliant time – until the Troubles started and I was told I might have to carry a gun to go to work.

No thank you. So there I was, out of work after a sparkling 11-week career. As it happened, a reporter's position opened up at the *Spectator* and a letter arrived inviting me for an interview. I had met Miss Roycroft several times before; she introduced me to the newspaper business through *Groomsport Gleanings,* a column I wrote about life in the village – mainly church events, Boys' Brigade notes, birthday celebrations, births, deaths, etc.

The interview was a piece of cake, I think; I really can't remember a thing, but somehow I ended up with a job. It was January 1970. When Miss Roycroft told me I was being taken on as a junior reporter she said: "This is not a nine-to-five job, if that's what you're looking for, it won't work."

At the time it didn't mean much, but after 40-plus years

in the newspaper business I could count on the fingers of one hand the years I actually spent working something like nine-to-five. I've worked shifts from 2pm, 7pm, midnight and my all-time favourite, 3.45am.

I did actually start at 9am on a drizzly Monday, met some of the staff in the front office and the back shop, was given a camera and told to drop down to Trinity Church to take a photo of ... I stopped hearing shortly after camera. I'd never had a camera. No problem. A few seconds of instruction in the intricacies of photography from Brian Orr (he was one of the other lucky guys to attend Avoca, but a year ahead of me) and off I trotted.

Several hours later I was back in the office with something in the camera. Good first day, I thought. Until Miss Roycroft said I was to take the camera home and then show up at the Bangor Horticultural Society meeting at 7.30. At what? I'm sure I had to look that up in the dictionary. Again, good first day.

Then there was Day 2. In at nine, take the camera and notebook to... and come back to the Bangor Council meeting at 7pm. Of course, I missed the 6.35 bus from Groomsport and didn't think there was much point in showing up more than an hour late. Wrong! Next day, Annie suggested I could have walked it in 40 minutes (35 if I'd pushed it).

Ian Alexander sat beside me – chastised and feeling sheepish – to offer some sage advice... don't miss Council meetings when Annie is holding court. (Some months later she honoured me by assigning me to the Council meeting in her absence – she was taking an extremely rare week off.)

Life in Bangor in 1970 was... different. The Troubles were not our direct concern. That was Belfast; people had to travel there to work, even shop, but it wasn't a big problem for Co. Down. But eventually things changed.

The early days on the job were a dream; it was a new world every day. Covering sports, reviewing plays at the Little Theatre, fetes at the Clandeboye Estate, the magistrate's court every Wednesday where I would occasionally meet some of my friends (not socially) – and those great horticultural meetings.

Then, it all began to take off in early 1972. Two car bombs went off in the centre of town and caused extensive damage, but no loss of life. I don't even think there were any injuries. Bangor had met the Troubles.

Main Street was cordoned off, but the press pass got me through. I remember standing just about where the Flagship Centre is now – with the camera – waiting to capture history as some of Bangor's severely damaged buildings were being demolished. It took a while to get things going and I always thought it was because no one wanted to rip apart the heart of the town.

Other memories are even more disturbing. Police officers killed in the line of duty elsewhere in the Province, but who lived in Co. Down. The public was curious – who was this person? What were they like? The toughest part of the job was always having to interview the survivors. It's never something you forget.

The death, the suffering, the destruction hit us every so often.

In early 1973, a 24-hour loyalist protest brought industry to a halt again plus more violence and disruption to the town. Mob-rule took over. Police were stoned on the streets; houses were hit by petrol bombs; shots and small explosions were reported in several areas.

The crowd decided to protest outside the police station and I found myself in the middle of an unruly mob – me and my trusty camera. The fence surrounding the police station at that time had to be 20 feet tall, but several people decided to climb up to plant flags on the top. A few people noticed I was taking photographs and, eventually, I was surrounded. I managed to distract them by pointing out that the police had

Bangor Police Station with its 20ft fence *Picture courtesy of North Down Museum*

photographers on the station roof and they were getting much better portraits of anyone facing the station. Before they could figure out if I was telling the truth, I decided to slip away. Just as I reached the *Spectator's* outer door – which was locked, great – half-a-dozen people caught up with me and demanded the camera. I had them talked down to just taking the film when two police officers appeared and the group disbanded. Never did get a chance to give them the blank roll; I'd managed to rewind the film and throw in a fresh roll as I hurried back to the office. It wasn't even wound around the spools, but who was to know?

Amid all the nonsense, there was always some fun. The boys from the *Spectator* composing room used to kick a ball around at the back of the building; Jim Gore, the Savage brothers, Joe Cairnduff would watch and laugh. I was the crazy reporter playing wearing a shirt and tie.

Little things, as they were thought of at the time, turned out to be very special. For many weeks on Thursday afternoon I was seconded to the delivery department; there really wasn't one at the Spec. – it was composed of anyone not fully occupied at that particular time. But it was terrific.

I'd jump in the van with a load of papers and disappear. Bangor to Crawfordsburn, to the Ponderosa (as many of us referred to Kilcooley), the Clandeboye Shopping Centre, Clandeboye Estate, Conlig, Ballyholme, Groomsport, Donaghadee and I think Millisle – that may not have been on the route but I just liked the place so I may have gone there anyway.

And then there was Bangor Football Club. They tormented Bangorians season after season. My Dad – William John McDowell Gibson, born in Abbey Street – used to lift me over the wobbly turnstiles in the early Sixties but I would have more fun chasing the seagulls than watching the ones on the pitch. Many years later, club chairman Bertie Murphy – who owned a shop in Groomsport – realised I was the Peter Gibson who wrote for the *Spectator*. My life was hell; I even started shopping elsewhere.

Bertie was a genial and generous man and it was probably one of the happiest days in his life when Bangor finally won a trophy – the County Antrim Shield. I had travelled to the mid-week replay against Ards (the third!) – with my camera – and filed a report and photos for the paper later that week. Bertie was so impressed with my efforts that he gave me a free 99 cone the next time he saw me.

In those days the Northern Ireland team would 'train' at Castlereagh Park in Newtownards (come on, these guys didn't need to train, it was just a get-together). So one slow Tuesday afternoon I popped over to watch a training session. Derek Dougan, Pat Jennings and the one-and-only George Best all running around on one of the greatest football surfaces in the Province. And me, watching from only a few feet away.

That's when I made history.

I tell my Canadian friends that I played football with George. The squad had been divided into small groups playing touch football, when George bounced the ball off someone's leg and it left the square they were supposed to be playing in. When it bounced in my direction, George said, "Kick us that ball back, will ye?" So I flicked it up with my right foot and kicked it to George. He caught it and took the throw-in. Pure history, in my mind.

And then there was Northern Ireland politics. I've never been big on politicians, even in my 36 years in Western Canada where I've met or lunched with a couple of Prime Ministers, several provincial premiers and a few city mayors – even shared drinks with one of Alberta's most famous mayors who ended up premier, the great Ralph Klein from Calgary, who was in the news business before politics. Just Google the name.

But there will never be another place in the world to rival Northern Ireland in the Seventies for politics and politicians.

No matter what you thought of them, we had the most diverse group of representatives perhaps ever assembled. Bernadette Devlin, the Rev. (Dr.) Ian Paisley, John Hume, Gerry Fitt (a distant relative of mine – an older, Protestant lady – had a housing problem and took it to his constituency office. Problem was fixed the next day), Gerry Adams. An endless list.

I was even 'thrown out' of one of the Rev. Paisley's meetings in Bangor in the early Seventies. He was top news and I would cover his meetings for the *Spectator* and the Belfast dailies and TV stations. So, on one of his visits to Bangor, I was dispatched to the meeting – with the trusty camera – to record more history. I was clicking away before the Rev. Paisley appeared on stage and kept clicking as his thunderous voice silenced the audience and he, as always, took control. Several minutes and many camera clicks later, he paused. And looked directly at me. Now imagine the following words spoken by the Rev. Dr. Ian Paisley as he glared at a 20-something-year-old reporter/photographer... "Young man, are you quite finished taking my photograph?" It only took a few seconds to comprehend he was looking in my direction and an even shorter time to understand that the two burly characters marching down the aisle toward me weren't coming over to invite me out for dinner or a drink. So I sat down.

I had four great years at the *Spectator*, learning every day. I met thousands of people; most of them under happy circumstances – like horticultural society meetings. In time I decided Northern Ireland wasn't working for me and sought some more newspaper experience before a planned move to Canada. I landed a job in the subs room at the *News Letter* in January 1974 to gain some insight into the editing and layout side of the business. I believe it was Cowan Watson, the paper's editor, who told me during an interview that I probably wouldn't have made it through the door if I hadn't worked at the *Spectator* for four years under Annie Roycroft's leadership. She was a remarkable woman, to whom I – and many other ink-stained wretches – owe a lot.

I was only allowed to call her Annie when I left Canada in

Peter with his sons (from left): Allen, John and Kevin

1980 to return 'home'. I had a job at the *Belfast Telegraph,* but it didn't sit well with me. On a visit to the *Spectator* Annie suggested I take over the sports section so she could concentrate on the rest of the paper. I think it worked out well for both of us, but in January 1981 I returned to Canada.

I enjoyed the Seventies in my business and there is one situation from my early career in Bangor at the *Spectator* that still makes me smile. A lovely lady staggered into the office under the weight of a giant sunflower plant – complete with pot – and was convinced it should be documented as some sort of record.

It was impressive, so I located the trusty camera and asked the lady to set the plant on the floor and stand beside it. She had to be over six feet tall, so I thought it would add some perspective. After taking several photos she seemed quite disturbed and said: "Listen, I think you are just trying to humour me. Do you expect me to believe you can get this huge plant into that tiny camera?"

See, the horticultural theme was always going to haunt me.

Ah, the memories.

John Savage
remembers...

After all these years I still haven't quite worked out why I set my sights on being a journalist. It may be due to the fact I was useless, and still am, at more practical pursuits. I did once make a bread board during wood-work class in school. I brought it home to my Mum, but it broke in half within days. I also managed to assemble a bird box, but it disintegrated when I attempted to nail it to a tree.

As a teenager, my passions were music, football and motorcycle racing, so perhaps that's how my attraction for journalism began. Having cousins who were several years older, I'd been brought up on a diet of The Beatles, Rolling Stones, Dusty Springfield and The Kinks. At home we listened to Paul Robeson, Nat King Cole, Hank Williams and Harry Belafonte. I neither sang nor played any instrument, aside from the recorder, so I guess I wanted to write about the records I bought in Woolies and avidly read about in the *NME*.

I still vividly recall watching, on monochrome television, as England defeated West Germany in the 1966 World Cup Final, and having adopted West Ham United as 'my' team, after I watched my first FA Cup Final on telly in 1964, and the European Cup Winners' Cup Final the following year, I wanted to be the next Malcolm Brodie.

My paternal grandparents lived in Abbey Street and Dad

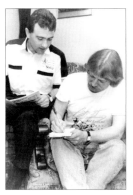

John with motorcycle racing legend Robert Dunlop

John Savage was born in Bangor in 1955 and spent his formative years in his home town, before his family relocated to Craigantlet. He attended school in Holywood, before he 'escaped' to Bangor Technical College. He joined Spectator Newspapers as a trainee reporter in 1972 and was subsequently transferred to the *County Down Spectator's* sister title, the *Newtownards Chronicle*.

He was quickly established as senior journalist with the *Chronicle*, before he was appointed deputy editor, and in 1985, following the death of Norman Boal, he was appointed editor of the *Chronicle*, a position he holds to this day. John is one of the longest serving weekly newspaper journalists in Northern Ireland and one of the longest serving weekly newspaper editors in Northern Ireland.

He is also acknowledged as one of the most respected motorcycle racing journalists in the UK, and has been the recipient of several major awards within the motorcycling fraternity, having established a following far beyond the *Chronicle's* circulation area and as a contributor to many books, magazines and publications.

Aside from motorcycle racing, John is a lifelong West Ham United supporter and is an avid music enthusiast, most notably of David Bowie, to the extent that he regards his 'Bowie collection' as his legacy! He and his wife Dawn have a son, Jonathan, and two daughters, Sara and Rachel, together with two grandchildren, Faith and Alex.

took me to my first motorcycle race in Castle Park in 1964. I was hooked; I wanted to be the next Jimmy Walker.

By my early teens, I'd decided I didn't want a job in which I had to employ the impractical uselessness of my hands. My brain was fairly functional though. I read and wrote a lot, therefore I decided I would like to pursue a career as a reporter. Enquiries to then *County Down Spectator* editor Annie Roycroft informed me that I required 'shorthand, typewriting and a good standard of English'.

My only avenue to obtain the requisite qualifications was to study at the 'Tech'. I spent an enjoyable two years at Bangor Technical College, during which Mr Taggart despaired at my sometimes irregular attendance, Miss Watson made sure I achieved more than adequate shorthand and typewriting qualifications, while Mr Tohill helped me to spell write, I mean right! As one of only two blokes on a floor jam-packed with girls it was a tolerable time.

When I turned up at the *Spectator* office for my job interview, I was given a shorthand/ typewriting test and spelt 'definately' wrongly. Annie Roycroft informed me that was promising, as she had rarely encountered a journalist who could spell 'definitely' correctly.

The date 4 July 1972 will forever be etched in my memory. It was my first day as a cub reporter with Spectator Newspapers and Annie welcomed me with the question: "Do you know the significance of today's date?" Sheepishly I replied: "It's American Independence Day." "No," she retorted: "It's the day you *lose* your independence!"

My time as a trainee reporter with the *Spectator* was to set the template for the rest of my life, an invaluable period of learning, both about life and journalism, before I was seconded to the *Newtownards Chronicle,* the *Spectator's* sister title, a temporary deployment which was to become permanent.

Thankfully, Bangor escaped much of the Troubles which beset Northern Ireland during the Seventies. Nevertheless, as the Province stood on the brink of civil war, there were some horrific occurrences which left a lasting impression.

As a still teenage journalist, I was dispatched to Whitehill to interview the family of young Michael Browne, who had been brutally murdered after an 11th Night bonfire. It was a life-changing experience I will never forget, but one which taught me to adopt a policy I have stood by ever since: Never ask a journalist to do a job you haven't done, or wouldn't do, yourself.

Following the departure from the *Spectator* of Peter Gibson, a former colleague to whom I owe much, I assumed responsibility for covering Ards and Bangor football matches, although the latter was not a particularly desirable occupation for a 'dyed in the wool' Ards supporter. Somehow I managed to keep my objectivity largely intact and I enjoyed my brief time reporting at Clandeboye Park, with the likes of ace goalscorer Gordon Stewart, together with dogged defenders 'Snowy' Murphy and Billy Finlay amongst those who did the 'yellow and blue' great justice. Retrospectively, I would reluctantly concede my 'derby' match reports were probably distinctly 'red and blue'.

I vividly recall leaving Clandeboye Park one Saturday afternoon and witnessing a pall of smoke over Bangor. Perplexed, I hastened my way down Clandeboye Road and Church Street, to be met by my girlfriend in Abbey Street, where she had taken refuge in the home of a colleague, who worked with her in what was then Templeton's supermarket in Main Street, beside the *Spectator* office. The town centre had been evacuated as Bangor had fallen victim to a series of IRA incendiary bomb attacks, which caused considerable devastation.

While I avidly digested newspapers, I'd never harboured a particular interest in politics, or the legal system, until I began my career in the *Spectator*, but that was quickly to change. I soon found myself covering the local courts, with Joy Bannister 'showing me the ropes'. Joy was a patient and talented mentor and it came as no surprise when she succeeded Annie Roycroft as editor of the *Spectator* and then proceeded to carve out a successful career as a talented science fiction and crime novelist.

The late Martin McBirney was Resident Magistrate in Bangor and Holywood, where the court was held on Fridays in the Orange Hall, and it was incumbent upon me to bring 'His Worship' a copy of the *Spectator* each week, handing it up to the 'bench' from the press desk. It was with horror that I learned in 1974 he had been shot dead by the IRA at his Belfast home. A great man's life taken by some of the scum who attempted to destroy this hapless little corner of the island at that time.

As for politics, my brief time covering Bangor Borough Council afforded me an opportunity to learn the rudiments of local government. Few of the Councillors left a lasting impression on me, but those who did included Andy Templeton, perhaps best known for his newsagents/confectionery shop in Abbey Street; George Green, quite a formidable character to a rookie reporter; and Bertie Mc-Connell, a gentleman and genuine humanitarian.

However, the most erudite politician I encountered during my sojourn working in Bangor was Jim Kilfedder, who encapsulated North Down's maverick brand of unionist politics and once embarrassed me during an election campaign on a 'Market Day Wednesday', when he spotted me crossing from Castle Street to Warden's Corner and announced through his megaphone: "Good afternoon, John. I trust the *Spectator* will be giving me good coverage this week!"

Our paths crossed many times subsequently, and my respect for Jim never diminished. When he was elected Speaker of the original, doomed Northern Ireland Assembly, Jim personified all the integrity of not only a politician, but also a statesman, when he hosted a private reception for the late, great motorcycle ace Joey Dunlop and his wife Linda at Parliament Buildings — a ground-breaking event, organised by then Assembly member and Ards Councillor Simpson Gibson, with some assistance from myself. It was the first time a sportsperson had been formally hosted at Stormont and as Jim and Ian Paisley, Joey's local MP, greeted us before we entered the dining room, 'The Doc' asked Joey for his autograph. The humble world champion embarrassingly obliged, with an entourage of 'top brass' from the Honda factory in Japan proudly looking on.

Back at the *Spectator* Annie Roycroft encouraged me to

watch how the pages were compiled. In those days, before the advent of computer technology, the finished articles were printed out, trimmed with a surgical scalpel, then waxed on the reverse and basically stuck onto a full-page grid sheet. I spent many moments on Wednesdays alongside compositors like John Dickson or Jim Gore as they 'pasted' my football reports onto the back page. At the time I didn't appreciate how beneficial that experience would be, but, as my career progressed, and now in an era when journalists don't only write and edit reports but also compile pages on computers, it was an invaluable insight.

The ineptly misnamed Troubles meant there was little 'live' music in the Province during the early Seventies, with 'big name' groups not prepared to risk life and limb to make the trip across the Irish Sea. The likes of Chips were the big draw at Milanos, but Chips and Milanos weren't my cup of tea. The Queen's Court Hotel was my entertainment venue, and when Mungo Jerry came to play, the queue for admission stretched all the way along Queen's Parade and up Southwell Road. Such was our desire to see 'live' groups we had watched on *Top of the Pops,* we even queued to see Mud. Mind you, after a few Crème de Menthe, even Les Gray and his troubadours sounded good.

Those days are fondly remembered: downing a few lagers and 'Torrey Canyons', a cocktail which was all the rage at the time, in the Queen's Court with the late Jon Antony, the doyen of DJs back in the Seventies; enjoying a few beers in Furey's pub, at the corner of Main Street,

KING'S CLUB
at the QUEEN'S COURT HOTEL
FRIDAY JULY 6th
Chart Toppers MUD
SATURDAY JULY 7th
DOMINO (ex Dunno)
Plus DISCO Plus D.J. JON ANTONY Plus REVEALING ELAINE
COMING SATURDAY JULY 14th
EMILE FORD and CHECKMATES
● LATE BARS ●

DJ Jon Antony (right) met up with old friend Tony Blackburn, when the Radio 1 DJ appeared at the Coachman on 17 October 1979. *305/14-8*

John with wife Dawn at a garden party hosted by the Queen at Hillsborough Castle

with fellow reporter Philip Conaty, who died much too young; browsing in Smyths record shop and proudly departing with the likes of *The Slider* by T. Rex or *Aladdin Sane* by David Bowie; playing Space Invaders upstairs in the Midnite Lounge; picking up cut-price 45s in the Co-Op's excellent record department; sharing a burger with mates and girlfriends on Queen's Parade and in Isabeal's in Main Street; and being dragged along to the Tonic/ Odeon Cinema to see the likes of Dick Emery, Glen Campbell and the Bay City Rollers.

My memories of Bangor in the Seventies remind me of my first ever Chinese meal in a restaurant in High Street which, I think, is now occupied by a charity shop: more sweet than sour.

As my late father's favourite singer put it: 'Unforgettable.'

Michael Megarry
remembers...

My favourite quote about journalism comes from American political satirist P. J. O'Rourke: "I am a journalist and, under the modern journalist's code of Olympian objectivity (and total purity of motive), I am absolved of responsibility. We journalists don't have to step on roaches. All we have to do is turn on the kitchen light and watch the critters scurry,"and it summarises more eloquently than I can about why I started on the path to word-smithing glory.

I have two ladies to thank for setting me on that path – Miss Ferris, my legendary English teacher at Bangor Secondary School, and my late mother Betty. Miss Ferris introduced me to Annie Roycroft, where it all began in 1973 at the tender age of 16, while my mother battled – literally, sorting bullies and other teachers along the way – to get me in the right stream to focus on the opportunity ahead.

It started with a happy coincidence of being the part-time and very amateur PRO for the Air Training Corps Squadron 825 (which is still in existence and thriving as far as I know). Whether it was the drive to capture ATC activities in the written word, or the fact it allowed me to shirk some of the parade duties, it positioned me for my first foray into journalism. I remember to this day the sheer joy of seeing a few paragraphs of written text

1972-1973: Dishwasher, shelf stacker, gardener – anything to make a few bob!

1973-1978: Journalist with the *County Down Spectator* – everyone should start their working life this way!

1978-1981: Journalist with the *Belfast Telegraph* – from general news to feature writing to cinema column.

1981-1982: Press Officer with the Northern Ireland Tourist Board – getting married meant he needed more than a journalist's salary! And he wanted a challenge. Michael worked with Eric Thurley and the late Ian Hill on his first real communications strategy – bringing journalists into Northern Ireland to see its beauty for themselves.

Michael Megarry (back, third from left) is pictured with 'Tech' staff and fellow GSCII students in 1974. Back (from left): Mr W. F. Crowe, teacher of Bookkeeping and Commerce, Pamela Arlow, Lorna McFadden, Mr Tom Place, teacher of Arithmetic, Shorthand and Typewriting. Front: Pamela McIntyre, Heather Burns, Lana Heaney and Grainne Strain. Missing: Linda Davidson and Margaret Marshall. *30/12a/87*

His main role was creating and producing the quarterly newspaper *Tourist News*.

1982-1987: Public Relations Manager for the Leeds Permanent Building Society, then the fourth largest in the country, since swallowed up by the Halifax. There Michael managed also to acquire a degree level communications qualification, something that had eluded him earlier. "Six O-Levels, supplemented by shorthand and typing, just don't cut it in the corporate world!" he says.

1987-1991: Director of Communications for Coopers & Lybrand, now part of PriceWaterhouseCoopers – at the heart of City, Finance and Corporate life.

1991-1996: Board Director at global public relations agencies, including Burson-

appearing on page 23 of the *County Down Spectator* – they were my words!

Like others before me and since, Annie set me on the right course. At that time journalism was still seen as a trade with a three-year apprenticeship. I needed to acquire some skills first – so I attended Newtownards Technical College to be honed in shorthand and typing, skills I still use today. You'll see this as a remarkably similar story in the background of most of the journalists at the *Spectator* and, as mentioned too by John Savage, being in a class of girls for a time didn't do any harm at all.

My introduction to life as a cub reporter was first to Bangor Magistrate's Court, under the tutelage of Joy Bannister, then a senior reporter, and then to a meeting of North Down Borough Council with Annie herself. I remember the utter professionalism of both in accurately reporting the facts – a great grounding for the new boy.

To be honest, the years that followed at the *Spectator* are a little bit of a blur. That may be something to do with the fact it's now coming on for 40 years ago since I took that first step. But it was also that when working to weekly deadlines, packed full of activities in a bustling community – from weddings to obituaries, from ruby anniversaries to football matches – time just flew by.

My years at the *Spectator,* formative and exciting as they were, coincided with key events: the turbulent era of the Troubles – and Bangor was not unaffected – through to broader international events such as the oil crisis. That was the backdrop and they did impinge from time to time.

In those first years I was a photo-journalist too. I remember the advice from Annie – long captions which name everyone in a large group means they will buy the paper! With Praktica camera slung round my neck and a yellow Mini *Spectator* van at the ready, I was king of the turf.

The Praktica was not the most reliable. I remember something of a scoop for news in the 70s when incendiary devices were planted in several stores in the town. They were found and bravely defused by police officers. I arrived as they were leaving with the devices and took what I thought were some stunning images of heroes and the bombs they had defused. This turned to complete chagrin when I realised the camera had malfunctioned. Fluffed it!

I remember too that we had our lighter moments in the *Spectator* newsroom. On one occasion a Bangor policeman had uncovered some bomb-making material in the back of a car and Annie won the prize for the longest and tongue-twistiest headline: "Bangor Bobby Bags Bootful of Bombs". That made it to the equivalent of the *And Finally* section of the UTV news.

Gaining experience and a little maturity (allegedly) meant being given space in the paper for personal interests. This amounted to running the entertainment column for a time – I remember great shows at the Tonic Cinema, and sometimes good movies too. Getting to the front of queues helped to impress some girlfriends at the time as well. As a by the way, it also led to an interesting period moonlighting as manager for a pop band, but that's another story.

Annie was keen to get me to focus all my time on writing though. I recall she phoned the owner of the town's

Marsteller and Edelman.

1996-present: Royal Dutch Shell plc. He joined the communications team initially to look after what was colloquially known as 'the Nigeria issue' – supporting communications around Shell's presence there. Successive positions followed looking after communications issue management for Africa and the Americas, high-level representation in the Middle East based in Dubai, and currently Vice-President, Global Internal Communications, based in the Head Office in The Hague, Netherlands, where Michael is working with the CEO to create a new behaviour culture amongst the company's 100,000 staff.

He adds: "I'm married to an amazing wife, Angie, with two beautiful daughters, Charlotte and Sophie; with an incredible Dad, John, who has always supported me and continues to carry the Megarry flag in beautiful Bangor."

Winston Hotel to explain why I wouldn't be returning to my spare-time job washing dishes. And she was right.

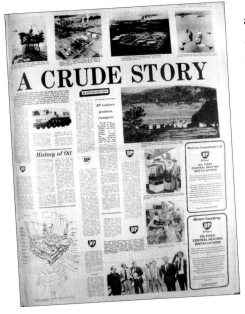

A CRUDE STORY

I progressed to writing my own column about the local pop scene, cringingly called *Michael Megarry's Meanderings* – and that about summed them up.

I was delighted too to follow my hobby, aided by my father John, of writing about model aircraft. Created quite a following – especially as in week one I centred on a helicopter that anyone could build and fly. Actually, it was two 12-inch rulers held together in the centre by two elastic bands. Simple, but effective – although there were some reports of minor injuries in school playgrounds!

Professionally, I branched out into other areas, encouraged by Annie. One of my favourite stories of the time was strangely prescient if you look at my CV – an article on BP's offshore operations which got tagged as *A Crude Story*. Little did I know that one day I would be working in the energy industry, if not for BP.

I moved on from the *Spectator* in 1978 to become a journalist at the *Belfast Telegraph*. It ended something of an era for me – a great team led by Annie, one of the most professional and loyal editors I have come across, either then or since; Joy, as a great tutor; enjoying the company of fellow journalists David Crossen, the late Philip Conaty, and Peter Russell (who moved from typographer to journalist); and then there was that little yellow *Spectator* van.

And as we say in good journalistic circles – ends…

Former *Spectator* reporter Michael Megarry, now Vice-President, Global Internal Communications with Shell, takes a look at one of the last broadsheet editions of the *Spectator* in June 2011, together with his family (from left): wife Angie, and daughters Sophie (10) and Charlotte (12).

Mervyn Jess
pays tribute to Philip Conaty

The phrase "larger than life" is often used to describe someone's character. In the case of Philip Conaty it was right on the money. I first 'experienced' Philip when I was a cub reporter with the *Newtownards Chronicle*. This was during the late Seventies and Philip was a senior member of the editorial staff at the *Chronicle's* sister paper, the *County Down Spectator*. He would sometimes appear in the *Chronicle* newsroom for one reason or another and when he did his character would fill the already cramped editorial space.

As a young trainee reporter on a weekly newspaper I was astonished by Philip's penchant for expensive motor cars. He always seemed to be driving the latest model of the top brands, changing cars about once a month. Then I discovered he was the *Spectator's* Motoring Correspondent.

Philip Conaty

He was a big lad and to some people he could appear quite intimidating. I got to know him better as our journalistic paths crossed over the next 15 years, and that first impression became more modified. He wasn't someone to trifle with and he didn't suffer fools gladly, but beneath

Mervyn Jess, a Senior Broadcast Journalist (News and Current Affairs) with the BBC in Belfast, was born in Comber in 1958 and attended Comber Primary School, Comber Secondary Intermediate School and Bangor Technical College.

Although his first published work was for the *County Down Spectator*, he commenced his career in journalism with sister paper the *Newtownards Chronicle* in 1977. Three years later he joined Downtown Radio as a news reporter.

Mervyn, who moved to the BBC in 1988, reports primarily for BBC Newsline, along with BBC Radio Ulster News and BBC News Online. He is also a

Another interest ... The cast from *The Long Night*, one of three one-act plays presented to friends and associates of Bangor Drama Club in their own miniature theatre in March 1975. Back (from left): Simone Farbus, Philip Conaty, Cherrie McIlwaine, Niall Gilbert, James O'Fee. Front: Louise Farbus, Ann Polson, Marjorie Eadie, Oona Harris and Maureen Grant. 9918-102

published author (*The Orange Order*, O'Brien Press, 2007).

He is married to Lynn and they have two daughters. Mervyn's outside interests include music (playing and listening), soccer (mostly watching these days), reading and hillwalking.

Mervyn Jess today

that sometimes gruff exterior lay a softer more sensitive side that would only fully be revealed to his colleagues at his funeral service.

I eventually followed Philip into the world of broadcast journalism when I was employed as a news reporter with Downtown Radio at the start of the Eighties. He was one of the Assistant News Editors at the Independent Radio station. The ANEs effectively ran the news desk during what were particularly brutal and busy times. Hardly a day went by without some sort of Troubles-related story breaking.

The Downtown Radio News desk was the Troubles touchstone for the Independent Radio News network and it seemed for every other local independent radio station in the English-speaking world, who called us for the on-the-scene voicers. Philip took it all in his stride before moving on to join the British Broadcasting Corporation's television newsroom in Belfast. It was here a few years later that our paths crossed once again. The story was the same, only the medium and the SOC – standard out cue – had changed.

Philip ruled the BBC TV bulletins desk with a rod of iron and a can of Diet Coke. It was here he finished his news days, retiring early because of ill health. There was one last gathering of all his colleagues at an informal leaving party for Philip in Bangor's Royal Hotel and that was a night to remember but not to report.

At his funeral those same people gathered once again to pay their last respects. It was during the funeral service that Philip had the last laugh when the minister announced the final hymn, written by a certain Mr P. Conaty. After a congregation-sized sharp intake of breath... you could have heard a pin drop.

Philip Conaty died on 8 February 1997, aged just 42. The hymn mentioned by Mervyn Jess was written for Philip's wedding in June 1979 to Anne, who still lives in Bangor.

Peter Russell
remembers...

Looking back, I suppose Bangor and the *Spectator* had both been going through a process of change during this time. For Bangor its glory days as a seaside resort were gone and the process of finding a new identity had begun; for the *Spectator* it was embracing the new technology that was to sweep aside so much of the old ways in the printing industry.

The paper had installed an ultra-modern press, but for a period we set the type for the pages by a combination of old-style hot metal and the new computer technology. The final pages were prepared with proofs of the type being literally cut and pasted at our offices on Main Street – which were located where the check-outs now are in the Asda supermarket.

I suppose the 'news' which was the staple diet for the *Spectator* during this time, remains, by and large, the same today — births, deaths, court appearances, protests by various residents' groups, etc. Our editor was the great Annie Roycroft. She would hand out the markings to reporters at the beginning of each week. I would then spend my week (and a great part of many weekends!) covering a range of stories.

Reporters at that time were required to take photographs, so some markings would involve getting shots of cheque presentations and such-like. I remember one colleague (who

Peter Russell pictured for the *Spectator* in late 1979

After leaving the *County Down Spectator*, Peter Russell spent some time working in the radio industry. He now divides his time between writing, painting and developing internet projects.

shall remain nameless) being sent to take a photograph one evening at the Royal North of Ireland Yacht Club at Cultra in Holywood. The reporter duly arrived, knocked on the door before venturing inside. No one was about so our trusty journo took a seat to await developments. Minutes later a woman arrived and rather indignantly pointed out that the clubhouse was the building next door!

Most Wednesdays I would spend my day covering North Down Magistrate's Court where, in my time, the Resident Magistrate was Mr Wishart Mills. He was a kindly man who dispensed justice in a firm but fair manner. I remember after one sitting, during which he had signed an eviction order for a troublesome family on one of the local housing estates, he overheard me express reservations to a police officer about his decision. Mr. Mills engaged me in a brief discussion on the issue before 'sentencing' me to six months!

The news team would also cover the local entertainment scene. At this time Caproni's was still open at Ballyholme, but for younger people the place to be was the Queen's Court Hotel, on Queen's Parade, where the marvellous DJ Jon Antony was in charge.

Members of popular Bangor band Chalkie in July 1975. From left: Pat Duignan, Drew Harrison, Peter Gregory, David Reid and David Barton. 7//15-112

The Queen's Court was also a place which generated quite a few stories, many of which appeared in the courts section of the paper.

For the under 18s there were the Blue Lamp Discos – a community relations initiative involving the RUC. The aim was to provide teenagers with entertainment and this was to prove extremely successful in Bangor where hundreds of kids attended. Some of the events were held in what had been the old Milanos Ballroom on the Seacliff Road.

I remember the Blue Lamp also provided a springboard for local musical talent. Bangor-based group Chalkie got their break there before enjoying success in the Northern Ireland entertainment scene.

Two particular stories remain firm in my mind from this period. The first involved Monty Python's *Life of Brian* film. Amazingly, Belfast Council banned the film from cinemas in the city and there was a fear that Councillors in Bangor would also be tempted to consider themselves a better judge of such things than Barry Norman.

I decided something had to be done to challenge what I saw as being an abuse of power. I started the 'Let Brian Live' campaign which called on *Spectator* readers to sign a petition urging the Council to let the film be shown in Bangor.

Before launching the campaign I had gone to see Sid Scott who owned the local Tonic Cinema. I asked him for a guarantee that if the campaign proved popular he would resist all pressure and show the movie. Sid agreed to my plan and generously offered free seats for people who helped me run the campaign.

Thousands of readers backed the effort. We handed in our petition at the Town Hall and any Councillors who had been thinking of pressing for a ban were forced to retreat.

Life of Brian was then shown in Bangor to packed houses and no doubt many people made the journey from Belfast to see what was forbidden to them in their own city.

The second story I remember concerned the *Belfast*

Telegraph. On 15 September 1976, a bomb exploded at the *Telegraph* premises in Belfast. Fourteen people were injured, one of whom lost his battle for life four days later.

It appeared the bomb was aimed at destroying the paper's pressroom and stopping production. There was no way the newspaper could be printed on its home press that day and this is where the *Spectator*, to its eternal credit, stepped in with an offer of help.

A contingent of *Telegraph* staff arrived at our offices and using our equipment put together a paper. We all lent a hand. I helped out at our printworks and together we produced that day's edition of the *Belfast Telegraph,* thus ensuring the newspaper was not silenced by the bombers.

What a day.

David Crossen
remembers...

If the Sixties was the party, the Seventies was the hangover – but what a hangover. Reading accounts of Bangor in the Sixties makes me envious for those buoyant, carefree, innocent times that I only experienced as an echo.

We moved to Bangor as the Seventies decade dawned. The icons of the Sixties were fading fast. Pickie Pool was no longer the place to spend lazy, sunny summer afternoons. The Rumbling Tum and Cloud 9 had closed their psychedelic doors; Queen's Parade was tired and terminally ill.

Perhaps the figure that best sums up the fading optimism of the Sixties was Jolly Jack. Remember him? Head

Jolly Jack Tar

into the urine-scented portals of Barry's Amusements and on the left, in a grimy glass cage, there he sat: Jolly Jack Tar, The Laughing Sailor.

My friends and I would roll our penny in with a delicious sense of irony. A mechanical whirring sound would be followed by hideous shrieking and Jolly Jack would begin rocking back and for-

David Crossen is married to Edna and lives in Queensland, Australia. They have two grown-up children, Louise and Laura.

David began his career at the *County Down Spectator.* He moved to London where he worked on regional papers and on Fleet Street, before returning to Northern Ireland to take up a role on the *Belfast Telegraph.*

In 1986 the *Sydney Morning Herald* took him to Australia where he now lives. He has been Deputy Editor of the *Brisbane Sunday Sun,* Editor of *Brisbane News,* Features Editor of *The Courier-Mail* and Deputy Editor of the *Sunday Mail.* He is now Editor-in-Chief of Quest Newspapers' Sunshine Coast division.

Minnie Delino aged 82 in 1979. *121/16-6*

ward, glassy-eyed and demonic with his hair hanging precariously from the corner of his shiny dome, suspended by one impossibly resistant blob of glue. In the background, Minnie Delino would bark and rattle her great bunch of keys.

There is nothing sadder than a seaside town in the rain – and on many rainy nights my friends and I would huddle with our bottles of QC Wine, Olde English Cider, Clan Dew... at the McKee Clock shelters, up The Vennel, the Ballyholme shelters, in Castle Park...

I told my Australian son-in-law we used to drink on a Saturday night at the badger's den. He thought I was talking about some olde worlde pub – no, literally a badger's den. In Castle Park. My first experience of drunkenness was there (Olde English Cider) and I will forever associate it with the Rolling Stones' song *Wild Horses,* which someone had on an early cassette player. Ah, the memories.

Talking of badgers... I remember during my early days at the *County Down Spectator,* the owners kept a pet badger called Snooky in their back garden. Snooky was often the subject of columns written for the paper by Lolita Alexander. Then one day Snooky went missing. A 'Find Snooky' campaign was launched by the paper. One day we received a mysterious phone call. If we wanted to find Snooky we should look in our post box – in the doorway of the old *Spectator* offices in Main Street. I was sent with the key to investigate. Inside the post box was the pelt of a badger's head. The work of a disgruntled reader perhaps? The official account has Snooky simply wandering back into the wild. His true fate is lost in the mists of time.

During my early teens I worked as a glass washer at The Helmsman bar in High Street. I was there for the grand opening and it would

be hard for people who remember its descent in the Eighties to realise how upmarket and, yes, glamorous it was then – all polished wood and glass, soft carpets and cocktail shakers. Our woodwork teacher at the secondary school had made a beautiful, sleek model of a sailing

ship which took pride of place under a spotlight in a glass case.

One night after my shift I left the older members of staff to enjoy their well-earned free drink and headed off into the night... up Main Street, Abbey Street, the Newtownards Road, heading home to Church Avenue. After I went to bed there was an almighty rumble and the window panes shook. A massive bomb had demolished virtually all of Main Street and parts of Abbey Street. The bomb had been placed by the IRA in a stolen car. I had walked past it.

My years at the *Spectator* as a young, wet-behind-the-ears reporter have proved invaluable to me as a journalist. Two great characters stand out from that time – editor, Annie Roycroft, and owner, David Alexander Senior. Every journalist should be so lucky to have had Annie as their first editor. She was a hard task master, but with a heart of gold and utterly fearless. It's strange to think that in a profession dominated today by women, Annie was the only female editor at the time in Northern Ireland – perhaps one of very few in the UK.

I realised from watching her that being an editor was not just about words, stories and pictures. Political and

The Crossen Diary

"SPECTATOR" reporter David Crossen has been given a column of his own, to be known as the Crossen Diary. He is just home from Reading Festival, on which he will report next week.

MOVIES ON MONDAY

David, an avid film fan, is looking forward to visiting the North Down Movie Makers on their opening night at Newtownards Camera Club rooms, South Street, on Monday.

The club, formerly known as the YMCA Cine Society, have altered their name for the new Cine season for which a varied and interesting programme is planned.

On Monday night members will show films from the past few weeks, including documentary, travel and comedy. They have the added attraction of sound and should be of interest to all, especially 8 mm Cine minded people.

Anyone interested in joining the club can get details from the hon. secretary, Robert Johnston, phone Bangor 66586, or go along on Monday at 8.

David Crossen today

commercial pressures are a daily fact of life and I saw her handle these with great courage and integrity, managing to steer the paper away from extremes on all sides. A lesson learned, I hope.

David Alexander Senior was a genuine eccentric, as was his wife Lolita (I once heard Annie deliver a superb Freudian slip when she complimented Lolita on her overdraft. She meant overcoat). David Senior drove a beautiful pale blue Jaguar automatic sedan with leather seats and wood trim and his son David, if memory serves me well, drove an E-Type of the same colour. Sometimes I would be sent out with David Senior to deliver papers along the Ards Peninsula. He was a hesitant driver and short-sighted so my role when we came to junctions was to yell out if there were any cars coming. Unfortunately, he was rather deaf as well. We were both lucky to survive.

One final anecdote concerns another character from that era. Major Affleck worked at Bangor Town Hall and was a tall, well dressed man of military bearing. His brown polished shoes would creak as he strode across the tiled floor.

My father was once discussing men who carried their military rank into civilian life.

Me: Yes, there's a man at the Town Hall called Major Affleck.

My father: What did he call you that for?

Me: Eh? Call me what?

My father: A giraffe neck.

Think about it.

Colin Bateman
remembers...

Ah, the teenage years... to go from a vaguely nerdy boy with a pudding bowl haircut obsessed with Marvel Comics and science fiction, to a vaguely nerdy and spotty teenager obsessed with punk rock and Strongbow Cider, while still managing to hold on to the pudding bowl haircut. I would have had it spiked up, but Mummy wouldn't let me. That tells you everything you need to know about how much *Anarchy in the UK* there was going on in my house.

Seventeen-year-old Colin Bateman's first *Spectator* photograph. *480/17-8*

Teenage drinking went on down in the Ballyholme Shelters, starting out with a small bunch of friends in the long gone White Shelters on the promenade, and then gradually migrating to the Blue Shelters in Ballyholme Park with a much bigger group of friends.

It was funny to watch – one week everyone was in flares and anoraks, and a week later we were all in drainpipes and Harrington jackets covered in punk badges, dancing around to the Pistols and The Clash and The Stranglers and then being lippy to the cops who came to quieten us down.

Through those 70s though, I always wanted to be an au-

Acclaimed as one of the UK's top crime writers, Colin Bateman was born in Newtownards (in 1962) and reared in Bangor, where he attended Ballyholme Primary School and Bangor Grammar School.

After a spell at 'The Tech' learning shorthand and typing he joined the *County Down Spectator* at 17, rising to the position of deputy editor and, following a brief break, remaining on the staff into the late 1990s.

A collection of his columns was published in 1989 as *Bar*

Stool Boy. But it was his debut novel *Divorcing Jack*, in 1995, which set him on the road to a career as a professional writer. It won a Betty Trask Award and was adapted into a 1998 film starring David Thewlis. He has since written over 30 novels. In 2010 he was made a Doctor of Letters by the University of Ulster for his services to literature.

He created the *Murphy's Law* television series for the BBC (2001–2007), which starred Ulster actor James Nesbitt. The 90-minute pilot was seen by more than seven million people, and led to three TV series, on which Colin was the chief writer.

In more recent years he has added children's books to his ever-expanding CV. *Titanic 2020* was shortlisted for the 2008 Salford Children's Book Award. Colin says his children's books are written "purely for fun" and take him back to the days when writing was just a hobby.

Nowadays he devotes a considerable amount of time to visiting schools and talking to the children about the importance of books and reading.

He describes writing as "the best job in the world, apart, obviously, from being centre forward for Liverpool. I still have lingering hopes of that one."

Colin Bateman today

thor, but that's almost impossible to do when you're a teenager, you haven't enough experience. But there was a way for me to write and get paid for it – becoming a journalist on the local paper. My Dad hoodwinked me into going in to meet the editor of the *Spectator* at the tender age of 14 – little did I realise it was a job interview.

Annie Roycroft sat me down and told me to write 300 words on why I wanted to be a journalist. I hadn't given it a moment's thought, but I did it all the same, and in the process probably created my finest work of fiction. And it worked – I walked out with a job offer, if I would go to 'The Tech' for a year and learn how to type and take shorthand.

Three years later, just as the 70s were coming to an end, still in my narrow trousers, I walked into the Speccy to begin my life as a cub reporter. It should have been a disaster – I was very shy, and very quiet, and was somewhat paranoid about using the phone (it was an open-plan office and everyone could hear me making a fool of myself as I tried to conduct interviews), but somehow, somehow, I managed it – and within weeks I had my first by-line in the paper, on an article about the Sex Pistols and how hypocritical Woolworths were now selling their once-banned album.

I was going to say, "And I've never looked back", but I look back all the time. The Seventies were good. Bangor was mostly peaceful, I'd a great bunch of mates and we had fun. People make as much of a fuss these days about teenage drinking, but it was GREAT; the music was brilliant once we got rid of all that hippy nonsense, and as for the girls…

Yes, exactly, what girls…?

Never mind the Sex Pistols

FRESH controversy has been raised locally surrounding Punk Rock group the Sex Pistols, with a reader of the 'Spectator' angrily complaining about local displays of the group's first L.P., 'Never Mind the Bollocks, Here's The Sex Pistols.'

The Bangor man came across the album while browsing in Woolworth's Department Store, and was outraged that it should be displayed where children - and indeed adults - might see it.

The record itself was first released in 1977 in a blaze of publicity and controversy and was soon the subject of an obscenity trial, from which it emerged unscathed and perfectly legal. The title of the record was not the only thing to annoy certain members of the public. The inclusion of the group's first two singles, 'Anarchy in the U.K.', banned and then deleted by their record company, and 'God Save the Queen', the single banned nationwide because of its anti-monarchist lyrics but described by the Sex Pistols as an attack on the hypocrisy of the Jubilee celebrations, also roused the general public to anger. Despite such setbacks, the album entered the National album charts at No. 1, the first record to do so since the time of the Beatles.

In Bangor, the record was stocked by only a few of the more daring shops, but most prevented its display and indeed would not allow any of the group's records controversial or not, to be stocked for some time.

Now, nearly two years after the release of the record, all the fuss has died down and it has made its way to the 'respectable' shops which would not might easily see it in passing.

Although it might be considered offensive, the record is not the only shop; almost every record shop in Bangor has supplies.

The record is not, however, displayed prominently where younger children - and adults - legal and extremely popular, especially among teenagers.
— COLIN BATEMAN

Coming Attractions

Belfast promoter Eamonn McCann is bringing top band Planxty to the Ulster Hall, Belfast, on Tuesday, November 27. Tickets are on sale at Harrison's Tapes, Belfast, and the support will be American folk singer Jim Page. The Ulster Hall is also the venue for Joe Jackson on Thursday, December 20. Tickets will be on sale shortly.

Where it all began – Colin Bateman's first by-lined article in the *County Down Spectator*, published on 9 November 1979

Spectator Stalwarts
in the Seventies

The editor and deputy editor pairing of Annie Roycroft and Joy (now author Jo) Bannister remained largely constant during the 1970s, with the reporting team being joined by a succession of very capable teenagers at various points during the decade.

In addition to the reporters who recount their memories of the Seventies in this section was former Bangor Grammar School pupil Paddy Price, who joined the paper in 1976 and combined general news reporting with regular motoring and fashion columns.

One of the paper's most popular columnists was Lolita Alexander, born of English parents and raised in Spain, who was married to company director David S. Alexander. Her weekly *Come Here Till I Tell You* (and particularly the exploits of Snooky the badger) attracted a legion of readers over many years.

Annie Roycroft

Joy Bannister

Lolita Alexander

Paddy Price

Deirdre Atkinson

Spectator editor Annie Roycroft was renowned for nurturing the writing talents of young recruits to her reporting team. One such trainee reporter, who joined the paper's staff in the autumn of 1973, was teenager Deirdre Atkinson.

Tragically, the young Belfast woman would lose her life at the age of just 26, along with her five-year-old son David, in a road accident near Killyleagh on 28 February 1981.

Deirdre Atkinson is pictured in 1974 interviewing former *Spectator* reporter Jack Ledgerwood, then on the Press Association staff at Westminster, who also passed away in the 1980s. *2/9a-80*

Although her stay at the *Spectator* was short, just a year, Deirdre's legacy is an extensive selection of by-lined stories and feature articles which indicate her obvious enthusiasm for writing.

Reflecting at the end of 1973 on the year she joined the *Spectator*, Deirdre wrote: "After drifting in and out of the things I never wanted to do, and being singularly unsuccessful in the things I wouldn't have minded doing, I weighed up the pros and cons of doing nothing at all.

"I was, I thought, brilliantly clever, unconventional, extremely gregarious and had a genuine flair for writing, which due to complete laziness was wilting, to say the least.

"As I was about to sign myself away into the convent-like confines of the Civil Service, to emerge sometime later mechanised, responsible, stiff upper-lipped, decent and impersonal, like so many indifferent secretaries in the Ministry of It's Nothing To Do With Us, Try Next Door, I fortunately saw an advertisement calling for juniors in the *Spectator.*"

When the headmaster of Bangor Grammar School instructed his staff to send home a number of pupils because their hair was too long, Deirdre observed: "Are they [headmasters] to be allowed to threaten a pupil's further education because his hair is too near his collar – or are civil liberties only for adults?"

She added: "Many of our teachers are not much older than Sixth Formers and it is ludicrous to expect a pupil to accept old authoritarian forms of discipline from a master in the same generation as himself."

And reflecting on the importance of sound and the spoken word, she wrote: "A poet without words could not impart his conception of beauty to those around him... perhaps the only ironic advantage of a silent world would be not to hear the battle bugles, the sound of a rocket attack, the scream of a soldier in agony and the terrible sound of the tears of a million people."

The compiler of this book expresses his sincere thanks to Deirdre's mother Vivienne for allowing this tribute to be included in *Bangor in the Seventies.*

Maxine Mawhinney

And finally...
It's doubtful whether any former *Spectator* reporter has such an extensive and accomplished work CV as Maxine Mawhinney, who is widely recognised as one of the most experienced journalists in the UK. In a career spanning more than 30 years she has reported from across the world.

Hailing from the Lisburn Road in Belfast, Maxine attended several schools in the city before the family's move to Donaghadee, which saw her enrolling at Regent House in Newtownards.

After completing the intensive course run by the National Council for the Training of Journalists at the Belfast College of Business Studies in 1978, Maxine joined the *Spectator* as a junior reporter, covering an extensive range of stories and features, with a special interest in the local entertainment scene and educational matters.

Her broadcasting career began in the early 1980s at BBC Northern Ireland in radio and television before she moved to Ulster Television and then

Maxine Mawhinney pictured for her *Spectator* column in late 1979

Ulster Magician of the Year 1978 Vivian Woods, who followed up this success six months later by being named Irish Magician of the Year, demonstrates a guillotine trick to *Spectator* reporter Maxine Mawhinney. *323/1-4*

on to ITN in London.

When Sky News began in 1988 she was appointed Ireland Correspondent, returning to Northern Ireland during a turbulent period in the Troubles. She reported on the bombings and shootings, as well as political and economic progress north and south of the border.

Maxine then spent two years in Tokyo as the Asian News Editor for Reuters TV, covering the assassination of Rajiv Ghandi, elections in India, Pakistan and Malaysia and the first Asian Games in China, among many other major stories. She also reported from the Falkland Islands.

In October 1992 she became Washington Correspondent for British breakfast television station GMTV when it launched and reported from the United States for four years, including coverage of the Waco Siege, the Oklahoma Bomb, O. J. Simpson and the Clinton Presidency.

On returning to the BBC in 1996 she became a presenter on BBC World TV in London, where she anchored single-handed throughout the night when Princess Diana died. This was broadcast live across the world (a role she portrayed in the 2006 feature film *The Queen,* starring Helen Mirren).

Maxine Mawhinney – a familiar face on our television screens

Maxine then moved to BBC News 24 (the BBC continuous news channel) when it launched and she is now one of the main presenters on BBC News. She also presents BBC One national news bulletins.

In an echo of her own early days in the business, Maxine is now heavily involved in the training of the next generation of journalists and broadcasters. She is the on-air trainer of presenters and reporters for the BBC College of Journalism.

She has received several awards for her work – two from the American Committee for Excellence in Journalism and one from Lincoln University School of Journalism, USA, for foreign coverage of American affairs.

Members of Maxine's family still live in Donaghadee.

A last word
from Terence Bowman

In the introduction to *Bangor in the Seventies* I refer to the sense of loss I believe sums up the 1970s for a sizeable proportion of the town's residents. For a mercifully small yet still significant number of families and individuals it was the heart-rending loss of a loved one as the result of the Troubles. For others it was the demise of so many long-established places of employment through either terrorist action or the growing trend among big manufacturers to shift their production overseas – without a care (from either the terrorist or the manufacturer) for the devastating impact this would have in countless local homes.

Among the consequences was the never-ending brain drain that took so many of our brightest young people off to a new life in Britain or beyond, never to return. In truth, every family in Bangor will have their own story of how things changed for them during the 1970s. For some their loss will have had very little to do with either the Troubles or unemployment, but it will have been felt just as keenly.

For me, after a Sixties childhood which, as this book's predecessor will testify, still evokes so many happy memories, nothing defines the first half of the new decade more than the sudden death of my father Hugh, at the age of just 49.

My 14th birthday was a matter of weeks away when, on 5 March 1971, my easy-going – some might say spoilt – life came to an end. *Dad died tonight:* three words, a mere 14 letters between them, which still have the power to stop me in my tracks as they stare out from the scribbled pages of my Letts pocket diary for that year.

Looking back more than 40 years later it seems somewhat bizarre I should have taken the time, within hours of hearing such shocking news, to write even

Terence's father Hugh is pictured at the Taj Mahal in India during a visit he made in January 1971 – just weeks before his death – to attend the fourth Commonwealth Legal Conference in Delhi.

a brief entry in a diary used more for recording soccer scores and favourite television programmes than anything else.

I remember how we were watching a John Wayne western, *The Comancheros,* when my mother opened the door late in the evening to admit Dr Browne, bearer of the news that my father had died from the stroke he'd suffered the previous day. To this day I've never wanted to watch the end of that film.

Such thoughts are all part of the tangle of emotions sparked off by my Dad's death, and which, to this day, still have the habit of nagging away at me.

By way of example, not long after I'd passed my 50th birthday, I agreed to take part in Radio Ulster's long-running *Days Like This* series, in which members of the public recalled a meaningful day in their lives. I selected 15 May 1971, which over the years I'd come to look upon as a turning point in the grief process.

It's a story I never cease to enjoy telling. During that summer term, and regardless of the worsening Troubles, our Bangor Grammar School under-14 cricket team was still playing away fixtures against rival schools in Belfast. The opposition that morning was Inst. at Osborne Park, in the south of the city, and, although we lost the game, the location provided the perfect springboard for our grand adventure.

Ulster 71, which had just opened, comprised a vast exhibition area along the Stranmillis Embankment and spreading into Botanic Gardens, highlighting all that was good about Northern Ireland at a time when all that was bad tended to dominate the headlines. A bunch of barely teenage schoolboys, with money in their pockets and not a teacher in sight, trooped down the Stranmillis Road in the pouring rain, attracted by the huge funfair and amusements, the hotdogs and the hamburgers.

Then it was on to Windsor Park for Northern Ireland's Home International against England – the one everyone claims to have been at – where George Best's moment of genius saw the ball hitting the back of the visitors' net after just 12 minutes. World Cup hero Gordon Banks had begun to toss the ball in the air to kick it down field. Quick as lightning, Best dashed in, managed to get his foot to the ball first, wheeled round the 'keeper and headed it into the open goal. The referee ruled that Best must have done something wrong – nobody could be that good – and disallowed the goal.

That was the yarn I was all set to tell on *Days Like This,* yet the more the interviewer gently probed, the more my thoughts turned to my Dad, who had taken me to Windsor Park a couple of years earlier and had then settled into the fortnightly routine of taking me to Clandeboye Park for Bangor's home matches. The last time was just days before his death. I was close to tears as I recalled a long-hidden memory of wishing he'd been there on the terraces that afternoon, sharing my Mum's ham sandwiches and joining in the raucous barracking of the England players.

A phrase I caught on the radio a while back – "the missing conversations between a son and his father" – aptly pinpoints the dimension absent from my life then … and oh how I envied all my schoolfriends who still had both their parents.

Looking back, it seems like the four years to 1975 went by like a blur, one school day merging into the next, exams followed by more exams, summer breaks over all too quickly, discovering X-rated films at the Tonic or the Queen's, *Top of the Pops* on a Thursday night… being in awe of other boys for their seemingly effortless ability to get dates with our Glenlola counterparts.

Of course, as those cricketing adventures would suggest, it wasn't all gloom. I also enjoyed the companionship of good friends during those difficult times – Tommy, Sam, Geoff, Peter, Gavin, David and Michael, you can all take a bow – and my Mum, somehow managing to suppress her own grief, took my brother Geoffrey and me on some terrific holidays abroad. Yet, there remained the empty seat at the dinner table. Although rarely the subject of conversation, because of the pain we all still felt, Dad was never far from our thoughts.

Ultimately it required radical action – more radical than I ever believed myself capable of – to draw myself free from such emotionally destructive negativity. But it also meant bidding farewell to Bangor, the place of my birth.

My brother was already studying Law at Queen's when I began my A-Levels in September 1973. During those final two years at school I had little reason to believe I wouldn't be following in his footsteps, indeed in the footsteps of my Dad, whose career as a leading barrister, and quite likely a senior judge of the future, had been cut short by his death.

Yet somewhere along the way I'd also heard about the year-long pre-entry course run by the National Council for the Training of Journalists at the College of Business Studies in Belfast. Over the years I'd contributed some school-related stories which were published in the *County Down Spectator* and while I'd no great desire to work so close to home, Annie Roycroft certainly deserves the credit for encouraging my interest in journalism.

I decided to take the plunge, exercising what I've described before as "the right of the second son to be different." My mother was surprised, to say the least, but took some slight comfort from my promise that if it didn't work out I would still go to Queen's, albeit a year later.

A couple of days before my first A-Level examination I took time out from revision to travel to Belfast for the NCTJ course test and interview. It wasn't until the day of my last exam that I learned I'd been accepted – one of just 10 out of hundreds of applicants. By the end of the course, in June 1976, several had dropped out and seven of us were looking for work.

Times were different then and we were all but promised a job. In my case it took what seemed a very long three weeks and three unsuccessful interviews before I was offered a position as a junior reporter at the *Mourne Observer*. I was 19 and, without realising it then, a 35-year career at the paper lay before me.

Needless to say, the 40-mile move to Newcastle, while certainly providing the initial thrill of a new job in new surroundings, wasn't the panacea I'd hoped it would be. I was living in digs and working long, very demanding hours, which all too often provided the lame excuse I needed for my almost non-existent social life away from the paper.

Yet fate intervened and it was a journey through life that thankfully I would not take alone. Returning home to Bangor one Saturday evening to meet up with an old schoolfriend, I found myself, quite unexpectedly, as part of a foursome. Averil, whom I'd never met before, was equally unaware of that evening's plans but we both surprised ourselves by hitting it off right from the beginning.

Very quickly we became inseparable soul mates, to the extent that few of our friends were particularly surprised when our thoughts turned to marriage. That day came on 25 August 1979 – the Bangor teenager who'd moved to Newcastle in search of work and a new life three years earlier had returned to his native town to meet and subsequently marry the girl of his dreams.

The Eighties were just around the corner and just as Bangor could look forward to better times ahead, including that long-anticipated seafront marina, so too my own decade was ending on a happy note.

In time the pain of losing my Dad diminished; I enjoyed regular encounters with his former colleagues at local court sittings and hearing their tales about overnight adventures away from the pressures of a demanding profession. All the same, what wouldn't I have given for those "missing conversations between a son and his father."

Averil at Christmas 1978

Terence and Averil on their wedding day in
August 1979

Thirty years on – Terence and Averil celebrate their wedding anniversary

Dear Reader,

I hope you have enjoyed this publication from Ballyhay Books, an imprint of Laurel Cottage Ltd. We publish an eclectic mix of books ranging from personal memoirs to authoritative books on local history, from sport to poultry, from photographs to fiction and from music to marine interests – but all with a distinctly local flavour.

To see details of these books, as well as the beautifully illustrated books of our sister imprint Cottage Publications, why not visit our website **www.cottage-publications.com** or contact us on +44 (0)28 9188 8033.

Timothy S Johnston

BALLYHAY BOOKS